LIBRARY OF HEBREW BIBLE/ OLD TESTAMENT STUDIES

710

Formerly Journal for the Study of the Old Testament Supplement Series

Editors
Laura Quick, Oxford University, UK
Jacqueline Vayntrub, Yale University, USA

Founding Editors
David J. A. Clines, Philip R. Davies and David M. Gunn

Editorial Board
Sonja Ammann, Alan Cooper, Steed Davidson, Susan Gillingham,
Rachelle Gilmour, John Goldingay, Rhiannon Graybill, Anne Katrine Gudme,
Norman K. Gottwald, James E. Harding, John Jarick, Tracy Lemos,
Carol Meyers, Eva Mroczek, Daniel L. Smith-Christopher,
Francesca Stavrakopoulou, James W. Watts

PSALMS AND THE USE OF THE CRITICAL IMAGINATION

Essays in Honour of Professor Susan Gillingham

Edited by

Katherine E. Southwood and Holly Morse

LONDON • NEW YORK • OXFORD • NEW DELHI • SYDNEY

T&T CLARK
Bloomsbury Publishing Plc
50 Bedford Square, London, WC1B 3DP, UK
1385 Broadway, New York, NY 10018, USA
29 Earlsfort Terrace, Dublin 2, Ireland

BLOOMSBURY, T&T CLARK and the T&T Clark logo
are trademarks of Bloomsbury Publishing Plc

First published in Great Britain 2022
Paperback edition published 2023

Copyright © Katherine E. Southwood, Holly Morse and contributors, 2022

Katherine E. Southwood and Holly Morse have asserted their rights under the Copyright, Designs and Patents Act, 1988, to be identified as Editors of this work.

All rights reserved. No part of this publication may be reproduced or transmitted in any form or by any means, electronic or mechanical, including photocopying, recording, or any information storage or retrieval system, without prior permission in writing from the publishers.

Bloomsbury Publishing Plc does not have any control over, or responsibility for, any third-party websites referred to or in this book. All internet addresses given in this book were correct at the time of going to press. The author and publisher regret any inconvenience caused if addresses have changed or sites have ceased to exist, but can accept no responsibility for any such changes.

A catalogue record for this book is available from the British Library.
Library of Congress Control Number: 2021951985.

ISBN: HB: 978-0-5676-9632-8
PB: 978-0-5677-0618-8
ePDF: 978-0-5676-9633-5

Series: Library of Hebrew Bible/Old Testament Studies, volume 710
ISSN 2513-8758

Typeset by Trans.form.ed SAS

To find out more about our authors and books visit www.bloomsbury.com and sign up for our newsletters.

Contents

List of Tables and Figures	vii
Contributors	ix
Preface	xi
INTRODUCTION	1

Part I
IMAGINING ANCIENT ORIGINS OF THE PSALMS

THE SPREADING VINE OF RECEPTION (HISTORY) STUDIES
  Daniel J. Crowther — 7

WHO'S KISSING WHO? REFLECTIONS ON PSALM 2.11-12
  H. G. M. Williamson — 25

JOAB'S CURIOUS ROLE AND DAVID'S VIVID IMAGINATION IN PSALM 60:
THE PSALM'S TITLE AS A PERTINENT TOOL FOR EXEGESIS
  Stefan M. Attard — 42

THE TWO 'SOLOMON' PSALMS:
PSALM 72 AND 127 IN THE LIGHT OF THE SOLOMONIC ATTRIBUTION
  Katharine J. Dell — 68

IMAGINING PRAYER:
DEEPENING AWARENESS OF AUDIENCES IN THE PSALMS
  M. I. J. Daffern — 81

Part II
THE PSALMS AND THEOLOGICAL IMAGINATION

PSALMS AND PERFORMANCE:
ON THE DIFFERENCES OF REHEARSED AND LITERARY
OLD TESTAMENT PRAYERS
  Erhard S. Gerstenberger — 99

'UNTIL THE MOON IS NO MORE':
PSALM 72 AS POLITICAL IMAGINARY
   Marcel V. Măcelaru   118

LITERAL AND ALLEGORICAL READINGS OF THE PSALMS:
IMAGINING THE PSALMIST
   John Barton   138

NATURAL THEOLOGY?
GERARD MANLEY HOPKINS AND PSALM 19
   Peter Groves   146

Part III
REIMAGING THE PSALMS IN LITERATURE,
MUSIC AND VISUAL ARTS

THREE RENDITIONS OF THE THREE BREATHS IN PSALM 39
   John Jarick   163

HANDEL-ING THE PSALMS:
RECEPTION-HISTORICAL REFLECTIONS ON HANDEL'S CHANDOS ANTHEMS
   Deborah W. Rooke   176

VISUALIZING PSALM 23:
PASTORAL IDYLLS, PROTECTORS AND SHADOWS OF DEATH
   Natasha O'Hear   193

Index of References   227
Index of Authors   233

Tables and Figures

Every effort has been made to trace copyright holders and to obtain their permission for the use of copyright material. However, if any have been inadvertently overlooked, the publishers will be pleased, if notified of any omissions, to make the necessary arrangement at the first opportunity.

Figure 1.1. BL Or: 14057/2, item 114.
    By permission of the British Library   21

Figure 3.1. The structure of Psalm 60   44

Figure 3.2. The geographical location of the places mentioned   46

Table 3.1. The chiastic structure of Ps. 60.13-14   47

Figure 12.1. *Utrecht Psalter*; Ms. 32, fol. 13r., 33 × 25.8 cm.
    Utrecht University Library   201

Figure 12.2. *Stuttgart Psalter*; Cod. bibl. fol. 23, f. 28v,
    26.5 × 17.5 cm. Wuerttembergische Landesbibliothek   203

Figure 12.3. *Parma Psalter*; fol. 29a, c. 1280, 13.5 × 10 cm.
    From the facsimile of the *Parma Psalter*,
    www.facsimile-editions.com/en/pp/   205

Figure 12.4. *Luttrell Psalter*; fol. 45v, 35 × 24.5 cm.
    Credit: British Library, London, UK. © British Library Board.
    All Rights Reserved/Bridgeman Images   208

Figure 12.5. *Luttrell Psalter*; fol. 46r, 35 × 24.5 cm.
    Credit: British Library, London, UK. © British Library Board.
    All Rights Reserved/Bridgeman Images   208

Figure 12.6. Arthur Wragg, *Psalm 23*; 18.
    5 × 12 cm in Arthur Wragg, *The Psalms for Modern Life*.
    London: Selwyn & Blount, 1933   211

Figure 12.7. Marc Chagall, *Psaumes de David*; 29.5 × 22 cm.
    © ADAGP, Paris. Localisation: Nice, musée national
    Marc Chagall, Photo © RMN-Grand Palais,
    (musée Marc Chagall) / Adrien Didierjean   213

Figure 12.8. Dürer, *Knight, Death and the Devil*;
   24.3 × 18.8 cm. Credit: Cabinet des Estampes et des Dessins,
   Strasbourg, France/Bridgeman Images   216

Figure 12.9. *The Pilgrim's Progress*. Credit: Lebrecht Authors/
   Bridgeman Images   218

Figure 12.10. W. R. Smith after John Martin,
   The Valley of the Shadow of Death.
   © Photo: Royal Academy of Arts, London   220

Figure 12.11. Roger Fenton, *The Valley of the Shadow of Death*;
   1854, 27.6 × 34.9 cm. Credit: Private Collection/
   Bridgeman Images   221

CONTRIBUTORS

Stefan M. Attard, University of Malta

John Barton, University of Oxford

Daniel J. Crowther, University of Oxford

M. I. J. Daffern, University of Cambridge

Katharine J. Dell, University of Cambridge

Erhard Gerstenberger, University of Marburg

Peter Groves, University of Oxford

John Jarick, University of Oxford

Marcel V. Măcelaru, University of Arad

Holly Morse, University of Manchester

Natasha O'Hear, University of St Andrews

Deborah W. Rooke, University of Oxford

Katherine E. Southwood, University of Oxford

H. G. M. Williamson, University of Oxford

Preface

The Revd Cannon Professor Susan (Sue) Gillingham (DD) retired in September 2019 from a long career based at Worcester College, University of Oxford. Sue went to a grammar school in Bradford, and then on to the University of Nottingham where she did a degree in Theology. After this, she went on to do a PGCE and a Masters in Exeter. She spent several years teaching in secondary schools in Plymouth, Witney, and High Wycombe before moving on to Oxford. Sue joined the Theology Faulty in the 1980s and had to juggle childcare for her two small daughters alongside writing her doctoral thesis. Nevertheless, she submitted her doctoral thesis, supervised by Ernest Nicholson, in 1987, after which she became a post-holder in 1995.

Sue's career in Old Testament research and teaching has, unquestionably, gone from strength to strength. She was faculty chair from 2004 to 2008, made a Reader in 2008, a Professor in 2014, received the Doctor of Divinity (DD) in 2015 – the second woman ever to receive such an award – and was awarded a Professorial Distinction in 2016. Sue was the President of the Society for Old Testament Studies very recently (2018–19). She is the Director of the Psalms network at The Oxford Centre for Research in the Humanities. Sue was ordained as a Permanent Deacon in June 2018 and was installed as Canon Theologian of Exeter Cathedral shortly there after. But aside from being an excellent scholar and one of leaders in the field of Psalms research, Sue has also been an inspiring person to work with, both as a colleague and prior to that when I was a student at Oxford. Indeed, the Oxford University Student Union presented Sue with the award for the 'Most Acclaimed Lecturer of the Year' in 2018, a clear demonstration of the admiration and respect that she generates not only as a researcher, but also as a teacher and a mentor.

Over the course of Sue's career, she has amassed a significant volume of publications. In addition to over fifty articles in edited volumes and journals, Sue's bibliography includes many monographs, such as her 1998 book, *One Bible, Many Voices*, which has been highly influential for the field of methodology. Similarly, her 2002 work on *The Image, the Depths and the Surface: Multivalent Approaches to Biblical Study* continues scholarly dialogue about approaches to the interpretation of biblical texts.

More recently, Sue's highly ambitious three-volume, detailed commentary entitled *Psalms Through the Centuries* focuses on the reception history of the Psalms (2013, 2018, 2021). In it, Sue draws together a wide range of material and selects discerningly when choosing what material is most important to include and analyse. She encourages biblical reception critics to develop a multivalent approach to biblical interpretation that creates real opportunity for the horizon of the ancient text to meet with the horizon of later interpreters and the contemporary reader. For Sue, careful analysis of the biblical text, along with its earliest history and traditions, goes hand in hand with exploration of imaginative appropriations of the Psalms. It is really Sue's unique vision and unstoppable energy as a biblical scholar and pioneer of the importance of reception history for biblical texts which generates this collection of essays in honour of her.

Prior to her work in Oxford, Sue studied at a theological college. In her first year – when women could only be deaconesses – she was the first woman ever to be admitted to an Anglican theological college and she studied alongside ninety (male) ordinands. Similarly, when Sue came to Oxford she was the only female student at Keble College and in the Faculty (most women had only started to be admitted as graduates in all subjects a year earlier). In addition, she was the only woman with a small baby. As a doctoral student with children, Sue survived by teaching for two full days in order to pay for the nursery before she could spend another two days (and often nights!) on research. Sue was also the second ever female tutorial fellow to be appointed at Worcester College, and was one of only two women on a sizeable Governing Body. Maybe it is these early, perhaps rather isolating, experiences as a woman in several male-dominated environments that propelled Sue to her characteristically robust and unwavering support for the many female scholars who work in the field. As one of my colleagues here in Oxford commented, 'Sue is particularly supportive to female scholars. She has been instrumental in advising and supporting many now well-known and respected women in their careers. In this way she has changed the discipline for the better.'

I end with a quotation from an adaptation of a Psalm sent to me in response to a recent request I made to my colleagues for reflections about Sue, partly in preparation for writing the preface to this volume. What I was sent, in response, is an excerpt of an after-dinner speech entitled the 'Sue Psalm' (presented to her by the Worcester College Theology community): 'Glory be to the Susan, and to her scholarship, and to her love for her students. As it was thirty years ago is now and ever shall be, Sue without end. Amen.'

Katherine E. Southwood

INTRODUCTION

As a highly varied, challenging and inspiring text, the book of Psalms has provoked numerous imaginative interpretative and cultural responses. This co-edited volume seeks to address some of the multi-vocality of the Scripture by drawing together a range of scholars' voices working from diverse standpoints in the study of the Bible and theology. The collection of essays presented in the volume speak to the plurality of ways in which the Psalms as individual texts, and the Psalter as a whole, pose textual, historical, theological, and artistic questions for the reader today, as well as throughout history.

This edited collection also offers readers a unique opportunity to map the diverse methodological approaches that are available in Psalms studies and biblical studies, and highlights the mutually beneficial relationship that can be formed between imaginative application of different critical approaches and theoretical frameworks in order to continue to illuminate the myriad facets of the book of Psalms. In doing so, collectively, the chapters in this book aim to provide readers with fresh new insights into the context surrounding the composition and reception of the Psalms, the relationships between the Psalms, and the audiences who have engaged with the material in both critical and creative ways through the ages. Equally, the volume pays detailed attention to specific interpretative problems which emerge in the Psalms, both linguistic and theological, and the impact they have had on readers of the biblical text. This will enable readers to create a more sophisticated historical reconstruction of how the Psalms were used originally, and their appropriation in later times, which does not limit readers' reflections on the material to specific critical approaches or time periods, but which instead opens up challenges and possibilities through emphasizing the need in critical Psalms scholarship for vitality and imagination.

Much attention has been devoted to the Psalms in biblical and theological scholarship. This volume carves out a distinctive niche in scholarship through choosing an innovative research agenda which deliberately brings 'critical approaches' and 'imaginative work' together. This volume is, we hope, a fitting celebration of Susan Gillingham's own critical imaginative approach to biblical studies, and in particular her reception critical work on the Psalter, through which she persuasively argues that writing and early reading and performing of the Psalms is the foundation for all subsequent cultural imaginings of these texts.[1] Even as later reinterpretations of the Psalms in art, music, and literature might appear to move away from the biblical text through their incorporation of more of the interpreters' own additions, expansions, and elaborations, Gillingham's method of study reminds the biblical critic to keep the earliest, ancient text in view when engaging with its subsequent afterlives.[2] In doing so, she encourages biblical reception critics to develop a multivalent approach to biblical interpretation that creates real opportunity for the horizon of the ancient text to meet with the horizon of later interpreters and the contemporary reader. For Gillingham, careful analysis of the biblical texts, its earliest history and traditions, goes hand in hand with exploration of imaginative appropriations of the Psalms. This volume, then, as a collection, represents the collaborative critical imagination of Psalms studies, as it fosters a dialogue between close reading and an informed imagination that provides an engaging and refreshing approach to researching ancient texts.

Gillingham's work in the field of reception is also very clear in its view that to study later interpretations of the biblical texts, in literature, music and art, 'offers a change of perspective because its encounter with so many cultures through time and space means that the framework of interpretation is much broader'.[3] The biblical text, and the Psalms in particular, are rich in possibility for reinterpretation in different eras, morphing the ancient words into countless creative new forms of artistic and theological forms that speak in new voices to new audiences. Scholarship that helps us to understand how we 'see' and 'hear' the Psalms through art and music allows us to access new meaning-making processes that take place through the encounter with biblical texts, and offer possibilities for understanding the Psalms in new and creative ways, ones that provide imaginative

---

1. Especially Susan E. Gillingham, *Psalms Through the Centuries: Volumes 1 and 2*, Blackwell Bible Commentaries (Chichester: Wiley-Blackwell, 2008/18). The third volume, on Pss. 73–151, is nearing completion and scheduled for publication in 2022. In addition to these volumes, Gillingham has published a prolific number of articles and essays in Psalms studies.

2. S. Gillingham, 'Biblical Studies on Holiday? A Personal View of Reception History', in *Reception History and Biblical Studies: Theory and Practice*, ed. Emma England and William John Lyons, LHBOTS 615/Scriptural Traces 6 (London: Bloomsbury T&T Clark International, 2015), 19–20.

3. Ibid., 17.

insight into the potential of the Psalter, both in the past and the present.[4] This volume, by attending to the reception of Psalms in literature, music, visual art and theology, aims to provide further insight into the project of reading the Psalms anew through their reception history.

At the heart of Susan Gillingham's approach to the critical imaginative project of reception historical research is scholarly collaboration. This collaboration can work in a number of ways: on a single shared research project; with different disciplines and areas of expertise; at conferences on particular biblical texts or characters; among communities other than the Academy. This book, which collects together work focused on the Psalms from scholars working in a range of biblical studies and theological contexts, intends to offer support to Gillingham's observation about the rich potential that is brought about by reception historical studies, and its encouragement of collective critical approaches to scholarship.

This collection of articles on the Psalms and critical imagination is organized into three parts: 'Imagining Ancient Origins of the Psalms'; 'The Psalms and Theological Imagination'; and 'Reimaging the Psalms in Literature, Music and Visual Arts'. In Part I, Daniel Crowther, H. G. M. Williamson, Stefan Attard, Katharine J. Dell and Megan Daffern reflect on the earliest origins and audiences of the Psalms, critically engaging in crucial issues of translation, historical-critical curiosities and the potentially rich meeting of 'author focused' studies of biblical text, and reception history. These five chapters cover a range of topics in historically and textually focused Psalms study, introduced by Crowther's chapter which reflects on the historical nature of reception studies, and the necessity of following a text's journey from its beginnings as a piece of writing, so that a reader might best comprehend the language and structure of the text, and the ways in which this influences subsequent interpreters. This sets the scene for the following four chapters, beginning with Williamson's response to the question 'Who's Kissing Who? Reflections on Psalm 2.11-12', followed by the Attard's exploration of the role of Joab in the superscription of Psalm 60, and Dell's discussion of the Solomonic attribution of Psalms 72 and 127. Part I is concluded by Megan Daffern's essay, which focuses on the performative power of the Psalms, and in particular Psalm 31 and its imagined ancient audience, using Audience Design principles to frame the essay.

Part II of this volume, 'The Psalms and Theological Imagination', expands the focus on the Psalms' earliest writing and reading context to include reflection on the way these texts have shaped theological

---

4. Ibid., 22.

imaginations. The first offering in this part of the book, by Erhard Gerstenberger, continues a focus established in Daffern's paper, tackling the question of the relationship between Psalms and performance through an examination of the Psalter in the context of both ancient and contemporary prayer. Continuing the consideration of power and the Psalms, Marcel V. Măcelaru's essay discusses the text and reception of Psalm 72 to argue for its function as a 'political imaginary', which is developed within the Psalm through its focus on king and kingship. John Barton's essay turns our attention to early Christian imaginings of the Psalmist, and investigates the interpretative processes that led to the transformation of the Psalter into a text that might be seen to 'contain the whole of the Christian truth' within the readings and writings of the Church Fathers. In the final essay of this section of the collection, Peter Groves writes on the merging of creativity and theology in the poetry of Gerard Manley Hopkins. Here Groves argues that Hopkins' nature sonnets provide a synthesis of the nineteenth-century debate concerning the natural world, with Hopkins presenting creation as a source of revelation that leads to deeper understanding as one moves from created to Creator, in the process illumining human selfhood most profoundly in the incarnate presence of Christ, the self-maker, in creation.

Part III, which reflects on the richness of 'Reimaging the Psalms in Literature, Music and Visual Arts', opens with an essay by John Jarick that reflects on the threefold deployment of הבל in Psalm 39 and the reception of 'breath' in three modern poetic retellings of the Psalms by Leslie Brandt, Juanita Colón, and Edward Clark, arguing that consideration of the reception of the *hebel* motif can enhance contemporary understanding of the biblical text. From literature, the volume now moves on to a consideration of the Psalms and music, with Deborah Rooke's paper on the Psalms in Handel's Chandos Anthems, exploring the tension between the ancient origins of the Psalms, and their Christianized eighteenth-century appearances in – or omission from – Handel's compositions. The collection concludes with Natasha O'Hear's work on powerful visual reimagings of Psalm 23 in medieval manuscripts which represent the Psalm in its entirety, and select artworks which focus on the image of the 'valley of the shadow of death' (Ps. 23.4). Engaging with a wide assortment of artistic portrayals prioritizing the positive and/or negative textual elements of the psalm (including the shepherd, the landscape, and the shadow of death) reveals a constructive range of how various communities understood and used Psalm 23 historically, while simultaneously expanding our present-day imaginations and inspiring meaningful, illuminating encounters of Psalm 23 itself.

Katherine E. Southwood and Holly Morse

Part I

IMAGINING ANCIENT ORIGINS OF THE PSALMS

THE SPREADING VINE
OF RECEPTION (HISTORY) STUDIES

Daniel J. Crowther

Reviewing the Foundations of Reception History

Reception history approaches provide a (relatively) neutral space for the study and evaluation of past confessional and non-confessional interpretations of Scripture.[1] Since the focus of reception history studies is the reader (receiver) in interaction with the text, the reception historian suffers no qualms in following a trail of interpretation deep into the context of the reader – whether this be puritan piety, Islamic culture, new atheism or Jewish mysticism. The first aim of the reception historian is, therefore, to comprehend how a text can mean what it has meant to its past readers. Psalm 124 is a good example. Psalm 124 has been received as a song of hope by Jews who had been forcibly baptised in fifteenth-century Spain, as battle hymn by Huguenots of sixteenth-century France, and as a psalm for the celebration of the 5th of November (and the failure of the Catholic Gunpowder Plot) by eighteenth-century Englishmen.[2] Such studies make

---

1. Susan E. Gillingham, *One Bible, Many Voices: Different Approaches to Biblical Studies* (London: SPCK, 1998); Emma England and William John Lyons, ed., *Reception History and Biblical Studies: Theory and Practice*, LHBOTS 615/ Scriptural Traces 6 (London: T&T Clark, 2015), esp. Chapter 3, James E. Harding, 'What Is Reception History, and What Happens to You if You Do It?', 31–44.

2. See Frank E. Talmage, 'Apples of Gold: The Inner Meaning of Sacred Texts in Medieval Judaism', in *Jewish Spirituality: From the Bible through the Middle Ages*, ed. A Green (London: Routledge & Kegan Paul, 1986), 312–55, esp. p. 330 for reference to Ps. 124; W. Stanford Reid, 'The Battle Hymns of the Lord: Calvinist Psalmody of the Sixteenth Century', *Sixteenth Century Essays and Studies* 2 (1971): 36–54, esp. pp. 47 and 53 for reference to Ps. 124; and J. R. Watson, 'The Hymns of Isaac Watts and the Tradition of Dissent', in *Dissenting Praise: Religious Dissent*

for a lively and interesting classroom, but they are often seen as an extra-curricular 'additional extra' to the chief task of biblical studies, that is, 'Biblical Studies on holiday'.[3]

In the self-effacing words of Saul Lieberman (1898–1983), 'nonsense is nonsense, but the history of nonsense is science'.[4] Lieberman coined this adage in the cause of reception history in order to create a space for the hearing of Jewish Kabbalah mysticism within the hearts and minds of students at the Jewish Theological Seminary (New York). It seems Lieberman's adage worked: he is fondly remembered by the seminary and his adage is often repeated (frequently with variation). Lieberman's use of this adage was ironic. The connection between Jewish mysticism and the text of the Hebrew Bible is not being upheld. But the hope behind the adage is that once Jewish mysticism has been better understood within its context, opinions about it will be revised. This is reception history at work. In another context, Isaac Watts ascription of Psalm 124 for the celebration of 5th of November appears nonsensical. Yet, if the full reception history story is told throughout Jewish and Christian history, the relationship between text and context might well begin to emerge. Watts might even be commended for creating a meaning from Psalm 124 for his congregation in his day that was 'dynamically equivalent' to how Psalm 124 may have generated meaning for Second Temple Jewish worshippers in theirs.[5] The reception history task is not necessarily to be sympathetic, but rather to understand how others have thought: so as to be able to compare one's own methodology and one's own thoughts in the light of theirs. It is upon these Gadamer-esque hermeneutical foundations that Jonathan Roberts understands reception history approaches to stand firmly.[6] In the words of Professor Gillingham, everyone should accept that 'we all do reception

---

and the Hymn in England and Wales, ed. Isabel Rivers and David L. Wykes (Oxford: Oxford University Press, 2011), 33–69, esp. p. 63 for reference to Ps. 124.

3. Cf. Susan E. Gillingham, 'Biblical Studies on Holiday? A Personal View of Reception History', in England and Lyons, eds., *Reception History and Biblical Studies*, 17–30.

4. As quoted by Yaacob Dweck, *The Scandal of Kabbalah: Leon Modena, Jewish Mysticism, Early Modern Venice* (Princeton: Princeton University Press, 2011), 1, with reference to Gershom Scholem, *Major Trends in Jewish Mysticism* (New York: Schocken, 1995), vii.

5. See, for example, Keith F. Pecklers, *Dynamic Equivalence: The Living Language of Christian Worship* (Collegeville: Liturgical Press, 2003).

6. Jonathan Roberts, 'Introduction', in *The Oxford Handbook of the Reception History of the Bible*, ed. Michael Lieb, Emma Mason and Jonathan Roberts (Oxford: Oxford University Press, 2011), 1–8.

history in one way or another'.⁷ These hermeneutical foundations also lie behind the interesting terminology of 'reception history exegesis' with its emphasis on both the negative and the positive lessons of reception history.⁸ Negatively, we do reception history studies to discover the bias of our heritage (that is, to free ourselves from our heritage). Positively, we do reception history studies to expand our horizons (that is, to explore the potential for diverse meaning in the text that stands before us).

Reviewing a Reception History Journey

Professor Gillingham's approach to the reception history of the Psalms has 'naturally' evolved over the years. This evolution can be seen in the comparison of the first two volumes of her magnum opus, *Psalms Through the Centuries*.⁹ In the first volume (2008), she states that 'our account begins where most commentaries end: the debates about the dates, authors and provenances of individual psalms are of minimal concern, because our emphasis is on the reception of individual psalms once the Psalter had become a recognized collection'.¹⁰ So, the focus of this work is not upon issues of the text or its translation, but upon subsequent mainstream and unusual Jewish and Christian interpretations of the canonical Psalter: first in various homilies and commentaries and then in liturgy, literature, art and music. A similar focus on the interpretation of the post-canonical text also dominates her extensive works on individual psalms.¹¹ All this

    7. Gillingham, 'Biblical Studies on Holiday?', 30.
    8. Paul M. Joyce and Diana Lipton, *Lamentations through the Centuries*, Wiley-Blackwell Bible Commentaries (Chichester: John Wiley, 2013), 17–21; see also John F. Sawyer, *Isaiah through the Centuries*, Wiley-Blackwell Bible Commentaries (Chichester: John Wiley & Sons, 2018), 4–8.
    9. Susan E. Gillingham, *Psalms Through the Centuries: Volumes 1 and 2*, Blackwell Bible Commentaries (Chichester: Wiley-Blackwell, 2008/18). The third volume (Pss. 73–151) is to be published in 2022.
    10. Gillingham, *Psalms Through the Centuries*, 1:6.
    11. Cf. Susan E. Gillingham, 'Psalm 8 Through the Looking Glass: Reception History of a Multifaceted Psalm', in *Diachronic and Synchronic: Reading the Psalms in Real Time: Proceedings of the Baylor Symposium on the Book of Psalms*, ed. Joel S. Burnett, W. H. Bellinger Jr., W. Dennis Tucker Jr. (London: T&T Clark International, 2008), 167–96; 'An Introduction to Reception History with Particular Reference to Psalm 1', *Revue Des Sciences Religieuses* 85, no. 4 (2011): 571–99; 'The Reception of Psalm 137 in Jewish and Christian Tradition', in *Jewish and Christian Approaches to the Psalms: Conflict and Convergence*, ed. Susan E. Gillingham (Oxford: Oxford University Press, 2015); 'Psalms 105 and 106 and the Participation in History through Liturgy', *HBAI* 4, no. 4 (2015): 450–75.

follows the norm: reception history studies deal with the after-life of the text, Biblical Studies with its formation and philological identity.[12]

The second volume (2018) very gently breaks this convention because in this work the reception history commentary of each psalm begins with issues of authorship, text, canon and intertext, before going on to the translations and only then the multifarious interpretations – both Jewish and Christian. As a result of this methodology, subsequent interpretations are typically related directly to textual issues, intertextual choices and the way in which the earliest translations witness to the 'original' form(s) of the text. Only after these connections have been established are the roles of each psalm in liturgy, literature, art, music and (finally) modern theological movements discussed.[13] The tight interwoven nature of each of the brief three-thousand-word pieces on each psalm conveys the extent to which issues of authorship, text, canon and context are inextricably part of its reception history. For example, the opening verse of Psalm 51 relates its contents to a specific event in the life of David in a way strongly suggestive of his authorship.[14] However, the closing cry of this psalm is for the walls of Jerusalem to be built up so that the sacrifices can be restored. This part of the prayer is consistent with a post-exilic setting, not a Davidic one. So, it is possible to read the opening verse of the psalm as part of the reception history of a post-exilic psalm; or to read the last two verses as part of the reception history of a Davidic psalm; or, indeed, to read both the beginning and the end verses (and perhaps some select verses within the psalm) as part and parcel of a more complex reception history journey that has itself moulded the content of the Psalm.

The strength of the argument for the involvement of reception history in every aspect of Biblical Studies is cumulative. As one reads through the reception history of psalm after psalm in the second volume, it becomes increasingly difficult to make any case for the separation of issues of reception history from those of the text. In the case of each psalm, its

---

12. For example, Yvonne Sherwood, *A Biblical Text and its Afterlives: The Survival of Jonah in Western Culture* (Cambridge: Cambridge University Press, 2000), and all the volumes in the Wiley Blackwell Bible Commentary Series that specifically focus upon reception history.

13. This approach addresses nine aspects of the reception history of each psalm (Text, Intertext, Translations, Interpretations, Liturgy, Literature, Art, Music, Modern Theology). This gives the obscure mnemonic 'titillammt'. However, if the word 'Tune' is used for music and 'Exegesis' for Modern Theology, then the mnemonic can become the rather more memorable 'titillate.'

14. 'To the leader, a psalm of David. When Nathan the Prophet came to him after he had "come to" Bath-Sheba.'

textual and its reception history begin with a song. It may have been quite some time before the words of the song came to be written down, perhaps in many different forms.[15] How this text was then edited and how it circulated in different collections of songs prior to its adoption in the Psalter are also issues of reception history.[16] So, in Gillingham's commentary issues of reception history are inseparable from issues of text, intertext, canon, translation and transmission; which, in turn, turn out to be inseparable from later issues of interpretation.[17] The point is that Professor Gillingham did *not* set out to write a reception history commentary that encroached on every issue of Biblical Studies. According to Volume 1, the opposite seems to have been the case. Instead, in the case of the Psalter, the trail of reception history naturally leads one to layers of reception history that predate the earliest well-established canonical standard texts: such as the opinion of the translators of the Septuagint or of the community at Qumran – both of whom seem to have used Psalters at variance with the Psalter of the Masoretic text.

The resulting commentary is, in effect, a signpost to an integrated reception history approach to Biblical Studies. Even though the case for such an integrated approach is, perhaps, most obvious regarding the Psalter, I see no reason why the approach should not extend to the whole Hebrew Bible. The observations made will not differ from those that have been already observed by the practitioners of, for example, text criticism or canonical criticism. But the focus will be quite different. Whilst the text critic might wish to discard any alterations to the text that their placements in the canon may have inspired (such as the title of the psalm), the reception historian treasures them as potential explanations of its subsequent identity and interpretation. Whilst proponents of canonical criticism might seek to simplify (or ignore) complications with the process in which the canon and its canonical text has been determined, the reception historian seeks to understand how many of the later interpretations are connected to the canonical complications that may well indeed define the identity of the text as scripture.

---

15. Possible examples include: Pss. 8, 18, 2 Sam. 22 and Ps. 144; Pss. 14 and 53; Pss. 40.13-17 and 70; Pss. 57, 60 and 108; and 1 Chron. 16 and Pss. 95 and 96.

16. For example, the Elohistic Psalter (Pss. 42–83) and the Psalms of Ascent (Pss. 120–134), as well as the five books (Pss. 1–41, 42–72, 73–89, 90–106 and 107–150).

17. For example, 'Psalm 27, like 19, seems to be another example of two psalms brought together as one' (Gillingham, *Psalms Through the Centuries*, 2:170); the discussion of Pss. 9 and 10 as one psalm (ibid., 83–9); and the frequent references to inter-connections of vocabulary and ideas that are offered to explain the canonical order.

Textual criticism and canonical criticism do not represent the limits of the reach of the spreading vine of reception history. Volume 2 is a signpost to much more than this. In a recent paper addressing the image of the sun as a bridegroom in Psalm 19, Professor Gillingham has followed the trail of reception history back to before the time of composition of the psalm![18] In this paper, this psalm's personalization of the sun is read in the context of (1) the impact of sun-worship in late second-millennium Egypt to the time of David, (2) the impact of Assyrian sun worship in the time of Hezekiah and, then, (3a) the impact of both of these back-histories to the Jews in exile (perhaps in Egypt) and (3b) to later Jews worshipping in Second Temple of Jerusalem. Each of these imagined worlds-behind-the-text generates a different imagined 'original' reception for the text which in turn assigns a different meaning to the 'original text' in its 'original context'. Since we do not know when Psalm 19 was written, each of these imagined receptions could be the 'background pre-history' of the text, if a late date for its composition is supposed. Many of these could, however, equally well be described as part of its reception history if an early date was accepted for the composition of the whole or parts of the psalm.

This adventurous methodology proves to be more robust than might be expected. For even if Psalm 19 was composed in the Second Temple period, most likely its composer(s) and its subsequent readers would have been culturally influenced by prior uses of divine sun imagery – whether consciously through a broad education, or subconsciously through the impact of past cultures upon the vocabulary and thought world of later generations. In this scenario, the distinction between the 'world behind the text', the 'original meaning of the text in its original context' and reception history ('the world before the text'?) becomes blurred to extinction. Reception pre-history and reception history blend into one. Reception history studies become passé. It's all a reception story now!

The potential for this methodology only expands when other psalms are considered, such as Psalm 29. Since the discovery of Ugarit in 1928, many scholars have proposed that the imagery of Psalm 29 should be read in the context of Ugaritic temple poetry.[19] But the city-state of Ugarit

---

18. Susan E. Gillingham, '"Like a bridegroom" and "like a strong man": The Reception of Two Similes in Psalm 19:5', in *Fromme und Frevler Studien zu Psalmen und Weisheit: Festschrift für Hermann Spieckermann zum 70 Geburtstag*, ed. C. Körting and R. G. Kratz (Tübingen: Mohr Siebeck, 2020), 41–54.

19. For a comprehensive bibliography up to 1970, see Peter Craigie, 'Psalm 29 in the Hebrew Poetic Tradition', *VT* 22 (1972): 143–51. In this article, Craigie questions the proposal of Ginsberg – supported by scholars such as W. F. Albright and F. M.

was destroyed approximately two hundred years before the proposed accession of David to the throne of Judah and Israel. The consideration of Ugarit can be helpfully described as an imagined possible reception pre-history.

Theodore, the fifth-century Bishop of Mopsuestia (near Antioch), proposes that Psalm 29 should be read in the context of Hezekiah, not David:

> After the effect of God's anger that consumed the Assyrians (one hundred and eighty-five thousand fell, and the rest fled, thus ending the siege), it behoved blessed Hezekiah as part of his attention to the divine cult and his divine piety to perform rites of thanksgiving with victims offered to God because against hope all troubles had ceased, thanks to God. For this reason, therefore, blessed David sings this psalm in the person of the same Hezekiah.[20]

Theodore's approach and subsequent commentary provide a refreshing insight into the potential import of the words of Psalm 29. It can be helpfully applied to many other psalms regardless of whether (or not) this exercise is considered to involve an imagined pre-history, an imagined authorial context, or an imagined reception history or some combination of all three of these. Theodore himself applies it to Psalms 28, 30, 32, 33 and 34, 48 and 75.[21]

In this light, any category distinction between an exegesis of the text of the Hebrew Bible based on its imagined ancient context and the observation of later interpretation in different contexts must be suspect. It is all part of one reception *story*. This story can be allowed to begin in the period before its composition, to cover the entire period of its possible composition and extend to many different periods and contexts after its canonization. In her Festschrift paper for Hermann Spieckermann cited above, Professor Gillingham relates the worship of the sun god Aten in

---

Cross – that Ps. 29 is a Canaanite psalm that has been Yahweh-ized and adopted into the Psalter. If Ginsberg is correct, then the inclusion of Ps. 29 in the Hebrew Psalter is an act of reception history. If Craigie is correct, then the composition of Ps. 29 by a later Israelite has been deeply influenced by prior Canaanite poetry: that is, its reception pre-history.

20. R. C. Hill, *Theodore of Mopsuestia, Commentary on Psalms 1–81* (Atlanta: SBL, 2006), 265.

21. Cf. ibid., 271 (Ps. 30); 279 (Ps. 32); 285 (Ps. 33); 315 (Ps. 34); and 621 (Ps. 48).

Egypt, and the worship of Shamash in Assyria through the medium of Psalm 19 to the medieval piety of the Eadwine Psalter and the twentieth-century art of Marc Chagall. There is no good reason why the puritan pietism of Isaac Watts could not also have been included.

For me, the argument that most recommends the spreading vine of reception studies is that there does not appear to be an obvious agenda behind the takeover. Professor Gillingham does not seem to be actively championing reception history approaches over and against more traditional approaches to Biblical Studies for any ideological purpose. It seems to be more a case of unintended mission creep – the unforeseen spreading of the creepers of the vine – and it seems to be bearing fruit.

Sifting Through What Remains of Biblical Studies

As we gaze upon the spreading vine, the question arises as to whether there are any aspects of Biblical Studies that might be usefully declared to be beyond its tendrils: or to be, perhaps, suffocated (rather than stimulated) by its spreading vine. According to informed opinions, textual criticism and canonical criticism are already inextricably intertwined, and fruitfully so.[22] According to the above, the archaeology of the context in which the text developed is also interwoven with its reception history both as a developing text and as a text in its final form. Given the reader-centred focus of reception studies, if anything should be beyond the reach of the vine, it should be found amongst more author-based approaches to the text. Since there is no consensus regarding the process of composition, or authorship, of any book in the Hebrew Bible, author-based approaches are effectively limited to the study of the text itself: that is, the language that the author has used and the structure that the author has given to the text.

---

22. Eugene Ulrich, 'The Old Testament Text and Its Transmission', in *The New Cambridge History of the Bible* (Cambridge: Cambridge University Press, 2013), 83–104; *The Dead Sea Scrolls and the Developmental Composition of the Bible*, VTSup 169 (Leiden: Brill, 2015); John Barton, 'Historical Criticism and Literary Interpretation: Is There Any Common Ground?', in *Crossing the Boundaries: Essays in Biblical Studies in Honour of Michael D. Goulder*, ed. Stanley E. Porter, Paul M. Joyce, and Davie E. Orton, BibInt 8 (Leiden: Brill, 1994), 3–15; *The Spirit and the Letter: Studies in the Biblical Canon* (London: SPCK, 1997); *The Old Testament: Canon, Literature and Theology: Collected Essays of John Barton*, SOTSMS (Aldershot: Ashgate, 2007).

Philological Approaches to the Hebrew Bible

Philological or linguistic analyses of the Hebrew scriptures typically focus upon the linguistic possible meanings of the words, clauses and sentences both individually and in relation to one another. The foundational resources for these analyses are, aside from the text itself, the various established lexicons and grammars of the Hebrew Bible alongside a burgeoning corpus of research-based studies recently overviewed in the *Encyclopaedia of Hebrew Language and Linguistics*.[23] The role of the reception studies of the Hebrew Bible in the formation of these resources and studies cannot, however, be overlooked. In regard to the lexicons and grammar, most (if not all) of their insights are dependent upon the Tiberian Masoretic vocalization, accentuation and punctuation (*neqqudot* and *ṭeʻamim*) that accompany the consonantal text. This distinguishes, for example, *piel* verbs from *qal*, defective plural endings (*-im*) from possessive suffixes (*-am*) and various forms of the verb *yire'* ('to fear') from forms of the verb *raʼah* ('to see'). It must be admitted, however, that the Tiberian Masoretic vocalization, accentuation and punctuation indicate the way in which the Tiberian Masoretes understood the Hebrew language of the text – and not necessarily the author. Furthermore, it is clear from other often older sources that the Tiberian Masoretic way of reading the text was not the only way in which the consonantal Hebrew words of the author have been read.

It is interesting to observe in Biblical Studies that whenever a linguistic insight is proposed that goes against the masoretic vocalization or punctuation, it is almost always substantiated by reference to other traditions (such as those given by the Dead Sea Scrolls, Josephus, Philo, the Septuagint or Old Greek, Vulgate or Old Latin, Targum, Peshitta or Samaritan Pentateuch). In other words, whenever the Tiberian reception tradition is rejected, it is perceived to be worthy of consideration if, and only if, the rejection can be substantiated by reference to another reception tradition. The present linguistic analysis of the Hebrew scriptures is, therefore, profoundly intertwined with reception research.

---

23. Cf. David J. A. Clines, *The Dictionary of Classical Hebrew*, 9 vols. (Sheffield: Sheffield Phoenix, 1993–2016); Wilhelm Gesenius, E. Kautzsch, and A. E. Cowley, *Gesenius' Hebrew Grammar* (Mineola: Dover, 2006); Paul Joüon and T. Muraoka, *A Grammar of Biblical Hebrew*, 2nd ed., SubBib 27 (Rome: Gregorian & Biblical, 2009); Geoffrey Khan, ed., *Encyclopedia of Hebrew Language and Linguistics*, 4 vols. (Leiden: Brill, 2013).

Structural Analysis

Structural analyses attempt to discern authorial intent by means of observing the way the authors of texts have structured their texts. Structural analyses of the Hebrew scriptures typically focus upon various kinds of parallelism, chiasmus, and concentric structures. Whilst observations on the structure of a text are ubiquitous in modern studies of the Hebrew text, it is difficult to define one corpus of foundational resources that directs these observations.[24] It is clear, however, that some of these resources do originate from the study of other forms of literature and rhetoric outside the sphere of the reception of the Hebrew Bible.[25] So, structural studies of the biblical text could, at least in theory, be conducted independently from the study of the reception of the biblical text. The question then becomes whether there is anything to be lost or gained by relating structural studies to reception studies.

Structural Analysis: Parallelism. The term 'parallelism' owes its origins to one of Robert Lowth's 36, wide-ranging eighteenth-century Oxford lectures (in Latin) 'On the Sacred Poetry of the Hebrews', specifically, his nineteenth lecture. The lectures were published in their original Latin form in 1753, and then translated and published in English in 1787. More recently they have been retranslated and published in an interlinear Latin and English.[26] An interesting anomaly in the first Latin printing of this work is that the Hebrew text is presented as unpointed consonants. At first sight, this presentation might suggest that the parallelism is fundamental to the consonantal text: and was observed apart from the Masoretes. On closer inspection, however, Lowth is found to follow the Masoretes in all but two of the 51 verses he selects to illustrate 'synonymous' and

---

24. Cf. Roland Meynet, *Rhetorical Analysis: An Introduction to Biblical Rhetoric*, JSOTSup 256 (Sheffield: Sheffield Academic, 1998); and Nils Lund, *Chiasmus in the New Testament* (Chapel Hill: University of North Carolina Press, 1942). Note that Meynet uses the paradigm of chiasmus in the New Testament for his recovery of chiasmus in the Old Testament whilst Lund uses the paradigm of chiasmus in the Old Testament for his recovery of chiasmus in the New Testament.

25. Cf. esp. the Greek tradition of Aristotle, *Rhetoric*, and Demetrius, *Style*.

26. Robert Lowth, *De Sacra Poesi Hebræorum Prælectiones Academicæ Oxonii Habitæ. Subjicitur Metricæ Harianæ Brevis Confutatio: Et Oratio Grewiana* (Oxford, 1753); Robert Lowth and G. Gregory, *Lectures on the Sacred Poetry of the Hebrews* (London: Thomas Tegg & Son, 1787); Robert Lowth and David A. Reibel, *De Sacra Poesi Hebraeorum: Praelectiones Academicae Oxonii Habitae* (London: Routledge/Thoemmes, 1995).

'antithetic' parallelism.[27] The implicit role of the Tiberian Masoretes in the work of Lowth is made explicit when he turns to observe 'synthetic' parallelism. This, according to Lowth, is parallelism that 'is very subtle and obscure, and must be developed by art and ability in distinguishing the different members of the sentences, and in distributing the points, rather than by depending upon the obvious construction'.[28] As a result of this subtlety all his 22 exemplar verses follow the Tiberian Masoretic delimitation.[29] Furthermore, in the Latin edition, his ultimate example of this subtlety adds a word (נסכתיו) into the Hebrew consonantal text in order to capture the nuance of the parallelism that is only given by the accents of the masoretic reading tradition:[30]

ואני נסכתי מלכי
נסכתיו על־ציון הר־קדשי:

I also have anointed my king;
I have anointed him in Sion, the mountain of my sanctity.

Lowth then closes his argument for synthetic parallelism with the words 'Which indeed the Masorites seem to have perceived in this as well as in other places'. A footnote then refers to a further six verses that illustrate the Masoretic witness and competence in this matter.[31] For the illustration of synthetic parallelism in un-pointed Hebrew, Lowth is required to change the Hebrew text to make plain the latent parallelism. The Tiberian Masoretic reading tradition gives this parallelism by use of a pause signalled by an *atnah ta'am* so that the verb of the first colon is heard in the second colon (by elision) and by lesser pauses after 'myself' and 'over Zion' signalled by other disjunctive *te'amim*.

---

27. Lowth and Gregory, *Lectures*, 200–211. Lowth, *De sacra poesi Hebræorum*, 177–91. The verses are Exod. 15.21; Ps. 136; 1 Sam. 18.7; Ps. 114; Isa. 60.1-3; Isa. 53.1-5; Hos. 11.8-9; Pss. 94.1; 94.3; Judg. 15.16; Nah. 1.2; Ps. 105.20; Isa. 49.7; Pss. 117.1; 93.3-6; Hos. 6.1-2; Isa. 31.4; Zech. 9.5; Ps. 33.13-14; Deut. 32.42; Isa. 54.5; 2.7; Prov. 27.6-7; 13.7; 28.11; Song 1.5; Judg. 15.14; 1 Sam. 2.4-7; and Isa. 54.7-8. Of these the only two divergences from the delimitation of the Masoretes are found in Isa. 53.2 and 53.4 (that is, two stichs out of 148).

28. Lowth and Gregory, *Lectures*, 213.

29. Ps. 19.8-11; Isa. 14.4-9; Ps. 77.18-19; Hos. 14.6-7; Job 5.19; Ps. 62.12; and Amos 1.3.

30. Lowth, *De sacra poesi Hebræorum*, 194.

31. Pss. 17.7; 32.3; 33.14; 102.8; and 137.2. Gregory's 1787 translation adds a further six verses from Ps. 116 to the five in Lowth (1753).

וַאֲנִי נָסַכְתִּי מַלְכִּי   עַל־צִיּוֹן הַר־קָדְשִׁי׃

And I myself, I have anointed my king: over Zion – my holy mountain.

The study of parallelism has, therefore, long been wedded to reception studies because its primary observer, Bishop Lowth, was indebted to the Masoretes both for his observation and for his proof of the phenomenon.

Structural Analysis: Chiasmus. Although observations of chiasmus have been ubiquitous ever since Nils Lund's seminal work was published in 1942,[32] it is often hard to distinguish between chiasmus that is read into the text and chiasmus that is part of the text. David deSilva 2008 article expresses the issue succinctly:

> The role of chiasmus as a structuring device in ancient literature continues to be a much-debated facet of literary and rhetorical analysis, with often overly exuberant discovery of complex chiasmi spanning whole books running far ahead of the methodological substructure needed to sustain a convincing demonstration of the same. This article analyses three recent attempts to propose a chiastic macro-structural analysis of Revelation and finds them to present fine examples of three recurring problems in the quest for the elusive chiasmus: (1) developing chiastic outlines by means of selective shaping of summary statements for major blocks of text; (2) discovering a chiasmus by means of selective reading of key terms; and (3) creation of a chiasmus by means of manipulation of formal markers. The article is offered in the hope that future proposals will take the methodological cautions proposed by critics of chiasmus to heart, as well as the standard rules of critical thinking (e.g., seeking for better alternative structuring devices alongside the quest for the hidden chiasmus).[33]

One of the most helpful 'critics of chiasmus', David Wright, has proposed a series of tests to help discern readers between a chiasmus imposed

---

32. Cf. Lund, *Chiasmus in the New Testament*. For examples of this ubiquity in New Testament Studies, see David G. Palmer, *Sliced Bread: The Four Gospels, Acts and Revelation, Their Literary Structures* (Cardiff: Ceridwen, 1988). For examples in respect to the Hebrew Bible, see Anthony R. Ceresko, 'The A:B:B:A Word Pattern in Hebrew and Northwest Semitic, with Special Reference to the Book of Job', *UF* (1975): 73–88; 'The Chiastic Word Pattern in Hebrew', *CBQ* 38 (1976): 303–11; 'The Function of Chiasmus in Hebrew Poetry', *CBQ* 40 (1978): 1–10. See also David A. Dorsey, *The Literary Structure of the Old Testament: A Commentary on Genesis–Malachi* (Grand Rapids: Baker, 1999).

33. David A. deSilva, 'X Marks the Spot? A Critique of the Use of Chiasmus in Macro-Structural Analyses of Revelation', *JSNT* 30 (2008): 343–71 (343).

upon the text and one intrinsic to it.[34] Wright's 2004 article is often referenced (as per deSilva), but his rules are rarely used (as also observed by deSilva). The claim is often made that these patterns would have been self-evident in a more oral society in which many readers would have known large parts of the scriptures by heart. But how can this be gauged?

Once again reception studies can come to the rescue. Regarding the Hebrew Bible, an extensive oral reception tradition has been preserved by the Tiberian Masoretes. If it can be shown that their reading tradition does recognize the phenomenon of chiasmus in some texts, any pattern of chiasmus that is elsewhere also recognized by the Tiberian Masoretes could be immediately declared significant. Furthermore, any chiasmus that was given no Masoretic recognition would be under suspicion. If other reception traditions had recognized the chiasmus (for example, the LXX), then it might be redeemed. But if an observed pattern had not had any impact on the way the Masoretes or anyone else read the passage, then it is hard to see how it could be held to be either 'self-evident' or 'intrinsic' to the text.

Psalm 67 provides a clear example of the Masoretic recognition of a chiasmus. The psalm is widely recognized in modern commentaries to have a chiastic structure.[35] The NRSV translation reads as follows:

<To the leader: with stringed instruments. A Psalm. A Song.>

May God be gracious to us and bless us and make his face to shine upon us, Selah

2   that your way may be known upon earth, your saving power among all nations.

3   Let the peoples praise you, O God; let all the peoples praise you.

4   Let the nations be glad and sing for joy, for you judge the peoples with equity and guide the nations upon earth. Selah

5   Let the peoples praise you, O God; let all the peoples praise you.

6   The earth has yielded its increase; God, our God, has blessed us.

7   May God continue to bless us; let all the ends of the earth revere him.

---

34. David Wright, 'The Fallacies of Chiasmus: A Critique of Structures Proposed for the Covenant Collection (Exodus 20:23–23:19)', *ZABR* 10 (2004): 143–68.

35. Cf. Marvin E. Tate, *Psalms 51–100* (Dallas: Word, 1990), 155; Willem A. VanGemeren, *Psalms*, vol. 5 of *The Expositor's Bible Commentary: Revised Edition*, ed. Tremper Longman III and David E. Garland (Grand Rapids, MI: Zondervan, 2008), 510; John Goldingay, *Psalms 42–89* (Grand Rapids, MI: Baker Academic, 2007), 299.

In this translation, it is evident that v. 5 repeats v. 3; the word 'earth' appears in v. 2 and v. 6 (and v. 7); and the combination of words 'God' and 'bless us' are present in v. 1b and v. 7. It is not clear, however, that these are significant or self-evident proof of chiasmus: the word 'earth' that defines the chiasmus of vv. 2/6, also occurs in vv. 4 and 7; the combination of 'God' and 'bless' that defines the chiasmus of vv. 1/7 also occurs in v. 6.

The first point to make is that the verse division – which is part of its reception history – enhances the realization of the chiasmus. The Tiberian presentation of the psalm is as follows:

	לַמְנַצֵּחַ בִּנְגִינֹת מִזְמוֹר שִׁיר:	
	יָאֵר פָּנָיו אִתָּנוּ סֶלָה:	אֱלֹהִים יְחָנֵּנוּ וִיבָרְכֵנוּ	2
	בְּכָל־גּוֹיִם יְשׁוּעָתֶךָ:	לָדַעַת בָּאָרֶץ דַּרְכֶּךָ	3
	יוֹדוּךָ עַמִּים כֻּלָּם:	יוֹדוּךָ עַמִּים ׀ אֱלֹהִים	4
וּלְאֻמִּים ׀ בָּאָרֶץ תַּנְחֵם סֶלָה:	כִּי־תִשְׁפֹּט עַמִּים מִישׁוֹר	יִשְׂמְחוּ וִירַנְּנוּ לְאֻמִּים	5
	יוֹדוּךָ עַמִּים כֻּלָּם:	יוֹדוּךָ עַמִּים ׀ אֱלֹהִים	6
	יְבָרְכֵנוּ אֱלֹהִים אֱלֹהֵינוּ:	אֶרֶץ נָתְנָה יְבוּלָהּ	7
	וְיִירְאוּ אֹתוֹ כָּל־אַפְסֵי־אָרֶץ:	יְבָרְכֵנוּ אֱלֹהִים	8

In contrast to the NRSV, the Masoretic presentation is emphatically chiastic on four accounts. First, the title of the psalm has been presented as a separate verse. This presentation allows the parallelism between v. 2 and v. 8 to be seen more clearly (vv. 1b/7 in the NRSV). Second, v. 5 stands out as being presented in three stichs, whereas all the other verses are presented as two: this underlines its status as the fulcrum of the chiasmus. Third, the status of v. 5 as the fulcrum is further emphasized by an unusual *shalshelet gadol* accent where a *revia mugrash* accent would be expected (as per the second stich of vv. 3, 4, 6, 7 and 8). Fourth, the interjection *selah* added to vv. 2 and v. 5 aids the chiasmus. The *selah* of v. 2 extends the line by two syllables which helps it feel longer and so to better parallel the longer v. 8 (which, in turn, has been given two *maqqefim* to make it feel shorter). The *selah* of v. 5 is appropriate to its role as a fulcrum verse.

As the picture used in Volume 2 of Gillingham's commentary so powerfully shows, following the Masoretes, medieval Jewish scribes developed a scribal artistic tradition of presenting the words of Psalm 67 in the shape of a menorah with the words of v. 5 forming its central stem and base.

Figure 1.1. *BL Or. 14057/2, item 114. By permission of the British Library.*[36]

Summary and Conclusion

In this study we observed that reception history studies have helped many modern readers of the Hebrew Bible to recognize the validity of many diverse interpretations of one text. Reception history studies have also inspired modern readers to be more self-aware about their own interpretative biases. When issues of date, authorship and process of composition are uncertain, the line between reception history studies and the archaeological exploration of the 'original' background of a text blurs to extinction. Given that the dates of authorship and composition of all the books in the Hebrew Bible are uncertain, this means that it is both unprofitable and impossible to separate issues of reception history from

36. BL Or. 14057/1 and 14057/2 form a collection of 123 *shiviti-menorah* illustrations. The name *shiviti* refers to a verse in Ps. 16 ('I have set myself before the LORD') under which the words of Ps. 67 are presented as a menorah. This particularly fine example occurs on p. 364 of Gillingham 2018. It can be viewed on-line with other examples of shiviti-menorah at http://www.bl.uk/manuscripts/Viewer.aspx?ref=or_14057!2_f001r.

issues that relate to its date, authorship and composition. Furthermore, it is unclear if philological studies of the Hebrew Bible can be declared to be independent of reader-focused reception studies. Since we depend on the Tiberian Masoretes both for the text of the Hebrew Bible and for an understanding of Hebrew language, these philological approaches are also in reality inextricably intertwined with the reception history of the text of the Hebrew Bible up to the medieval period. As a result, only structural analyses can truly be declared to be independent of a text's reception history. Ironically, even then the value of this independence must be questioned. It is hard to claim a particular structure to be integral to the meaning of a text if the understanding consequent from this structure cannot also be shown to have impacted any of the prior readings of the text.

May the spreading vine continue to flourish!

Bibliography

Barton, John. 'Historical Criticism and Literary Interpretation: Is There Any Common Ground?'. Pages 3–15 in *Crossing the Boundaries: Essays in Biblical Studies in Honour of Michael D. Goulder*. Edited by Stanley E. Porter, Paul M. Joyce, and Davie E. Orton. BibInt 8. Leiden: Brill, 1994.

Barton, John. *The Old Testament: Canon, Literature and Theology: Collected Essays of John Barton*. SOTSMS. Aldershot: Ashgate, 2007.

Barton, John. *The Spirit and the Letter: Studies in the Biblical Canon*. London: SPCK, 1997.

Ceresko, Anthony R. 'The A:B:B:A Word Pattern in Hebrew and Northwest Semitic, with Special Reference to the Book of Job'. *UF* (1975): 73–88.

Ceresko, Anthony R. 'The Chiastic Word Pattern in Hebrew'. *CBQ* 38 (1976): 303–11.

Ceresko, Anthony R. 'The Function of Chiasmus in Hebrew Poetry'. *CBQ* 40 (1978): 1–10.

Clines, David J. A. *The Dictionary of Classical Hebrew*. 9 vols. Sheffield: Sheffield Phoenix, 1993–2016.

Craigie, Peter, 'Psalm 29 in the Hebrew Poetic Tradition'. *VT* 22 (1972): 143–51.

deSilva, David A. 'X Marks the Spot? A Critique of the Use of Chiasmus in Macro-Structural Analyses of Revelation'. *JSNT* 30 (2008): 343–71.

Dorsey, David A. *The Literary Structure of the Old Testament: A Commentary on Genesis–Malachi*. Grand Rapids, MI: Baker, 1999.

Dweck, Yaacob. *The Scandal of Kabbalah: Leon Modena, Jewish Mysticism, Early Modern Venice*. Princeton: Princeton University Press, 2011.

England, Emma, and William John Lyons, eds. *Reception History and Biblical Studies: Theory and Practice*. LHBOTS 615/Scriptural Traces 6. London: T&T Clark, 2015.

Gesenius, Wilhelm. *Gesenius' Hebrew Grammar*. Edited and Enlarged by E. Kautzsch. Translated by A. E. Cowley. Mineola: Dover, 2006.

Gillingham, Susan E. 'Biblical Studies on Holiday? A Personal View of Reception History'. Pages 17–30 in *Reception History and Biblical Studies: Theory and Practice*. Edited by Emma England and William John Lyons. LHBOTS 615/Scriptural Traces 6. London: T&T Clark, 2015.

Gillingham, Susan E. 'An Introduction to Reception History with Particular Reference to Psalm 1'. *Revue Des Sciences Religieuses* 85 (2011): 571–99.

Gillingham, Susan E. '"Like a bridegroom" and "like a strong man": The Reception of Two Similes in Psalm 19:5'. Pages 41–54 in *Fromme und Frevler Studien zu Psalmen und Weisheit: Festschrift für Hermann Spieckermann zum 70 Geburtstag*. Edited by C. Körting and R. G. Kratz. Tübingen: Mohr Siebeck, 2020.

Gillingham, Susan E. *One Bible, Many Voices: Different Approaches to Biblical Studies*. London: SPCK, 1998.

Gillingham, Susan E. 'Psalm 8 Through the Looking Glass: Reception History of a Multifaceted Psalm'. Pages 167–96 in *Diachronic and Synchronic: Reading the Psalms in Real Time: Proceedings of the Baylor Symposium on the Book of Psalms*. Edited by Joel S. Burnett, W. H. Bellinger Jr., W. Dennis Tucker Jr. London: T&T Clark International, 2008.

Gillingham, Susan E. 'Psalms 105 and 106 and the Participation in History through Liturgy'. *HBAI* 4 (2015): 450–75.

Gillingham, Susan E. *Psalms Through the Centuries*. 2 vols. Wiley Blackwell Bible Commentaries. Chichester: Wiley-Blackwell, 2008/2018.

Gillingham, Susan E. 'The Reception of Psalm 137 in Jewish and Christian Tradition'. Pages 64–82 in *Jewish and Christian Approaches to the Psalms: Conflict and Convergence*. Edited by Susan E. Gillingham. Oxford: Oxford University Press, 2015.

Goldingay, John. *Psalms*. Vol. 2, *Psalms 42–89*. Grand Rapids, MI: Baker Academic, 2007.

Harding, James E. 'What Is Reception History, and What Happens to You If You Do It?'. Pages 31–44 in *Reception History and Biblical Studies: Theory and Practice*. Edited by Emma England and William John Lyons. LHBOTS 615/Scriptural Traces 6. London: T&T Clark, 2015.

Hill, R. C. *Theodore of Mopsuestia, Commentary on Psalms 1–81*. Atlanta: SBL, 2006.

Joüon, Paul, and T. Muraoka. *A Grammar of Biblical Hebrew*. 2nd ed. SubBib 27. Rome: Gregorian & Biblical, 2009.

Joyce, Paul M., and Diana Lipton. *Lamentations through the Centuries*. Wiley-Blackwell Bible Commentaries. Chichester: John Wiley, 2013.

Khan, Geoffrey, ed. *Encyclopedia of Hebrew Language and Linguistics*. 4 vols. Leiden: Brill, 2013.

Körting, C., and R. G. Kratz, eds. *Neuere Forschung zu Psalmen und Weisheit in Israel und dem Alten Orient*. Forschungen zum Alten Testament. Tübingen: Mohr Siebeck, 2020.

Lowth, Robert. *De Sacra Poesi Hebræorum Prælectiones Academicæ Oxonii Habitæ. Subjicitur Metricæ Harianæ Brevis Confutatio: Et Oratio Grewiana*. Oxford: Clarendon, 1753.

Lowth, Robert. *De Sacra Poesi Hebraeorum: Praelectiones Academicae Oxonii Habitae*. Translated by David A. Reibel. London: Routledge/Thoemmes, 1995.

Lowth, Robert. *Lectures on the Sacred Poetry of the Hebrews* Translated by G. Gregory. London: Thomas Tegg & Son, 1787.

Lund, Nils. *Chiasmus in the New Testament*. Chapel Hill: University of North Carolina Press, 1942.

Meynet, Roland. *Rhetorical Analysis: An Introduction to Biblical Rhetoric*. JSOTSup 256. Sheffield: Sheffield Academic, 1998.

Palmer, David G. *Sliced Bread: The Four Gospels, Acts and Revelation, Their Literary Structures*. Cardiff: Ceridwen, 1988.

Pecklers, Keith F. *Dynamic Equivalence: The Living Language of Christian Worship*. Collegeville: Liturgical Press, 2003.
Reid, W. Stanford. 'The Battle Hymns of the Lord: Calvinist Psalmody of the Sixteenth Century'. *Sixteenth Century Essays and Studies* 2 (1971): 36–54.
Roberts, Jonathan. 'Introduction'. Pages 1–8 in *The Oxford Handbook of the Reception History of the Bible*. Edited by Michael Lieb, Emma Mason and Jonathan Roberts. Oxford: Oxford University Press, 2011.
Sawyer, John F. *Isaiah through the Centuries*. Wiley-Blackwell Bible Commentaries. Chichester: John Wiley & Sons, 2018.
Scholem, Gershom. *Major Trends in Jewish Mysticism*. New York: Schocken, 1995.
Sherwood, Yvonne. *A Biblical Text and its Afterlives: The Survival of Jonah in Western Culture*. Cambridge: Cambridge University Press, 2000.
Talmage, Frank E. 'Apples of Gold: The Inner Meaning of Sacred Texts in Medieval Judaism'. Pages 312–55 in *Jewish Spirituality: From the Bible through the Middle Ages*. Edited by A. Green. London: Routledge & Kegan Paul, 1986.
Tate, Marvin E. *Psalms 51–100*. WBC 20. Dallas: Word, 1990.
Ulrich, Eugene. 'The Old Testament Text and Its Transmission'. Pages 83–104 in *From the Beginnings to 600*. Edited by James Carleton Paget and Joachim Schaper. Vol. 1 of *The New Cambridge History of the Bible*. Cambridge: Cambridge University Press, 2013.
Ulrich, Eugene. *The Dead Sea Scrolls and the Developmental Composition of the Bible*. VTSup 169. Leiden: Brill, 2015.
VanGemeren, Willem A. *The Expositor's Bible Commentary: Revised Edition. Vol. 5. Psalms*. Edited by Tremper Longman III and David E. Garland. Grand Rapids, MI: Zondervan, 2008.
Watson, J. R. 'The Hymns of Isaac Watts and the Tradition of Dissent'. Pages 49–67 in *Dissenting Praise: Religious Dissent and the Hymn in England and Wales*. Edited by Isabel Rivers and David L. Wykes. Oxford: Oxford University Press, 2011.
Wright, David. 'The Fallacies of Chiasmus: A Critique of Structures Proposed for the Covenant Collection (Exodus 20:23–23:19)'. *ZABR* 10 (2004): 143–68.

WHO'S KISSING WHO?
REFLECTIONS ON PSALM 2.11-12

H. G. M. Williamson

In her landmark reception-historical study of Psalms 1 and 2, Sue Gillingham gives attention to the treatment of Ps. 2.11-12 in the Septuagint and some other early Jewish and Christian sources, but it goes beyond her purpose to deal with the problems of the received Hebrew text as such.[1] Since I dare not suppose that I can add anything to her knowledge of the reception of these verses in general, I hope she will accept as a token of friendship and valued collegial collaboration over very many years this modest supplement to her presentation. After all, the history of text-critical research is its own, albeit narrow, form of reception history within the academy.

The question has long been debated whether textual criticism is an art or a science. The answer is that it is both. On the one hand, there are large quantities of empirical data that have to be collected and evaluated on the basis of well-established rules and principles. To that extent the technical sense of criticism is wholly appropriate. On the other hand, however, we are treating stages in the transmission of a text by human beings over a very long period of time, and this renders it subject to a myriad of foibles and weaknesses which cannot be predicted. From that perspective the use of imagination is also required, governed by whatever we can gather of the prevailing cultures at the time of composition and subsequently. Both these aspects of critical imagination are illustrated

---

1. S. Gillingham, *A Journey of Two Psalms: The Reception of Psalms 1 and 2 in Jewish and Christian Tradition* (Oxford: Oxford University Press, 2013). She adopts a comparable approach in her *A Reception History Commentary on Psalms 1–72*, vol. 2 of *Psalms Through the Centuries*, Wiley Blackwell Bible Commentaries (Chichester: Wiley-Blackwell, 2018), 25–43.

in the present test case. An attractive emendation was challenged long ago by a distinguished Oxford scholar whom both Sue and I admire. He pointed out a grammatical problem which looks like a strong objection to the emendation even though it has not been generally noted by subsequent commentators, perhaps because it was published in a lay-orientated book. The suggestion will be made here in response that an imaginative use of iconography and consideration of idiom can help overcome this otherwise strong critical argument.

The Masoretic text, excluding the very last clause of v. 12,[2] reads:

עבדו את־יהוה ביראה וגילו ברעדה
נשקו־בר פן־יאנף ותאבדו דרך כי־יבער כמעט אפו

and this is translated in the Revised Version as:

Serve the Lord with fear, and rejoice with trembling.
Kiss the son, lest he be angry, and ye perish in the way, for his wrath will soon be kindled.

These words are the conclusion of an address to the leaders of rebellious nations who are plotting to overthrow the rule of God's anointed king (presumably Davidic) on Mount Zion. This begins at the latest in v. 10 with an admonition whose speaker is not specified. Given that God is referred to in the third person in v. 11, it is presumably either the king himself or an anonymous figure whom we might most simply identify with the Psalmist (at least in the guise of a literary persona). To some extent a decision will depend on whether the king is also referred to in the third person at the start of v. 12. Commentators have long noted two difficulties with this text, and there is a third which, in my opinion, is equally significant, though it is less often included.[3]

The first difficulty is the awkward combination of 'rejoice' and 'trembling'. The usual explanation is that 'trembling' should here be

---

2. This clause is not directly relevant to my immediate text-critical purpose. It is one of several close links between Pss. 1 and 2 (which also include, of course, the reference to 'perishing in the way' in the previous line and Ps. 1.6); for an exhaustive survey of studies on this, see R. L. Cole, *Psalms 1–2: Gateway to the Psalter*, Hebrew Bible Monographs 37 (Sheffield: Sheffield Phoenix, 2013), 1–45.

3. Some commentators (especially in the early twentieth century) also argued from their understanding of poetic metre or the like that the text must be corrupt. Uncertainties about such factors mean that this should not be taken into consideration as determinative.

understood in the sense of reverence and awe in the presence of God,[4] as the parallel 'fear' can certainly be construed, but this is not attested anywhere else as being included within the semantic range of the word (Isa. 33.14; Ps. 48.7; Job 4.14; the same applies to the verb and one other noun related to the same root).[5] Thus, while one might be prepared to accept this anomaly as an unexpected quirk if it were the only difficulty in the verses in question, it is certainly sufficient to raise an initial question mark.

Second, it has long been noted that the use of the Aramaic word for 'son' (בר) at the start of v. 12 is unexpected, not least because the Hebrew word (בן) is used previously (with a suffix) in v. 7.[6] There have been two attempted explanations. Delitzsch offered the suggestion that it was an attempt to avoid the dissonance of בן פן[7] – unconvincing because the problem could easily have been avoided in other ways, such as the use of בנו rather than just בן. The more usual explanation is that in an address to foreign rulers the poet thought it appropriate to use a well-known foreign word.[8] This does not explain, however, why this single lexeme was selected for this treatment,[9] and it should further be noted, as we shall

---

4. E.g. A. F. Kirkpatrick, *The Book of Psalms with Introduction and Notes*, CBSC (Cambridge: Cambridge University Press, 1902), 11; see most recently F. Hartenstein in F. Hartenstein and B. Janowski, *Psalmen*, BKAT 15.1, Lieferungen 1–2 (Neukirchen-Vluyn: Neukirchener Verlag, 2015), 116–17, with particular attention to the context of an address to foreign rulers.

5. I am not aware of any detailed study of רעד and its derivatives, though the few remarks of M. V. van Pelt and W. C. Kaiser, *NIDOTTE* 3:1138, are fully in line with what I have written above: 'a condition of such immense terror as to produce physical trembling' (curiously, they make no reference to our verse in their entry).

6. It is also used in a Hebrew language setting at Prov. 31.2, though it has been suggested that 31.1-7 'bears the marks of extra-Israelite provenance' (see too מלכין in v. 3), W. McKane, *Proverbs: A New Approach*, OTL (London: SCM, 1970), 407. If so, it is scarcely a significant parallel.

7. F. Delitzsch, *Commentar über den Psalter*, 4th ed. (Leipzig: Dörffling & Franke, 1883), 79.

8. E.g. P. C. Craigie, *Psalms 1–50*, WBC 19 (Waco: Word, 1983), 64, though this argument has a much older pedigree; see, for instance, W. E. Barnes, 'The Text of Psalm ii 12', *JTS* 18 (1917): 24–9. See also more recently A. P. Ross, *A Commentary on the Psalms, Vol. 1*, Kregel Exegetical Library (Grand Rapids: Kregel, 2011), 198–9 and 212.

9. Admittedly, F. Baethgen, *Die Psalmen*, HAT 2/2 (Göttingen: Vandenhoeck & Ruprecht, 1897), 7, reminds the reader of the use of the apparently Aramaic spelling of the verb רעע in place of the expected Hebrew רצץ in v. 9, though that is not part of the address to the foreign rulers.

see, that it was not recognized in the earliest versions. The use of בר thus remains a problem.[10]

Third, in the text as it stands the subject of the clauses following 'lest' ought to be the 'son' at the start of the verse whereas it is universally and correctly identified otherwise as God. This less frequently discussed problem would have to be explained away as a syntactic anomaly whereby the subject is implied as carried over from v. 11 and that this is permissible given the obvious purport of the verbs in the line.

There are thus three problems with our verses. I agree that one or another might be tolerated with an element of good will if it stood alone, but three together in such a short space is enough to arouse suspicion in most commentators' minds that something has gone wrong with the text here.

Responses vary. One small group of commentators look for guidance to one or another of the ancient versions, not least because they all seem to be working on the basis of the present consonantal text.[11] Only P (and later Ibn Ezra) renders 'kiss the son', however. A few of them, such as certainly Symmachus and Jerome (in the *Psalterium iuxta Hebraeos*), and perhaps others as well, construed the challenging בר as the adjective בר meaning 'pure, clean', which has then, unusually, to be understood adverbially. This is either thought to qualify 'kiss' as part of a liturgical act, which has the disadvantage of not providing the transitive verb with

---

10. I note here, but do not consider it worth taking further, the possibility raised by S. Olofsson, 'The Crux Interpretum in Ps 2,11', *SJOT* 9 (1995): 185–99, that בר = 'open field' (as in Job 39.4), and that 'kissing the field' was an expression of homage (he fails to note that this is a relatively old suggestion, mentioned by several other scholars, starting with P. Haupt, 'The Poetic Form of the First Psalm', *AJSL* 19 [1903]: 129–42, cf. esp. p. 134). But as the Akkadian parallel cited (*našāqu qaqqaru*) shows, the idiom needs to state 'in the presence of PN' or equivalent in order to make sense; see *CAD* 11, 58.

11. This applies even to LXX and T, despite initial appearances; see the discussions in G. J. Norton, 'Psalm 2:11-12 and Modern Textual Criticism', *PIBA* 15 (1992): 89–111, and A. Pietersma, 'Empire Re-affirmed: A Commentary on Greek Psalm 2', in vol. 2 of *God's Word for our World: Theological and Cultural Studies in Honor of Simon John De Vries*, ed. J. H. Ellens et al., JSOTSup 389 (London: T&T Clark International, 2004), 46–62. Many suggestions have been made in the past as to a possible different Hebrew *Vorlage* that the LXX may have been working with; they have been most fully surveyed and discussed by Olofsson, 'The Crux Interpretum in Ps 2,11' (and he adds a further suggestion of his own), but these need be no longer entertained. Still less should we ourselves emend the text on this basis (e.g. C. A. Briggs and E. G. Briggs, *A Critical and Exegetical Commentary on the Book of Psalms, vol. 1*, ICC [Edinburgh: T. & T. Clark, 1906], 23–4).

an object, or is linked with a homonymous verb נשק, meaning 'submit', hence 'submit sincerely'.[12] This proposed meaning of the verb is far from certain, however, as will be noted further below.

Second, there are those who follow the 'philological' method of suggesting different meanings for otherwise familiar Hebrew words. The most ambitious is the article by Macintosh, whose arguments are too long and detailed to be fully summarized here.[13] The upshot is that first he proposes a different meaning for גיל. Along with some others back to at least medieval times, he proposes on the basis of Arabic evidence (root meaning: 'emotional or mental excitement') that, on the *'aḍdād* principle,[14] it may mean not only 'rejoice' but also its opposite, 'shew fear' or the like. Hosea 10.5 and Job 3.22 are cited as possible examples of the same meaning, though equally this is denied by others.[15] For the first two words of v. 12, Macintosh compares Gen. 41.40 and Arabic *nasaqa* to argue for the sense 'order oneself properly'. He then has to argue that בר should be deleted, perhaps as a mistaken dittograph of part of ברעדה.

In my opinion, for all the learning displayed in this article, it is eventually unconvincing because (i) the requirement conjecturally to delete בר in order then to fit the text to a solution based on a philological approach is weak from the point of view of method and unsupported by any evidence whatsoever; and (ii) it is suspicious that two common words in Hebrew in close juxtaposition with one another have both to be differently explained in ways which are in any case not certain. The case of גיל is the less difficult of the two, and on its own it might be possible to accept the proposal (which, as Macintosh documents, has a very ancient pedigree). However, it does not on its own solve all the problems of this passage, so that judgment should be suspended until we see if a different approach offers a more comprehensive solution.

The case of נשק is more challenging. Alongside a common verb meaning 'kiss', several other verbal roots have been proposed over the years. A second root, of far less frequent occurrence, has long been

---

12. So, for instance, J. Goldingay, *Psalms, 1: Psalms 1–41* (Grand Rapids: Baker, 2006), 93–4.

13. A. A. Macintosh, 'A Consideration of the Problems Presented by Psalm ii. 11 and 12', *JTS* NS 27 (1976): 1–14. On גיל, see also J. Reider, 'Contributions to the Scriptural Text', *HUCA* 24 (1952–53): 85–106 (esp. pp. 98–9).

14. For discussion, see J. Barr, *Comparative Philology and the Text of the Old Testament* (Oxford: Oxford University Press, 1968), 173–7. Without denying that this happens, he cautions that it is far from as frequent as has sometimes been implied.

15. See, for instance, D. J. A. Clines, *Job 1–20*, WBC 17 (Dallas: Word, 1989), 74.

recognized as meaning something like 'equipped with'; this too is included in all the major Biblical Hebrew dictionaries.¹⁶ Given that it is also related with Arabic *nasaqa*, it is curious that Macintosh does not include this in his discussion, if only to justify the proposed semantic range of the root. Equally, the meaning that Goldingay appeals to (noted above) is a development of a meaning that was first proposed by Driver in connection with Ezek. 3.13,¹⁷ though Driver did not favour it for our present verse, where he in fact wanted to emend בר to גבור, as also retained later in the NEB.¹⁸ The specific basis of this proposal has not attracted widespread support,¹⁹ and in fact it is only one of five possible roots listed in *DCH* (to which Goldingay appeals). *DCH*'s policy is to list all roots that have been suggested over the years without usually seeking to indicate which is to be preferred. In many cases they are mutually exclusive, so that the dictionary user has to choose which is to be preferred on other grounds. In the present instance it is not clear that these favour the proposal, not least because it is probable that we should combine Driver's approach with the second root ('be in order' *vel sim.*)²⁰ rather than postulate a third, so that the extension to the sense 'submit' (as assumed by both Macintosh

---

16. L. Sabottka, 'Ps 2,12: "Küsst den Sohn!"?', *Biblica* 87 (2006): 96–7, proposes that the verb is a privative *piel* of this second root, 'get disarmed', and that ב בר is used adverbially, 'sincerely'. Apart from the fact that this does not seem very plausible, it also suffers the defect of not addressing the difficulty in the preceding clause.

17. G. R. Driver, 'Ezekiel: Linguistic and Textual Problems', *Biblica* 35 (1954): 145–59 (esp. p. 147), though his proposal there is that the word must mean something like 'maintaining order' or 'keeping in line', which is not quite the way Goldingay uses it in relation to Ps. 2.12.

18. G. R. Driver, 'Difficult Words in the Hebrew Prophets', in *Studies in Old Testament Prophecy Presented to Professor Theodore H. Robinson*, ed. H. H. Rowley (Edinburgh: T. & T. Clark, 1950), 52–72 (esp. pp. 55–6); L. H. Brockington, *The Hebrew Text of the Old Testament: The Readings Adopted by the Translators of the New English Bible* (Oxford: Oxford University Press; Cambridge: Cambridge University Press, 1973), 120.

19. See, for instance, D. I. Block, *The Book of Ezekiel Chapters 1–24*, NICOT (Grand Rapids: Eerdmans, 1997), 132. It is ignored by W. Zimmerli, *Ezechiel 1: Ezechiel 1–24*, BKAT 13/1 (Neukirchen-Vluyn: Neukirchener Verlag, 1969), and M. Greenberg, *Ezekiel 1–20: A New Translation with Introduction and Commentary*, AB 22 (Garden City: Doubleday, 1983), 71. Ges¹⁸ also still includes it under the first root.

20. L. C. Allen, *Ezekiel 1–19*, WBC 28 (Dallas: Word, 1994), 13. *HAL* includes Ezek. 3.13 under the widely acknowledged second root. The etymological uncertainties are acknowledged also by L. Kopf, 'Arabische Etymologien und Parallelen zum Bibelwörterbuch', *VT* 9 (1959): 247–87 (esp. pp. 265–7), and by K. M. Beyse, *ThWAT* 5:676–80; consequently they both express the need for caution.

and Goldingay) is not supported. Given these uncertainties and the fact that Macintosh's approach in particular is rendered very doubtful by its inability to explain the presence of בר, and equally that Goldingay does not explain how 'pure' in the sense of 'clean' can here have the differently developed meaning of 'sincere', the so-called philological approach to the problems in our passage does not lead to a convincing outcome.

The third and most common response has been to propose a conjectural emendation. Several of the older commentaries each suggest one[21] (unless they simply delete נשקו־בר as a gloss[22]), but they all suffer from the disadvantage that they may treat one of the problems we have noted but do not solve the others as well. The same problem confronts more recent proposals[23] in addition to other questions that they raise. Thus, for instance, the rather wild reconstruction of v. 12a as תנו לשמו כבד by Morgenstern does not solve the problem at the end of v. 11,[24] and the same applies to Holladay's development of a suggestion by Dahood to read נשי קבר, 'you who forget the grave'.[25] Equally, we may dismiss as simply too far removed from textual probability the conjecture of Robinson to read וגלו ברעדה נשק ברזל, 'and remove with trembling weapons of iron'.[26]

21. To the commentaries we may also add the rather wild speculations of J. D. Prince, 'Notes on Psalm ii. 11-12 and on אֶרֶן, Isaiah xliv. 14', *JBL* 19 (1900): 1–4.

22. This is one possibility considered by B. Duhm, *Die Psalmen*, KHAT 14 (Freiburg: J. C. B. Mohr [Paul Siebeck], 1899), 10, following G. Bickell, *Dichtungen der Hebräer*, vol. 3: *Der Psalter* (Innsbruck: Wagner, 1883), 3 (a translation 'zum erstenmale nach dem Versmaße des Urtextes übersetzt', without any commentary or notes), and it is affirmed by T. K. Cheyne, *The Book of Psalms* (London: Kegan Paul, Trench, Trübner, 1904), 8; see more recently A. Deissler, 'Zum Problem der Messianität von Psalm 2', in *De la Tôrah au Messie: Mélanges Henri Cazelles*, ed. M. Carrez, J. Doré, and P. Grelot (Paris: Desclée, 1981), 283–92 (cf. esp. p. 286), and J. Vermeylen, *Jérusalem centre du monde: développements et contestations d'une tradition biblique*, Lectio Divina (Paris: Cerf, 2007), 80.

23. An exception here is I. Sonne, 'The Second Psalm', *HUCA* 19 (1945–46): 43–55, but his conjecture to read the end of v. 11 and the beginning of v. 12 as ולו ברעדה תשחוו (even with appeal to similarity of various letters in what he calls the 'old Aramaic alphabet') exceeds the bounds of plausibility.

24. J. Morgenstern, 'משקו־בר', *JQR* 32 (1942): 371–85.

25. W. L. Holladay, 'A New Proposal for the Crux in Psalm ii 12', *VT* 28 (1978): 110–12. In his commentary, *Psalms I, 1–50: Introduction, Translation, and Notes*, AB 16 (Garden City: Doubleday, 1965), 13, M. J. Dahood had thought that the first word was the construct plural of נשים, which he postulated was an alternative for אנשים, hence 'O mortal men' (literally, 'men of the grave').

26. A. Robinson, 'Deliberate but Misguided Haplography Explains Psalm 2 11-12', *ZAW* 89 (1977): 421–2.

For these reasons, by far the most widely adopted emendation is that usually ascribed to Bertholet,[27] even though, as he subsequently acknowledged, its most important element had been separately suggested before him by Sievers.[28] His suggestion was quite simply to postulate that נשקו־בר and וגילו ברעדה had mistakenly become inverted, so that we should restore ונשקו ברגליו ברעדה, 'and kiss his feet with trembling'. He drew attention to examples of this expression of obeisance in Akkadian texts.

The first advantage of this proposal is that it neatly deals with all three difficulties in the MT which I set out at the start of this discussion. Second, it keeps all the consonants in their present order (vowel letters are excluded from this exercise, of course), barring the postulation that the two halves of the clause had become inverted. And third, it refers to a well-attested gesture which seems eminently suitable to the context.[29] In addition to the textual sources I should add that on the Black Obelisk of Shalmaneser III there is an image of Sua of Gilzanu actually kissing the king's feet whereas Jehu of Israel is shown in a similar prostrate position but slightly in front of, and not touching, the king's feet.[30] However this difference is to be explained (see further below; note that both gestures are well attested as distinct in Akkadian[31]), and indeed, however uncertain the

27. A. Bertholet, 'Eine crux interpretum. Ps 2 11f.', *ZAW* 28 (1908): 58–9.

28. E. Sievers, 'Psalm 2', *ZDMG* 58 (1904): 864–6; A. Bertholet, 'Nochmals zu Ps 2 11f.', *ZAW* 28 (1908): 193. Unmentioned there is the fact that the emendation in a form even closer to that reached by Bertholet was also considered by M. J. Lagrange, 'Notes sur le messianisme dans les Psaumes', *RB* 2 (1905): 39–57 (esp. p. 40 n. 6). Note too that H. Zimmern was recorded in the 'Berichtigungen und Nachträgen' to the 14th edition of Gesenius's *Handwörterbuch* (Leipzig: Vogel, 1905), xiv, as anticipating the emendation advocated by Bertholet with reference to its Akkadian parallel.

29. Arguments based on literary structure (chiasmus between vv. 3 and 10–11) are surely a consequence of accepting the emendation rather than an independent argument in its favour, as suggested by P. Auffret, *The Literary Structure of Psalm 2*, JSOTSup 3 (Sheffield: JSOT, 1977), 38 n. 14 (cf. also p. 35 n. 2). Note that Cole, *Psalms 1–2*, 130–6, cites 'literary evidence' in support of MT!

30. For a translation of the relevant part of the text on the obelisk, see K. L. Younger in *CoS* 2:269–70.

31. *CAD* 11:58. Many texts citing each form of obeisance, including in the divine realm, are set out in M. I. Gruber, *Aspects of Nonverbal Communication in the Ancient Near East*, Studia Pohl 12/1 (Rome: Biblical Institute, 1980), 257–78; see too S. D. Sperling, 'A Study of Psalm 2', *UF* 43 (2011): 435–45 (esp. pp. 443–4). The gesture of kissing the ground in front of somebody is the closest parallel to the Biblical 'licking the dust': Isa. 49.23; Mic. 7.17; Ps. 72.9; Lam. 3.29; see Gruber,

recovery of 'history' from this carefully contrived monument as a whole may be,³² it serves as clear visual testimony to the gesture to which the texts also make reference.

Why, then, have others rejected this elegant solution, and how strong are their arguments? In the first place, some object to the anthropomorphism implied. In his article Macintosh says that 'to introduce so gross an anthropomorphism is implausible' (p. 13), while elsewhere he and others have stated that 'kissing God's feet...is plainly preposterous'.³³ Others argue comparably, if less stridently.³⁴ I fail to see the force of this objection. All language about God is necessarily anthropomorphic. To go no further than this very Psalm, God laughs, holds his enemies in derision, speaks, terrifies, becomes angry, and even 'begets' a son. In the Assyrian empire, at least, kissing God's feet was enacted in cultic settings in relation to idols.³⁵ The application of a human act of obeisance to the religious realm is fully in line with all forms of divine metaphor,³⁶ and in Hebrew texts similarly 'gross' anthropomorphic expressions have also survived and are not questioned on that ground, e.g. לחם אלהים (Lev. 21.6, 8, 17, 21, 22; 22.25). Although it is true, as some commentators stress, that the idiom is not attested elsewhere in the Hebrew Bible, there does not seem to be any reason why such a figure could not have been used by the psalmist.

Aspects, 285–91. No instance uses the verb 'to kiss', however, and only the Isaiah passage mentions feet. Although sometimes cited in relation to the conjecture on Ps. 2.12, these verses are therefore not a strict parallel.

32. See the brilliant analysis by C. Uehlinger as a case study in the course of his essay 'Neither Eyewitnesses, Nor Windows to the Past, but Valuable Testimony in its Own Right: Remarks on Iconography, Source Criticism and Ancient Data-processing', in *Understanding the History of Ancient Israel*, ed. H. G. M. Williamson, Proceedings of the British Academy 143 (Oxford: Oxford University Press, 2007), 173–228 (esp. pp. 201–10).

33. J. Emerton, D. Frost, and A. Macintosh, *'A Daft Text': The Psalter 1998* (Cambridge: Aquila, 1999), 15.

34. See, for instance, C. Vang, 'Ps 2,11-12: A New Look at an Old Crux Interpretum', *SJOT* 9 (1995): 163–84. He proceeds then to defend the present text as traditionally understood.

35. A. Berlejung, 'Kultische Küsse: Zu den Begegnungsformen zwischen Göttern und Menschen', *WO* 29 (1998): 80–97.

36. M. Brettler, *God is King: Understanding an Israelite Metaphor*, JSOTSup 76 (Sheffield: Sheffield Academic, 1989). Brettler does not include a discussion of our present idiom.

A second objection to the conjecture is that it is too 'radical' (or similar adjectives) in its departure from the MT.³⁷ That is certainly an objection that might be applied to some conjectural emendations that have even been made for this present passage. Again, in the case of this proposal, however, this objection is not valid. All that is suggested is that the two halves of the clause became inverted. Precisely how or why this happened cannot be determined with certainty, but perhaps by way of confusion between the repeated consonants ב and ר one half was accidentally omitted in the process of copying and then added in above the line as a correction. A later copyist then misunderstood where the supralinear element should be put back, so giving rise to the present text.³⁸ The inversion of textual elements in the Hebrew Bible is far from unparalleled. On the basis of parallel passages, manuscript evidence, and the like, Delitzsch pointed out long ago a considerable number of word and phrase inversions.³⁹ Since then, the evidence for this has been strongly reinforced by the biblical texts among the Dead Sea Scrolls, which show how often a word or more could be omitted and then copied back in supralinearly, while equally they include some examples where the order differs from MT.⁴⁰

The third objection is far more interesting than the first two. So far as I know it was first noted in an otherwise completely overlooked publication by the Oxford scholar S. R. Driver, though a few others have made the same observation since.⁴¹ Equally, however, it is interesting how many commentators appear unaware of the difficulty, and I have to admit that it had not occurred to me either until I was reading everything that Driver had written on the Psalms.⁴² Surveying the various proposals for the solution

37. E.g. N. deClaissé-Walford, R. A. Jacobson, and B. L. Tanner, *The Book of Psalms*, NICOT (Grand Rapids: Eerdmans, 2014), 67.

38. A rather more complicated, and therefore less attractive, suggestion about the textual history at this point (which nevertheless includes a way of eliminating the ב before רגלי) was advanced by R. Köbert, 'Zur ursprünglichen Textform von Ps 2,11. 12a', *Biblica* 21 (1940): 426–8.

39. F. Delitzsch, *Die Lese- und Schreibfehler im alten Testament* (Berlin: de Gruyter, 1920), 91–3. I, in fact, drew attention to this long ago when making a similar proposal in a different passage; see 'Word Order in Isaiah xliii. 12', *JTS* NS 30 (1979): 499–502.

40. E. Tov, *Textual Criticism of the Hebrew Bible*, 3rd ed. (Minneapolis: Fortress, 2012), 239, gives one or two examples.

41. See recently, for example, D. Barthélemy, *Critique textuelle de l'Ancien Testament*, 4: *Psaumes*, ed. S. D. Ryan and A. Schenker, OBO 50/4 (Fribourg: Academic Press; Göttingen: Vandenhoeck & Ruprecht, 2005), 5.

42. Driver's work on the Psalms has not usually been considered in scholarly circles because it nearly all appeared in works written for lay and church readerships.

of the problems in these verses, Driver comments briefly on what he calls an 'ingenious suggestion' that 'it is an objection to Bertholet's suggestion, not met by the parallels cited by him (נגע, דבק, אחז construed with ב), that נשק is construed often with ל (as well as with an accus.), but never with ב'.[43] Driver also notes that the expression does not occur elsewhere in Hebrew and he cautiously doubts that 'such an anthropomorphism would be used by a worshipper of Yahweh in Israel' (p. 66). His conclusion is that although the received text is not above suspicion, none of the alternatives is free from objection either. The question, then, is whether Driver's grammatico-syntactical observation is fatal to the proposal.

One of the first to pass comment was Gunkel, who simply proposed emending the preposition ב to ל as 'besser' (without explanation why).[44] This has been taken up by quite a number since, including *BHS*. It has to be said against this, however, that despite the strong advocacy of Closen,[45] ל is the letter of the Hebrew alphabet least likely to be miscopied because uniquely it rises above the line.[46] Equally, the occasional suggestion simply to delete the preposition as a scribal mistake (perhaps because of the first two letters of ברעדה) is unwarranted. The question is whether this unparalleled use of נשק + ב can be tolerated.

Since I cannot see any help with this from cognate languages, I propose instead that the unparalleled use of the preposition is linked to the unparalleled force of the verb in this idiom. Taking the most generous line of attribution to נשק I (i.e. discounting all suggestions of possible roots III, IV, and V simply for the sake of the argument at this point), there are 31

For a survey, see my article 'S. R. Driver on the Psalms', in *Fromme und Frevler: Studien zu Psalmen und Weisheit. Festschrift für Hermann Spieckermann zum 70. Geburtstag*, ed. C. Körting and R. G. Kratz (Tübingen: Mohr Siebeck, 2020), 303–15.

43. This was included in the text of a course of lectures on 'The Method of Studying the Psalter, with Special Application to Some of the Messianic Psalms', which Driver delivered to the Oxford clergy in 1908 and revised for the Oxford Summer School in 1909. This particular lecture was first published in *The Expositor*, 7th series, 9.1 (1910): 20–41 (see especially pp. 34–7). The lectures were republished posthumously, together with a number of sermons on individual Psalms and other work, at Driver's request by C. F. Burney in S. R. Driver, *Studies in the Psalms* (London: Hodder & Stoughton, 1915); see especially pp. 60–6.

44. H. Gunkel, *Die Psalmen*, Göttinger Handkommentar zum Alten Testament (Göttingen: Vandenhoeck & Ruprecht, 1926), 12.

45. G. E. Closen, 'Gedanken zur Textkritik von Ps 2,11b + 12a', *Biblica* 21 (1940): 288–309.

46. Among all the certainly attested confusions of letters that Delitzsch, *Die Lese- und Schreibfehler*, documents, virtually none that I can see ever involves a ל. The few suggestions on p. 117 are themselves not above question.

occurrences in the Hebrew Bible – 25 *qal*, 5 *piel* (including our present verse), and one *hiphil*. In the large majority of cases the object is introduced by ל (21 times), while four times we find the use of a verbal suffix. Only in two or three cases is there a direct accusative: 1 Sam. 20.41, in reference to reciprocal kissing between David and Jonathan (איש את־ רעהו), Hos. 13.2, people kissing calves (idols) without את, and probably the rather allusive Prov. 24.26[47] (again without את). In Ps. 85.11 the *qal* seems unusually to be used reciprocally without any object expressed, and at Ezek. 3.13 the *hiphil* is used with אל.

Thus only once do we have the object introduced by את, and that is probably to be explained as due to the standard idiom for reciprocity. Given that a verbal suffix can be used for an object otherwise introduced by a preposition, and as the other examples without ל are in poetry, where unmodified objects can be used, this means that, against what is usually stated, there is effectively no evidence of any weight to suggest that the verb can govern a direct accusative object. The object of נשק in Biblical Hebrew is always introduced by ל or an acceptable substitute except in one or two exceptional circumstances, for which alternative explanations lie readily to hand.

In terms of semantic usage, נשק is used primarily, of course, to express love in romantic, kinship, or friendship relationships. In addition it can be used as a term implying veneration in both secular and religious contexts.[48] Most of these are obviously far removed from the sphere of kissing feet in obeisance, but one or two have sometimes been drawn in for comparison, and these should be briefly considered.

In Exod. 18.7 Moses prostrates himself before Jethro his father-in-law and then kisses him, but this is clearly a mark of respect for a senior

---

47. See R. N. Whybray, *Proverbs*, NCBC (London: Marshall Pickering, 1994), 354.

48. In addition to the dictionaries, see the survey by K.-M. Beyse, *ThWAT* 5:676–80 (and more briefly C. J. Collins, *NIDOTTE* 3:196–7). Technical uses in specific instances have been suggested by A. Avioz, 'Why Did Joseph Kiss his Father (Genesis 50,1)? A New Proposal', *SJOT* 29 (2015): 241–6, and J. M. Cohen, 'An Unrecognized Connotation of *nšq peh* with Special Reference to Three Biblical Occurrences', *VT* 32 (1982): 416–24. It is a shame that in relation to Gen 41.40 he appears to have been unaware of K. A. Kitchen, 'The Term *nšq* in Genesis xli, 40', *ExpTim* 69 (1957–58): 30. If Kitchen's suggestion is right (and it has been accepted by several other commentators), it would bring the use much closer to the sense suggested by emendation in our verse, though as the object is not stated (as sometimes in the Egyptian parallel) it cannot help us with the particular question which is under consideration here.

member of the family with whom thereafter he enters into positive dialogue. In 1 Sam. 10.1 Samuel anoints Saul as prospective king and then kisses him. Gordon considers that this 'may betoken nothing more than affection',[49] but even if we wished to go a step further it is clearly a token of positive loyalty rather than enforced coercion. In 1 Sam. 20.41 David fell on his face to the ground and prostrated himself three times before Jonathan, but the kisses which follow are mutual, as we have already seen (איש את־רעהו), and so cannot be regarded in any sense as a token of one-sided submission. In 2 Sam. 14.33, it is David who kisses Absalom after the latter has done obeisance, clearly an affectionate response, and a few verses later in 15.5 the situation is the same in the interchange between various unspecified individuals and Absalom. In none of these cases, therefore, does the kiss carry the same freight as in the emended version of Ps. 2.12, and besides that none mentions kissing the feet.

At this point it may then be helpful to consider the force of the two inseparable prepositions ל and ב when used after the verb. Not infrequently these prepositions conceal an element of motion,[50] and ל with a kiss of affection in whatever sort of relationship would not be inappropriate as movement towards the one kissed is obviously implied. I propose that in the very different use of a kiss of the feet to express submission to an overlord the preposition ב is preferred by allusion to verbs of touching and holding (e.g. אחז, נגע, דבק)[51] and that this implies a similar gesture. On the Black Obelisk, whereas (as noted above) Jehu is depicted as bowing to the ground slightly in front of Shalmaneser III, Sua of Gilzanu is equally clearly close to the king's feet and his arms reach out in front of him, as if to grasp the king's feet. While no written explanation of this difference is provided, it seems natural to infer that the king had greater confidence in Sua, allowing him this closer contact without apparent apprehension. Submission may be forced in a way which engenders resentment or it may

---

49. R. P. Gordon, *1 & 2 Samuel: A Commentary* (Exeter: Paternoster, 1986), 116.

50. This so-called pregnant construction is well known; see, for instance, GK §119 *passim*, but esp. §*ee-gg*; J. C. L. Gibson, *Davidson's Introductory Hebrew Grammar – Syntax* (Edinburgh: T. & T. Clark, 1994), 147.

51. These verbs were in fact noted by Bertholet but dismissed by Driver as not apposite. My proposal is that closer consideration of the use of prepositions after a verb to indicate the virtual ellipse of a verb of motion or equivalent gives us reason to question Driver's hasty dismissal. We might add the *hiphil* of חזק to the list, and I am grateful to Dr E. Kozlova for reminding me that at Prov. 7.13 the woman grabs hold of the young man (והחזיקה בו) and then kisses him (נשק + ל). Here, the preposition relates to the verb in its commonest use, of course.

be 'voluntary' (whether welcome or a simple acknowledgement of the realities of power). Sua may fit better into this latter category.

This seems to me to fit the emended form of Ps. 2.12 very well. The previously rebellious rulers are urged to submit voluntarily to God. To express that the imperative verb urges them to kiss his feet and at the same time to hold them (implied by the preposition ב) in a way which hints at a degree of trust in their new lord. The use of 'kiss' in the Hebrew Bible with this sense is unparalleled, and the different preposition used fits well with it.

I conclude that in view of all the difficulties with the received form of the text and the unsatisfactory nature of other ways of handling those difficulties, the simple and explicable emendation remains the best solution. Objections that have been raised against it are far from decisive. Accepting it raises fewer difficulties than any alternative proposal. As Rowley summarized many years ago, it is 'the best suggestion yet made for curing the corruption of an acknowledged *crux interpretum*'.[52]

Bibliography

Allen, L. C. *Ezekiel 1–19*. WBC 28. Dallas: Word, 1994.
Auffret, P. *The Literary Structure of Psalm 2*. JSOTSup 3. Sheffield: JSOT, 1977.
Avioz, A. 'Why Did Joseph Kiss his Father (Genesis 50,1)? A New Proposal'. *SJOT* 29 (2015): 241–6.
Baethgen, F. *Die Psalmen*. HAT 2/2. Göttingen: Vandenhoeck & Ruprecht, 1897.
Barnes, W. E. 'The Text of Psalm ii 12'. *JTS* 18, no. 69 (1917): 24–9.
Barr, J. *Comparative Philology and the Text of the Old Testament*. Oxford: Oxford University Press, 1968.
Barthélemy, D. *Critique textuelle de l'Ancien Testament, 4: Psaumes*. Edited by S. D. Ryan and A. Schenker. OBO 50/4. Fribourg: Academic Press; Göttingen: Vandenhoeck & Ruprecht, 2005.
Berlejung, A. 'Kultische Küsse: Zu den Begegnungsformen zwischen Göttern und Menschen'. *WO* 29 (1998): 80–97.
Bertholet, A. 'Eine crux interpretum. Ps 2 11f.'. *ZAW* 28 (1908): 58–9.
Bertholet, A. 'Nochmals zu Ps 2 11f.'. *ZAW* 28 (1908): 193.
Bickell, G. *Der Psalter*. Vol. 3 of *Dichtungen der Hebräer*. Innsbruck: Wagner, 1883.
Block, D. I. *The Book of Ezekiel Chapters 1–24*. NICOT. Grand Rapids: Eerdmans, 1997.

---

52. H. H. Rowley, 'The Text and Structure of Psalm ii', *JTS* 42 (1941): 143–54, listing quite a number of others who had accepted Bertholet's conjecture in the meantime. More recently H.-J. Kraus has comparably termed it 'an evident textual conjecture'; cf. *Psalms 1–59: A Commentary* (Minneapolis: Augsburg, 1988), 124 (it is the ET by H. C. Oswald of *Psalmen, 1: Psalmen 1–59*, 5th ed., BKAT 15/1 [Neukirchen-Vluyn: Neukirchener Verlag, 1978], 144).

Brettler, M. Z. *God is King: Understanding an Israelite Metaphor*. JSOTSup 76. Sheffield: Sheffield Academic, 1989.
Briggs, C. A., and E. G. Briggs *A Critical and Exegetical Commentary on the Book of Psalms*. 2 vols. ICC. Edinburgh: T. & T. Clark, 1906.
Brockington, L. H. *The Hebrew Text of the Old Testament: The Readings Adopted by the Translators of the New English Bible*. Oxford: Oxford University Press, 1973.
Cheyne, T. K. *The Book of Psalms*. London: Kegan Paul, Trench & Co., 1904.
Clines, D. J. A. *Job 1–20*. WBC 17. Dallas: Word, 1989.
Closen, G. E. 'Gedanken zur Textkritik von Ps 2,11b + 12a'. *Biblica* 21 (1940): 288–309.
Cohen, J. M. 'An Unrecognized Connotation of *nšq peh* with Special Reference to Three Biblical Occurrences'. *VT* 32 (1982): 416–24.
Cole, R. L. *Psalms 1–2: Gateway to the Psalter*. Hebrew Bible Monographs 37. Sheffield: Sheffield Phoenix, 2013.
Craigie, P. C. *Psalms 1–50*. WBC 19. Waco: Word, 1983.
Dahood, M. J. *Psalms I, 1–50: Introduction, Translation, and Notes*. AB 16. Garden City: Doubleday, 1965.
deClaissé-Walford, N., R. A. Jacobson, and B. LaNeel Tanner. *The Book of Psalms*. NICOT. Grand Rapids: Eerdmans, 2014.
Deissler, A. 'Zum Problem der Messianität von Psalm 2'. Pages 283–92 in *De la Tôrah au Messie: Mélanges Henri Cazelles*. Edited M. Carrez, J. Doré, and F. Grelot. Paris: Desclée, 1981.
Delitzsch, F. *Commentar über den Psalter*. 4th ed. Leipzig: Dörffling & Franke, 1883.
Delitzsch, F. *Die Lese- und Schreibfehler im alten Testament*. Berlin: de Gruyter, 1920.
Driver, G. R. 'Difficult Words in the Hebrew Prophets'. Pages 52–72 in *Studies in Old Testament Prophecy Presented to Professor Theodore H. Robinson*. Edited by H. H. Rowley. Edinburgh: T. & T. Clark, 1950.
Driver, G. R. 'Ezekiel: Linguistic and Textual Problems'. *Biblica* 35 (1954): 145–59.
Driver, S. R. 'The Method of Studying the Psalter, with Special Application to Some of the Messianic Psalms'. *The Expositor*, 7th series, 9.1 (1910): 20–41.
Driver, S. R. *Studies in the Psalms*. London: Hodder & Stoughton, 1915.
Duhm, B. *Die Psalmen*. KHAT 14. Freiburg: J. C. B. Mohr, 1899.
Emerton, J. A., D. L. Frost, and A. A. Macintosh. *'A Daft Text': The Psalter 1998: A Critique of the New Psalter*. Cambridge: Aquila, 1999.
Gibson, J. C. L. *Davidson's Introductory Hebrew Grammar – Syntax*. Edinburgh: T. & T. Clark, 1994.
Gillingham, S. *A Journey of Two Psalms: The Reception of Psalms 1 and 2 in Jewish and Christian Tradition*. Oxford: Oxford University Press, 2013.
Gillingham, S. *A Reception History Commentary on Psalms 1–72*, vol. 2 of *Psalms Through the Centuries*. Wiley Blackwell Bible Commentaries. Chichester: Wiley-Blackwell, 2018.
Goldingay, J. *Psalms*. 3 vols. Grand Rapids: Baker, 2006–2008.
Gordon, R. P. *1 & 2 Samuel: A Commentary*. Exeter: Paternoster, 1986.
Greenberg, M. *Ezekiel 1–20: A New Translation with Introduction and Commentary*. AB 22. Garden City: Doubleday, 1983.
Gruber, M. I. *Aspects of Nonverbal Communication in the Ancient Near East*. Studia Pohl 12/1. Rome: Biblical Institute, 1980.
Gunkel, H. *Die Psalmen*. Göttinger Handkommentar zum Alten Testament. Göttingen: Vandenhoeck & Ruprecht, 1926.
Hallo, W. ed. *Context of Scripture*. 3 vols. Leiden: Brill. 1997–2002. [*COS*]

Hartenstein, F., and B. Janowski. *Psalmen*. BKAT 15.1, Lieferungen 1–2. Neukirchen-Vluyn: Neukirchener Verlag, 2015.
Haupt, P. 'The Poetic Form of the First Psalm'. *AJSL* 19 (1903): 129–42.
Holladay, W. L. 'A New Proposal for the Crux in Psalm ii 12'. *VT* 28 (1978): 110–12.
Kirkpatrick, A. F. *The Book of Psalms with Introduction and Notes*. CBSC. Cambridge: Cambridge University Press, 1902.
Kitchen, K. A. 'The Term *nšq* in Genesis xli, 40'. *ExpTim* 69 (1957–58): 30.
Köbert, R. 'Zur ursprünglichen Textform von Ps 2,11. 12a'. *Biblica* 21 (1940): 426–8.
Kopf, L. 'Arabische Etymologien und Parallelen zum Bibelwörterbuch'. *VT* 9 (1959): 247–87.
Kraus, H.-J. *Psalms 1–59: A Commentary*. Minneapolis: Augsburg, 1988.
Lagrange, M. J. 'Notes sur le messianisme dans les Psaumes'. *RB* 2 (1905): 39–57.
Macintosh, A. A. 'A Consideration of the Problems Presented by Psalm ii. 11 and 12'. *JTS* NS 27 (1976): 1–14.
McKane, W. *Proverbs: A New Approach*. OTL. London: SCM, 1970.
Morgenstern, J. 'נשקו־בר'. *JQR* 32 (1942): 371–85.
Norton, G. J. 'Psalm 2:11-12 and Modern Textual Criticism'. *PIBA* 15 (1992): 89–111.
Olofsson, S. 'The Crux Interpretum in Ps 2,11'. *SJOT* 9 (1995): 185–99.
Pietersma, A. 'Empire Re-affirmed: A Commentary on Greek Psalm 2'. Pages 46–62 in vol. 2 of *God's Word for Our World: Theological and Cultural Studies in Honor of Simon John De Vries*. Edited by J. H. Ellens et al. JSOTSup 389. London: T & T Clark International, 2004.
Prince, J. D. 'Notes on Psalm ii. 11-12 and on אֶרֶן, Isaiah xliv. 14'. *JBL* 19 (1900): 1–4.
Reider, J. 'Contributions to the Scriptural Text'. *HUCA* 24 (1952): 85–106.
Robinson, A. 'Deliberate but Misguided Haplography Explains Psalm 2 11-12'. *ZAW* 89 (1977): 421–2.
Ross, A. P. *A Commentary on the Psalms*. 3 vols. Kregel Exegetical Library. Grand Rapids: Kregel, 2011.
Rowley, H. H. 'The Text and Structure of Psalm ii'. *JTS* 42 (1941): 143–54.
Sabottka, L. 'Ps 2,12: "Küsst den Sohn!"?' *Biblica* 87 (2006): 96–7.
Sievers, E. 'Psalm 2'. *ZDMG* 58 (1904): 864–6.
Sonne, I. 'The Second Psalm'. *HUCA* 19 (1945–46): 43–55.
Sperling, S. D. 'A Study of Psalm 2'. *UF* 43 (2011): 435–45.
Tov, E. *Textual Criticism of the Hebrew Bible*. 3rd ed. Minneapolis: Fortress, 2012.
Uehlinger, C. 'Neither Eyewitnesses, Nor Windows to the Past, but Valuable Testimony in its Own Right: Remarks on Iconography, Source Criticism and Ancient Data-processing'. Pages 173–228 in *Understanding the History of Ancient Israel*. Edited by H. G. M. Williamson. Proceedings of the British Academy 143. Oxford: Oxford University Press, 2007.
Vang, C. 'Ps 2,11–12: A New Look at an Old Crux Interpretum'. *SJOT* 9 (1995): 163–84.
Vermeylen, J. *Jérusalem centre du monde: développements et contestations d'une tradition biblique*. Lectio Divina. Paris: Cerf, 2007.
Whybray, R. N. *Proverbs*. NCBC. London: Marshall Pickering, 1994.
Williamson, H. G. M. 'S. R. Driver on the Psalms'. Pages 303–15 in *Fromme und Frevler: Studien zu Psalmen und Weisheit. Festschrift für Hermann Spieckermann zum 70. Geburtstag*. Edited by C. Körting and R. G. Kratz. Tübingen: Mohr Siebeck, 2020.
Williamson, H. G. M. 'Word Order in Isaiah xliii. 12'. *JTS* NS 30 (1979): 499–502.

Zimmerli, W. *Ezechiel 1: Ezechiel 1–24*. BKAT 13/1. Neukirchen-Vluyn: Neukirchener Verlag, 1969.

Zimmern, H. 'Berichtigungen und Nachträgen'. In W. Gesenius, H. Zimmern, and F. Buhl. *Wilhelm Gesenius' Hebräisches und aramäisches Handwörterbuch über das Alte Testament*. 14th ed. Leipzig: Vogel, 1905.

Joab's Curious Role and David's Vivid Imagination in Psalm 60: The Psalm's Title as a Pertinent Tool for Exegesis

Stefan M. Attard

Introduction

Among the literary devices that, by their very nature, spark one's imagination we find similes and, to a larger extent, parables and metaphors. Their effect depends on the ability of the mind to associate ideas and thereby to perceive or even mentally create the reality referred to by the literary device. However, going beyond such specifically linguistic techniques and moving on to the realm of the redactors' activity, it becomes evident that their own association of ideas and correlation of concepts were based, to a large extent, on the biblical world they visualized in their mind and/or the biblical world they wanted to create for the reader. It will be argued that imagination had a decisive role in the formation of Psalm 60, including its title, and that this was a product of the faith of those responsible for its creation. Consequently, the reader-response approach which transpires through the present study is inspired by the imagination of author and redactor alike. In other words, the latter instigates readings that propel the interpreter beyond the confines of the text.

Psalm 60 is a poem immensely rich in metaphors, but a degree of complexity is added by its historical title which, it will be argued, plays a role in shifting the emphasis of the interpretation of the psalm.[1] Before

---

1. The focus of this paper is not on the apparent musical annotations which, for instance, was the concern of Herbert Gordon May, '"AL..." in the Superscriptions

the vast array of images and metaphors found in Psalm 60, the present study will limit itself to two avenues in its exploration of the role of the imagination, namely the title and the divine oracle. The latter has God as its referent, but it also bears upon the understanding of the title in which Joab is a protagonist. Prior to this present undertaking, it is necessary to offer a preliminary analysis of the psalm at large.

Genre, Structure and Analysis

It has been argued by G. S. Ogden that the classical formal elements of a lament are reproduced in this psalm in a different style and along a different pattern.[2] Psalm 60 may formally be classified as a collective lament, but it has a specific function in relation to its title. Though it is useful to understand the original *Sitz im Leben* of each psalm,[3] their forming part of the canonical text at times allows a particular genre to function on a very specific hermeneutical level that may differ significantly from the original intention of the psalm. Psalm 60 is a case in point. In this respect, J. Barton's remark hits the nail on the head: 'Genre distinctions can never be of more than secondary importance if one is dealing with the direct utterances of God'.[4] Here, the divine oracle – sandwiched between communal and individual interjections in a concentric manner – takes on a foundational role. The relevance of the psalm's structure ensues not only from formal characteristics but also from its content (see Figure 3.1).

---

of the Psalms', *The American Journal of Semitic Languages and Literatures* 58, no. 1 (1941): 70–83. Rather, it is the exegetical role of the Davidic biographical title that will be highlighted.

2. G. S. Ogden, 'Psalm 60: Its Rhetoric, Form, and Function', *JSOT* 31 (1985): 83–94 (esp. pp. 89–90).

3. Cf. C. Uehlinger, 'Antiker Tell, lebendiges Stadtviertel: Das Psalmenbuch als Sammlung von Einzeldichtungen und als Großkomposition', *BK* 56 (2001): 174–7.

4. J. Barton, *Oracles of God: Perceptions of Ancient Prophecy in Israel after the Exile* (London: Darton, Longman & Todd, 1986), 142. Hermann Gunkel and Joachim Begrich, *Einleitung in Die Psalmen. Die Gattungen Der Religiösen Lyrik Israels* (1933; repr., Götttingen: Vandenhoeck & Ruprecht, 1985), 138, highlight the oracle section when they state: 'In Ψ 60 ist ein Orakel 8-10 durch Klagelieder eingerahmt, die Gelegenheit ist ein unglücklicher Kriegszug'.

Title	
v. 1	Introductory tags, ending with ללמד, 'for teaching'[5]
v. 2	David's struggle and Joab's military action
Part I	
vv. 3-7bα	*Communal*: God's rejection (זנח v. 3) induces the lament [opens with אלהים] A request for salvation: הושיעה ימינך (v. 7)
v. 7bß	*Individual*: plea to be heard[6]
Part II	
vv. 8-10	*Divine oracle*: God as warrior and victor [opens with אלהים]
Part III	
v. 11	*Individual*: indirect plea to be led [opens with מי][7]
vv. 12-14	*Communal*: God's rejection (זנח v. 12); rhetorical question Affirmation of God's help in the light of man's empty salvation: תשועת אדם (v. 13)

Figure 3.1. *The structure of Psalm 60.*

Book II of the Psalter begins to treat the problem of the exile more explicitly. The theme of rejection that first appeared in Psalms 43 and 44 is found again in Ps. 60.2 (זנח, 'to reject'). Though David is portrayed as king, this reference is significant because his fate's association with the broken walls of Jerusalem in Psalm 51 (while still king) had already been affirmed. Together with Zech. 10.6, Ps. 60.3 is the only other time in MT that זנח ('to reject') and שוב ('to return') occur together.[8] The verb אנף ('to be angry', v. 3; ×14 in MT, rather than the more common אף) is used by Ezra (9.14) in his prayer concerning the exiles who had returned and yet

---

5. The term ללמד in the title may be related to Jer. 9.19 ('Teach [ולמדנה] your daughters how to wail; teach one another a lament') where the women cry because they have to leave the land. There, Egypt (מצור in Ps. 60.11 may be reminiscent of it, that is, of מצרים), Judah, Edom, Ammon, Moab are singled out for punishment (v. 25).

6. Following *qere* וענני as do several mss, versions and Ps. 108.7.

7. Ogden, 'Psalm 60', 83, groups v. 11 with vv. 8-10, probably due to his reading of the psalm in the light of Isa. 63.1-6.

8. A third lexeme, ענה ('to answer'), is used in both texts, further binding their reference to a common historical situation. Zechariah's words '*I will bring them back*...and they shall be as though *I had not rejected them*...and *I will answer them*' seem to be an answer to the complaint and the plea in Ps. 60.3, 7, much like Isa. 63.1-6 have been seen to be the divine response to Ps. 60.11 (and the psalm at large) by Ogden, 'Psalm 60', 91–3.

done detestable things, seeing that such actions could arouse God's anger.[9] שוב in MT usually has people as its subject and is used in significant post-exilic texts (e.g. Zech. 1.16; 8.15; Mal. 3.7) where God is said to return to his people, hence implying restoration.[10] The community complains that God has broken through it (פרץ, v. 3), presenting God as having made a breach in his people's city walls.

The land mentioned in Ps. 60.4 represents the condition of the one praying and his community – the verbs רפא ('to heal') and מוט ('to totter') are found in Ps. 30.3, 7, the latter having the psalmist as its subject. Psalm 60.5b should be read in the light of two texts: (1) Jer. 25.15-30 has God giving the cup of the wine of his wrath (כוס היין החמה) to be drunk (שקה) by the nations (v. 15), this bringing with it the bloodshed of the sword (cf. vv. 16, 27). Among them are mentioned the Philistines, Edom, Moab and the kingdoms of the north. With Psalm 60 it also shares the image of God who speaks from on high, from his holy place (Jer. 25.30; cf. Ps. 60.8). (2) In Isa. 29.1-16 God causes things to shake (רעש), metaphorically making his people drink wine that makes them stagger. Further on, Isa. 51.17, 22 speak of a cup that has the same effect, תרעלה, 'staggering', being used only here and in Psalm 60 in the entire MT. In the prophetic text, God promises restoration and comfort to his people.[11] Allusions to the exile are perceptible.[12] The divine action on land and people (vv. 4-5) differs, for the first is shaken and the second are intoxicated with wine,[13] but the effect is the same – the staggering of the people corresponds to the quaking of the land.

---

9. The first two occurrences of the word are in Deut. 1.37 and 4.21, where Moses states that because God was angry with him he would not enter the Promised Land. In Solomon's prayer, a direct link is made between God getting angry (אנף) and the people being taken captive to other lands (1 Kgs 8.46).

10. For A. Weiser, *Die Psalmen*, vol. 1, ATD 14 (Göttingen: Vandenhoeck & Ruprecht, 1987), 298, the oracle is about God's claim over the land of Canaan, that is the Promised Land.

11. The former oppression of Egypt and Assyria is mentioned in Isa. 52.4.

12. Against K. Seybold, *Die Psalmen*, HAT 1/15 (Tübingen: Mohr, 1996), 238, E. A. Knauf, 'Psalm 60 und Psalm 108', *VT* 50 (2000): 60, states: 'ein Gedanke an das "Exil" liegt noch nicht vor'. Yet, allusions to the time of slavery in Egypt may also be present. The difficult times experienced by the people are indicated in v. 5 by the word קשה (often used to refer to stiff-necked people) which is used in Exod. 1.14; 6.9; Deut. 26.6 to refer to that bondage.

13. See the notion of force-feeding in S. M. Attard, 'From Well-Fed Lions to Sitting Ducks: A Study of Complex Metaphors in Psalm 17', in *Networks of Metaphors in the Hebrew Bible*, ed. D. Verde and A. Labahn, BEThL 309 (Leuven: Peeters, 2020), 173–91 (esp. pp. 183–5).

The נס (v. 6, 'sign') given by God which is to be raised has been taken to be a sign to flee from before the enemy's bow. A.F. Kirkpatrick suggests following LXX, Vulgate, Symmachus and Jerome for this rendering.[14] Here, two observations may be made. Firstly, the bow may not be simply the weapon used in war. The geographical location of the adversary's cities in v. 10 create a bow-like formation which corresponds to another one represented by the locations mentioned in vv. 8-9, two of which are tribal allotments (Ephraim and Manasseh). Geographically, Judah, the third tribal allotment mentioned, occupies a central position (see Figure 3.2).

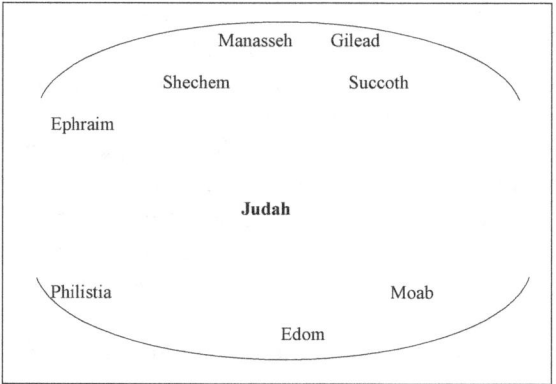

Figure 3.2. *The geographical location of the places mentioned*

Though ancient cartographers oriented their maps with the east pointing upwards,[15] the image displayed still holds, as the surrounding cities would flank Judah (and hence Jerusalem) on either side in two bow-like formations. Fleeing from the (lower) bow would bring the petitioners to Jerusalem, the place where God's decrees (cf. מחקקי, v. 9) are confirmed. This brings us to the second observation. Sticking strictly to the MT where

---

14. A. F. Kirkpatrick, *The Book of Psalms. Books II and III, Psalms XLII–LXXXIX* (1895; repr., Cambridge: Cambridge University Press, 1904), 340. G. R. Driver, 'Notes on the Text of Psalms', *Harvard Theological Review* 29 (1936): 171–95 (184), relates נס (which he gives as נַס, not נֵס) in v. 6a to the adjoining התנוסס (derived from נוס, 'to flee') and presumes that נס must here mean 'flight'.

15. For instance, see the map of the Mesopotamian city of Nuzi dating back to the third millennium BCE: J. Romero-Girón Deleito, *Historia de la Cartografía, La Evolución de los Mapas: Primera Parte. El Mundo Antiguo de la Prehistoria a Roma* (Madrid: Edición Personal, 2018), 44.

flight does not feature, the sign given by God could be a reference to the very word of God which is raised (נסס, v. 6) in his holy place and in which the believers find refuge.

Prior to the reporting of God's word in vv. 8-10 in the form of an oracle, factors such as a plea in v. 7 for God to help with his right hand evoke the song of Moses in the Exodus narrative (Exod. 15).[16] After the oracle, which will be treated later, the assonance between מָצוֹר ('fortified', v. 11) and מִצָּר ('from the enemy', v. 13) is noteworthy. One is left suspecting that the real aim of the psalmist is not really to *enter into* the city but to be set free *from* the enemy. That the psalm ends with God, and not the believers, who tramples the foes, confirms this reading. *BHS* indicates that a number of manuscripts read קמינו instead of צרינו in v. 14. This would render the phrase והוא יבוס צרינו, 'and he will trample down our foes', nearly identical to נבוס קמינו בשמך in 44.6 'in your name we trample down our assailants', where huge emphasis was laid on God as the only one who helped his people in battle. Though one need not emend צרינו,[17] such manuscripts hint at a relationship between the two psalms. That בוס is found only in Psalms 44 and 60 (and the composite Ps. 108) – the only two communal laments of Book II – supports this view. The last two verses of Psalm 60 constitute a final plea and form a chiastic arrangement that focuses on the indescribable difference between God and man (see Table 3.1).

v. 13a	v. 13b	v. 14a	v. 14b
מצר	אדם	אלהים	צרינו
foe	useless support	God the victor	foe

Table 3.1. *The chiastic structure of Ps. 60.13-14*

Once again, the concept of man's inability to ascertain victory which is so clearly stated in 60.13b is found in Ps. 44.7. Psalm 44.7 speaks of the uselessness of bow and sword, carrying on with a statement about victory over the foe (צרינו, v. 8; cf. 60.14b), and concluding, as does Psalm 60,

---

16. God's right hand (Exod. 15.12; Ps. 60.7); God leading the people (נחה, Exod. 15.13; Ps. 60.11); the mention of Philistia, Edom and Moab. F.-L. Hossfeld, 'Das Prophetische in den Psalmen. Zur Gottesrede der Asafpsalmen im Vergleich mit der des ersten und zweiten Davidpsalters', in *Ich Bewirke das Heil und Erschaffe das Unheil (Jesaja 45,7). Studien zur Botschaft der Propheten. Festschrift L. Ruppert*, ed. F. Diedrich and B. Willmes, FzB 88 (Würzburg: Echter Verlag, 1998), 236, relates Ps. 60.8-10 to Exod. 15.14-16.

17. צרינו is in parallelism with מצר in v. 13a.

with an affirmation of the agent of salvation (באלהים, 44.9; cf. 60.14).[18] After this short preliminary analysis of the psalm, it is timely to look into its relation to its detailed title and the historical occasion referred to therein.

Tension between Psalm Title and Communal Lament

Psalm 60 is particularly enigmatic in that a literary tension results from an apparent mismatch of its title and the content of its body, this having led to speculation concerning the genesis of this national liturgy. The combination of title and psalm proper disorients the reader as to which historical viewpoint to adopt. In fact, scholars have debated whether the actual psalm is meant to be interpreted as a prayer made *prior* to the report in the title or whether it should be seen as *following* those events.[19]

Pinpointing a Precise Historical Moment

The dissonance between the title and the psalm could be explained by positing a possible defeat, expressed in the very lament part of the psalm, which was subsequently followed by the victory alluded to in the title. Such an initial defeat has been suggested by B. S. Childs, who claims that the relation to 1 Kgs 11.15 where Joab buries the dead leads to such a postulation.[20] The insertion of Joab into the context of David's victory over the Edomites in the Valley of Salt (2 Sam. 8.13) would thus suggest that Psalm 60 is a lament because of the losses that had been incurred. However, nothing in the title points to any form of defeat, even if only transient.

---

18. Sawyer points out that ישע always has God as its subject except in a few cases where military aid is shown to be useless in saving, and cites Pss. 44 and 60, among a few others: cf. H.-J. Fabry and J. F. Sawyer, 'ישע *jšʿ*', *ThWAT* 3 (1982): 1035–59 (1055).

19. For instance, F. Delitzsch, *Biblical Commentary on the Psalms, Vol. 2* (Edinburgh: T. & T. Clark, 1880), 194, claims it was written before the victory in the Valley of Salt, and disagrees with the view that it was written after that victory but before conquering Edom. For a brief explanation of the distribution of Davidic titles in Pss. 51–72, see Frank-Lothar Hossfeld and Erich Zenger, *Psalms 2: A Commentary on Psalms 51–100*, ed. Klaus Baltzer (Minneapolis: Fortress, 2005), 3, 18–19. Here, the point is made that theological intentions outweigh chronological precision in order to show the progressive effect of David's sin and his ultimate reestablishment, despite continued dangers.

20. Cf. B. S. Childs, 'Psalm Titles and Midrashic Exegesis', *JSS* 16 (1971): 146–7.

The title showcases a victory wrought by Joab that may be related to the one that also features in 1 Kgs 11.5, which the LXX interestingly attributes to a *joint* operation with David (ἔκοψαν, 'they struck'). Psalm 60.2 possibly alludes to a two-stage invasion, since the victory obtained was in the *Valley* of Salt, but the desire expressed was that the *city* itself be captured. This may correspond somewhat to the initial assault upon Rabbath by Joab in 2 Sam. 12.26-29, where a final entry into the city was needed. His message to David – 'encamp against the city (וחנה על־העיר) and take it, lest I take the city and it be called after my name' (2 Sam. 12.28) – depicts the same situation of the psalm where David asks that he be brought to the fortified city (מי נחני עד־אדום, first person singular suffix in 60.11).[21] Edomites had been killed, but the city had not yet been captured. Yet, despite such possible connections, the military campaigns mentioned in 60.2 do not really account for the people's tragic state which is of cosmic proportions. Such a lament becomes pointless if Israel has struck down many enemies and is now moving on to capturing their major city. On the other hand, if the events of the title followed the lament, entry into the city *per se* was not granted, rendering vv. 11-12 unfulfilled.[22]

The sequence of the psalm titles from Psalm 51 onwards does not follow a chronological order, suggesting that the redactors' intent was not to construct an orderly historical sequence of events, but rather to convey a particular theological message. Each of the historical titles in this group of Davidic psalms commences with a temporal clause consisting in the preposition ב prefixed to an infinitive construct, hence referring to a particular duration of time ('when...'; 'while...'). The infinitive construct is a verbal form whose tense must be gleaned from the context. A perusal of the other psalms with historical titles reveals that these psalms are presented as being the *consequence* of the historical situation reported in the title. For instance, David's confession in Psalm 51 is to be located, at least theoretically speaking, at the moment when Nathan, who had just come to him (בוא + ב), was still in the king's presence. It is a result of Nathan's coming to him. If the same applies to our psalm which has ב + הצותו, 'When he struggled', in its title, the 'victories' mentioned

---

21. The return to the plural in vv. 12-13 may be a reference to David's armies and not necessarily to Joab's too (cf. 2 Sam. 12.31b).

22. Based on the discrepancies between the biographical notes and 1–2 Samuel, David Willgren, '"May YHWH avenge me on you; but my hand shall not be against you" (1 Sam. 24.13): Mapping Land and Resistance in the "Biographical" Notes of the "Book" of Psalms', *JSOT* 43 (2019): 417–35 (esp. 425) refutes the idea that these notes resulted from a midrashic-like activity that connected particular psalms to historical events recounted in 1–2 Samuel.

therein cannot be read as being the result of the lament and plea contained in the psalm itself. One would, once again, expect the psalm to be a response to the situation reported in the title, but this is not the case.

In this regard, it must be borne in mind that in narrative texts too, stories do not always follow a precise and logical narrative order. Rather, related scenes that were conceptually connected even though belonging to different time frames were sometimes juxtaposed. For instance: (1) in Joshua 2, Rahab the prostitute is said to have hidden the two spies in v. 4a and v. 6, which is after the messengers from the king of Jericho came to her in v. 3. The order should therefore be: vv. 1-2; 4a + 6; 3; 4b-16 (bar v. 6). (2) After David's return to Jerusalem with Goliath's head in 1 Sam. 17.54, in v. 55 we find Saul asking Abner, the commander of the army, about David's identity 'As Saul watched David going out to meet the Philistine...' This, naturally, had happened before David returned. The order should therefore be: vv. 32-40; 55-56; 41-54. (3) David's conversation with the Amalekite who killed Saul and the latter's consequent execution in 2 Sam. 1.13-16 must have happened immediately after this man gave the report to David which ends in v. 11. But this verse is followed by a description in v. 12 of the expressions of mourning that must have followed the execution. The order should therefore be: vv. 1-11; 13-16; 12. That the same procedure has been adopted for Psalm 60, despite it not being a narrative text, may not be surprising.

Since in 1–2 Samuel there is no precise corresponding event to the battles of David mentioned in the title,[23] it becomes apparent that the purpose of the title is not to throw light on any historical event as such. Rather, a putative historical setting was conceptualized by the redactors who intended the internal dynamic of the title to serve the purpose of teaching (ללמד, 'for teaching'). And that dynamic has to do with Joab's relationship to David, as will be seen shortly. Hence, the *raison d'être* behind the redactors' juxtapositioning of title and psalm must have been the following: (1) the suitability of the Davidic narrative as a broad historical backdrop against which to interpret the psalm; (2) a disregard

---

23. Kirkpatrick, *The Book of Psalms*, 338–9, notes that its historicity has been questioned, but sees the events as plausible in the light of 2 Samuel, 1 Chron. 18.12, and Joab's mention in the psalm title. However, he has to depend on the probability of textual error to account for the huge variation in casualties numbered. H. J. Kraus, *Psalms 60–150: A Continental Commentary*, trans. Hilton C. Oswald (Minneapolis: Fortress, 1993), 3, does not favour pinpointing the historical events to which the psalm may be linked, stressing the cultic function of the psalm. So also G. Ravasi, *Il libro dei Salmi. Commento e attualizzazzione, Vol. 2. 51–100* (Bologna: Edizioni Dehoniane, 2002), 213.

for the precise chronological order of the events recounted or alluded to in title and psalm; (3) an intention to highlight the figure of Joab for a specific purpose. The Davidic biographical tags turn out to have a double function, namely to broaden the imagination of the reader of the psalms in question, as well as to aid the hermeneutical enterprise that follows.

The Protagonists in Psalm Titles

The foregoing discourse shows that the correct interpretation regarding the chronological dilemmas created by Psalm 60 can only be arrived at by adopting a synchronic reading that brings the adjacent psalm titles into play. The element of distress, persecution and petition that mark the whole ensemble of the surrounding Davidic psalms is patent. Book II then ends with a prayer in Psalm 72 for the royal son, describing a kingdom which never really materialized to the extent envisioned.

Prior to Psalm 60, David suffers persecution at the hands of others. With the exception of Ahimelech, the personages mentioned or alluded to in the titles of the psalms before Psalm 60 are all portrayed negatively: Doeg, Saul, the Ziphites, the Philistines, and Absalom. The narrative is one of persecution, which Barbiero has correctly referred to as God's form of discipline intended to educate his people in view of their sin.[24] In Psalm 60, it is not as though David were faring well and simply needed some extra divine help in order to enter Edom. This psalm, like its surrounding compositions, portrays David as being in dire need of God. Any successes that might be hinted at in the title have no bearing whatsoever on the psalm.

Despite the report of Joab's seemingly gainful action, the title of Psalm 60 belongs in a sequence of titles that speak of David's persecution. The unresolved ending of the psalm, namely a mere plea for divine assistance, endorses the lament narrative of this whole group of Davidic psalms (Pss. 52–64).[25] This is enhanced by the perilous situation of David in Psalm 63's title due to Absalom's implied revolt.[26] The didactic function of Psalm 60 emerges more strongly, not in terms of a victory achieved after prayer, but rather in terms of God's absolute sovereignty and prerogative to grant salvation. In such a light, Joab is stripped of his military prowess

---

24. Cf. G. Barbiero, 'Il secondo e il terzo libro dei Salmi (Sal 42–89): due libri paralleli', *RivBib* 58 (2010): 152.

25. Cf. S. M. Attard, *The Implications of Davidic Repentance: A Synchronic Analysis of Book 2 of the Psalter (Psalms 42–72)* (Rome: Gregorian & Biblical Press, 2016), 225–8. Cf. also, p. 455: 'Ps 61–64 do not constitute a *return* to lament since Ps. 60 does not present David as having complete military success'.

26. Cf. Attard, *Davidic Repentance*, 244, 247, 272.

and turns out to constitute, paradoxically, part of the problem that needs to be addressed. One might ask even whether Joab's 12,000 slain men, contrasted to the 18,000 of David in 2 Sam. 8.13 and of Abishai in 1 Chron. 18.12, could not have been meant to deflate Joab's military achievements and, hence, to show why David had to depend on God alone for true help.

If the allusion to Absalom in the title of Psalm 63 has been deemed hermeneutically significant in creating a Davidic narrative, how much more is the specific mention of someone (i.e. Joab) in a title to be given due weight. Though one may contend that his presence simply serves to buttress the image of a David who now rules as a victorious king, I would like to advance the position that Joab's presence here is a disquieting matter and that the very nature of Psalm 60, a lament pleading for *divine* help, suggests that Joab's endeavours are, at best, of limited benefit to the king. The title, therefore, is not meant so much to highlight the victories of David as to make a statement about his dire need of God *in spite of* human help. J. Steinberg gives an interesting layout of the relation David had with various individuals in the different psalm titles.[27] Though in Psalm 60 he correctly identifies David's rulership over Israel and the neighbouring peoples, this is not, as such, the most significant element of the psalm. David's kingship at this juncture is indeed important, for subsequent psalms make reference to the king. Nonetheless, the composition's main intent is not to draw attention to David as king but as a believer in need of God. The real issue is that David, whether in his pre-monarchic years (in his persecution by Saul and others) or in his years of royal rule (Pss. 60; 63), always experienced difficulties from which God alone could liberate him. Steinberg is right in not identifying Psalm 60 as a 'David–Joab' psalm, in spite of the fact that, following the same logic of the other psalms, this would have been an obvious connection. After all, Joab does not directly persecute David here. But the king's association with Joab suffers considerable limitations (indeed Joab eventually becomes a threat to the monarchy) which only an intervention of God could remedy.[28]

---

27. Cf. J. Steinberg, *Die Ketuvim: ihr Aufbau und ihre Botschaft*, BBB 152 (Hamburg: Philo, 2006), 241: Ps. 51 (David–Bathsheba); Pss. 52–59 (David–Saul); Ps. 60 (David's royal rule); Ps. 63 (David–Absalom); Ps. 72 (David–Solomon).

28. Though set in a wholly different context, the message plainly set forth in Ps. 60 that human alliances (with Egypt) are of no use in assuring assistance and securing victory was also the message of Isa. 31.1-9 which states that 'the Lord of hosts will come down to do battle on Mount Zion and on its heights' (v. 4; then v. 9 speaks of a נס of God, just like Ps. 60.6). This follows upon Isa. 30.1-7 with its strong warning against seeking help (עזר, v. 7; cf. עזרה, Ps. 60.13) from Egypt.

Though the David–Joab connection would not merit David the criticism directed at Israel in 50.18 for association with wrongdoers, the psalm surely shows that that rapport was an unhappy one. The ensuing lament shows that, indeed, this was another low point in the life of David.

From this perspective, the term ללמד (60.1) cannot merely be taken to denote 'an instruction or direction to be issued in times of war'.[29] Despite the bellicose imagination triggered by the title and the oracle, the redactors' intent is not to present a David who prepares his people for war. Rather, this tag constitutes a pointer in the larger narrative of the Psalter to the exilic debacle on which the Davidic narrative threw light. ללמד usually has God as its subject, except in Psalm 51 and a few other psalms. Could this be a psalm wherein David is being taught by God?[30] Despite the annihilation of thousands of Edomites at this juncture in the meta-narrative of the Psalter, the problem of the exile has not yet been resolved. The oracle thus serves to point to God's own supremacy, much like the proclamation of the 'YHWH reigns' psalms in Book IV constitutes a resolution for the ever-present impasse of the Exile. In some way, Psalm 60 is the drama that David must rehearse before the tragic Psalm 89 opens him once again to a recollection of God's power in Psalms 93–99.

On the Hermeneutical Role of Joab

The title of Psalm 60 is the only one in which David is seen in association with someone else in terms of a common goal. The person is none other than Joab, the commander of David's army. Taken as a whole, it is intriguing that a psalm that opens with a notification of Joab's seemingly successful assistance to David should close with David's request for *God's* victorious intervention. The situation is all the more interesting in that God's help is invoked with regard to an attack on Edom, when the title reports that Joab himself had proved to be of help in defeating the Edomites.[31] Such a sense of incompleteness at the extremities of the psalm

---

29. R. Rendtorff, 'The Psalms of David: David in the Psalms', in *The Book of Psalms: Composition and Reception*, ed. P. W. Flint and P. D. Miller, VTSup 99 (Leiden: Brill, 2005), 53–64 (59–60).

30. If ללמד is meant to denote a didactic psalm by David to others, one might wonder why all the other psalms are not given this tag too.

31. In his study of psalm titles, V. L. Johnson, *David in Distress: His Portrait Through the Historical Psalms* (New York: T&T Clark, 2009), 123, observes that most commentators link this heading to the episode of 2 Sam. 8, adding that here it is David and not Joab who is said to have killed the Edomites (v. 13). The account of 1

elicits a particular understanding of human alliances and emphasizes their worthless character.³² Moreover, an examination of Joab's personal profile highlights the tenuous nature of the relationship between David and Joab. It would suffice to recall that Joab's involvement in the murder of Uriah (2 Sam. 11.14-21) came within a context where he, as commander of the army, fought on behalf of David. There, the help that Joab gave David in his evil scheming turned out to be detrimental to the king. The reality of Joab's vain help is intensified by the fact that he was the one who killed David's precious son Absalom with the intention of protecting David (2 Sam. 18.10-17). This is also confirmed by the statement in 2 Sam. 19.3 which speaks of the effect that Absalom's death wrought by Joab ultimately had on David and the people: 'So the victory that day was turned into mourning for all the people'.³³ Compounded by other factors, David's and Solomon's consequent displeasure with Joab is stated in no uncertain terms.³⁴

Perusing Joab's track record and his overall detrimental impact on David, the redactor's choice of this individual in the title of this psalm is

Chron. 18.12 has his brother Abishai as the victor in the Valley of Salt, which is the interpretation Josephus Flavius follows; cf. *Ant.* 7.109. That Joab is now portrayed as the protagonist would seem to constitute a conundrum, until it is accepted that his role here is not quite positive in his regard.

32. Cf. G. Barbiero, 'The Risks of a Fragmented Reading of the Psalms', *ZAW* 120 (2008): 89, relates the title of Ps. 60 to God's declaration that David had shed too much blood and waged too many wars, and would therefore not build the temple himself (1 Chron. 22.7-9). I have suggested elsewhere that actually the title may show David's moral superiority vis-à-vis Joab, for it is the latter who is described as having killed thousands; cf. Attard, *Davidic Repentance*, 272 n. 126. In the present study (see above), I have also put forward the idea that Joab's 12,000 are a far cry from David's 18,000, hence constituting a qualitative difference in their respective military ability. Whatever interpretation is preferred, Joab is shown to be inferior to David.

33. Since 1 Chronicles is a late opus, its hinting at the innocence of David with respect to the census taken (due to Joab's failure to fully obey David; cf. J. W. Wright, 'The Innocence of David in 1 Chronicles 21', *JSOT* 60 (1993): 97, who claims: 'Joab...weakened Israel to make David militarily vulnerable') may be related to the title of Ps. 60 which, like Chronicles, must have been inserted in a late phase of the Hebrew Bible formation (cf. Childs, 'Psalm Titles and Midrashic Exegesis', 143).

34. David then removed Joab from commander of the army and placed Amasa instead of him (2 Sam. 19.13) who was in turn killed by Joab (2 Sam. 20.8-10). Joab had also killed Abner son of Ner, the commander of Saul's army, for personal reasons of revenge, thus seriously upsetting David (2 Sam. 3.20-30; 1 Kgs 2.5-6). His tacit conspiracy in the usurping of the throne by Adonijah (1 Kgs 1.15-19) reached its climax in his being killed at Solomon's orders (1 Kgs 2.28-34).

highly significant.³⁵ From the canonical point of view, the huge blunder involving Bathsheba in Psalm 51, the first psalm to have a very specific Davidic historical note in the second Davidic group, can be considered to be related to Psalm 60 with its protracted Davidic historical note mentioning Joab whose undermining of Solomon, Bathsheba's son, ultimately became apparent.³⁶ In relation to this, in his final words to Solomon, the dying David instructed him not to allow Joab to go to Sheol in peace (לא־תורד שיבתו בשלם שאל, 1 Kgs 2.6) since he had dealt unkindly with David, Abner and Amasa (v. 5). The evil companion of Psalm 55 had taken it against his friends, and the wicked in the psalm are described as men of blood – בשלמיו (v. 21) ... אנשי דמים (v. 24) – this being comparable to David's description of Joab (וישם דמי־מלחמה בשלם, 1 Kgs 2.5). Possibly having 2 Sam. 3.39 in mind concerning David's anger towards the evildoer, Josephus placed these words on David's mouth: '...Joab, being mightier and more powerful than I, has escaped punishment until now'.³⁷

Noteworthy is the fact that, prior to 60.13, the last appearance of תשועה ('salvation') is precisely in 51.16 where the uniqueness of God's ability to save is affirmed by David himself: 'God, God of my salvation'. The central statement of the psalm, then, would concern precisely the locus of man's true help and salvation, highlighting God's unique and lasting help over and against that of man.³⁸ This message in the last מכתם psalm (Ps. 60) therefore builds upon the import of the last משכיל psalm where the image of the friend-turned-enemy (55.13-15) is an apt preparation for the deteriorated relationship between David and Joab that may be implied in Psalm 60.

Moreover, though the psalm title gives the impression that Joab wrought some profitable action on behalf of David, which action has been interpreted as beneficial to David's larger military campaigns,³⁹ the psalm notably concludes with a downplaying of man's salvation (תשועה). In fact,

---

35. Cf. Attard, *Davidic Repentance*, 199 n. 15.

36. The Midrash on Ps 60 – cf. W. Braude, *The Midrash on Psalms I*, YJS 13 (New Haven: Yale University Press, 1976), 515 – accords Joab a more benevolent role than is being proposed here, placing v. 3 on his lips and v. 4b on David's, this prayer being meant as a response to Joab's complaint.

37. Josephus Flavius, *Ant.* 7.386.

38. Johnson, *David in Distress*, 123, limits himself to noting how the title contributes to bringing God's role into the limelight: 'Obvious divine activity is sparse in the account of David's conquests in 2 Sam. 8 and the addition of this psalm makes the divine source of David's victories clear (vv. 7-10, 13-14)'.

39. Cf. Kirkpatrick, *The Book of Psalms*, 338, who follows Ewald.

תשועה would normally be wrought by God, not man.⁴⁰ It is as though the reader is alerted not to interpret Joab's intervention as being in any way valuable to David. The king finds himself between the rivalry of *'ĕdôm* (אדום) and the uselessness of *'ādām* (אדם), where the assonance of both lexemes suggests a conceptual connection. And the fact that Joab is the only *'ādām* mentioned in the psalm apart from the lyrical subject, David, the association of *'ādām* with him cannot be considered misconstrued.

Brueggemann comments on Mays' belief that the title of Psalm 30 alters its use in the Psalter. While agreeing with him, he also suggests that it is unlikely that the psalmists/editors had a rigid understanding of genre so characteristic of Gunkel and the post-Gunkel period. Whilst we may be uncomfortable with such a dissonance between title and genre, it may not have been the case with those responsible for the formation of the Psalter. For this reason, Brueggemann concludes that 'we may say simply that the psalm is richly polyvalent and could seed Israel's imagination in many ways, not only imagination tamed by genre'.⁴¹ This reasoning, clearly, can be applied to Psalm 60 too.

Despite the report of military victories, the negative impression of human warfare in the surrounding psalms (compare this to the response that Ps. 44 receives, particularly in Ps. 46, where military weapons are destroyed) and, particularly, the figure of Joab, are meant to raise suspicion as to the real value of the enterprise Joab himself is associated with. In this respect, it is significant that Psalm 60 is followed by yet more laments (Pss. 61–64) rather than by some celebration of victory achieved. Unlike 1 Chron. 18.12 and 2 Samuel 8 where it is Abishai and David respectively who overcome the Edomites, the portrayal of Joab as the protagonist in Psalm 60 suggests that the redactors had an agenda concerning him.⁴² Before even beginning to read the psalm proper, the world created by this protagonist who features in its title by name already anticipates the credo that would become more manifest in vv. 8-10, the oracle to which we now turn.

---

40. The account of Naaman the Syrian says that through him God had given victory to Aram (בו נתן־יהוה תשועה לארם, 2 Kgs 5.1). Also cf. 2 Kgs 13.14-17 where Elisha assures king Jehoash victory through the Lord's strength: 'The Lord's arrow of *salvation*, the arrow of *salvation* over Aram (חץ תשועה בארם)'.

41. Cf. W. Brueggemann, 'Response to James L. Mays, "The Question of Context"', in *The Shape and Shaping of the Psalter*, ed. J. Clinton McCann, JSOTSup 159 (Sheffield: Sheffield Academic, 1993), 33-4 (quote from p. 34).

42. Conversely, Delitzsch, *Psalms*, 2:193-4, sees Joab as fitting naturally here since he was Abishai's brother and the ultimate commander of David's army.

The Metaphorical Role of the Oracle

The inflated and colourful depiction of distress prior to the oracle in vv. 8-10 serves to accentuate the contrast created between the two sections, such that a grandiose image of God is bolstered. In fact, it is surprising that the psalmist can suspend his lament in order to recall or envisage a positive scenario that he can appropriate in his favour. In his *Texts Under Investigation: The Bible and Postmodern Imagination*, Brueggemann approaches the Bible as an 'army of metaphors' allowing the reader to interact with them.[43] The image is so apt here.

The Oracle and Its Effect

Psalm 60 is preceded by Psalm 59 which bears a request for the punishment of wicked nations (גוי, 59.6, 9). This request is granted by God's victory over various peoples in 60.8-10, and his imagined action is in response to his people having become the derision of the nations.[44] Kraus takes vv. 8-10 to be an oracle mediated through a priest or a cultic prophet, and attributes its origin to the Jerusalem שלום-prophetic tradition.[45] For Eaton it is the psalmist's (i.e. the king's) own citation of this oracle given at some earlier stage.[46] Gillingham has pointed out the difference between the MT and the LXX in the oracle of Psalm 2. In the latter, the oracle is part of the king's own speech, whereas in the Hebrew version it is God's speech addressed to the king.[47] In Psalm 60, all versions are in agreement, as is the corresponding 108.7 where the oracle is clearly delivered by God. The singular וענני 'answer me', which the *qere* proposes, overrides the plural form in the *ketiv* וענו, 'answer us'. The LXX ἐπάκουσόν μου

---

43. Cf. W. Brueggemann, *Texts Under Investigation: The Bible and Postmodern Imagination* (London, SCM, 1993), 90.

44. In Books II and III, לעג ('mocking', 'derision') is used in psalms that precede divine oracles or a positive divine image of sorts: 44.14 (with an allegorical representation of God in Ps. 45); 59.9 (with an oracle in Ps. 60); 79.4 and 80.7 (Pss. 81 and 82 being the divine oracles).

45. Cf. H.-J. Kraus, *Psalmen, Vol. 2*, 5th ed., BK 15 (Neukirchen: Neukirchen Kreis Moers, 1978), 588–9. He also sees an inviolable link between the reality of the Temple and questions related to the possession of the land on p. 589: 'Altisraelitische Vorstellungen von der Landverteilung (8) und Heilszusagen des Heiligen Krieges (8f.) haben sich mit dieser Theologie des königlichen Heiligtums zu Jerusalem verbunden'.

46. Cf. J. H. Eaton, *Kingship and the Psalms*, 2nd ed. (Sheffield: JSOT, 1986), 60.

47. Cf. S. Gillingham, *A Journey of Two Psalms: The Reception of Psalms 1 and 2 in Jewish and Christian Tradition* (Oxford: Oxford University Press, 2013), 28.

and Vulgate 'exaudi me' in both psalms confirm this reading. It is the king who makes this prayer, and it is to him that these words are addressed in the first place.

Following LXX ἐν τῷ ἁγίῳ αὐτοῦ and the Latin version of Jerome, Briggs takes בקדשו in v. 8 as referring to God's sanctuary and not to his holiness.[48] The previous time that God's address was introduced with the practical equivalent of אלהים דבר ('God spoke') was in 50.1, God's location being (the sanctuary of) Zion. Given the stance in Psalm 60 versus other tribes or peoples, the primacy of Zion would therefore be implied.

In v. 8, the mention of Shechem and Succoth seems to have two opposing implications. Judges 8.13-16 preserves the memory of an unpleasant encounter between Gideon and the disobliging people of Succoth who ended up being punished for their complacency. Conversely, Shechem had strong connections with Jacob and was the place of the renewal of the covenant. This difference is then extended to the next two groups of regions, there being a positive stance vis-à-vis Gilead, Manasseh, Ephraim and Judah in v. 9, and in v. 10 a subjugation implied with regards to Moab, Edom and Philistia (see LXX ὑποτάσσω, 'to subject').[49] In relation to this, a principal motif is the authority exercised over peoples, specified according to the different places. God's dealings with each region are unique, hence revealing diverse aspects of how he exercises his authority. Joab's circumscribed enterprise pales into insignificance compared to God's feats. Even if the title reported some form of success in Joab's battle, it must be remembered that any victory on the part of Israel was always seen as wrought by God himself – in

---

48. Cf. C. A. Briggs and E. G. Briggs, *A Critical and Exegetical Commentary on the Book of Psalms, Vol. 2* ICC (Edinburgh: T. & T. Clark, 1907), 59. The texts which M. J. Dahood, *Psalms, Vol. 2*, AB 16-17 (Garden City: Doubleday, 1966–68), 79, uses to support his claim that קדש (v. 8) refers to God's *heavenly* sanctuary do not seem relevant except for 20.3 (cf. 63.3; 68.25; 134.2; 150.1). It is true that the description of the different cities imbues God with gigantic qualities in relation to them, but this is a hyperbolic equivalent of the Zion-theophany of Ps. 50 where God stresses his sovereignty over the world and all within it.

49. A. Weiser, *Die Psalmen, Vol. 1*, ATD 14 (Göttingen: Vandenhoeck & Ruprecht, 1987), 285, says that the title refers to David's victory over Edom, Moab and the Philistines (and he cites 2 Sam. 8; 1 Chron. 18.3-13) but no perfectly corresponding event can truly be found. Cf. Knauf, 'Psalm 60 und Psalm 108', 59–62, who situates the composition of Ps. 60 in Jerusalem between 600 and 598 BCE following upheavals related to the Assyrian downfall, vassalage to Egypt, and the rise of Babylon.

1 Sam. 19.5, though David killed the Philistine, it is the Lord who gave the victory. What is more, Joab's killing of the Edomites coupled with David's request to finally enter Edom can be related to the account in 2 Sam. 12.26-29 where Joab spurred David on to take hold of Rabbath that it may be called by the king's name. Such an appeal seems to have been disregarded in this psalm, since God's sovereignty over the nations leaves no room for personal names of mere human beings to be placed over any city.

What begins as God's speech in v. 8 (דבר) concludes as a divine shout in v. 10 (*hithpolel* רוע).[50] This is anticipated in the last two verses of Psalm 59 by David's resolve to raise his voice in music and song: אשיר עזך ('I will sing of your strength', v. 17); עזי אליך אזמרה ('My strength, I will make music for you', v. 18).[51] In the same psalm, the ultimate victory wrought by God is expressed in anthropomorphic terms with God laughing at his enemies: אתה יהוה תשחק־למו ('You, O Lord, shall laugh at them', 59.9).[52]

What follows the divine words is deeply marked by them, as can be seen from the significant difference there is between the descriptions prior to the oracle and those after it. Initially, the believers' distress was stark and shocking, with images of earthquakes, forced drunkenness and pierced walls being employed. However, following the oracle, God is only asked to bring the psalmist to the fortified city of Edom (v. 11). There is no request for him to apply the wall-shattering power or intoxicating strength demonstrated against his people to now cause David to barge in through the walls of Edom. The oracle not only creates a picture of divine

---

50. Ravasi, *Il libro dei Salmi*, 2:225, reads *'alay* 'against me' as a *scriptio plena* of *'alê* 'over' and התרעע as a *hithpolel* infinitive construct with a first person singular suffix, rendering 'il mio grido di vittoria'.

51. The same can be said of the other Davidic titles: (1) David's seeking protection in Ahimelek's house (52.2) recalls David's prayer for the rebuilding of Jerusalem (51.20-21). (2) The Ziphites of 54.2 are already foreshadowed in those who devour God's people in 53.5. (3) The confidence transpiring from 55.24 is an antidote to David's capture by the Philistines in Gath in Ps. 56. (4) The same applies to 57.1 where the darkness of the cave, David's hiding place, is endured with the assurance that he will walk in the light of the living (56.14). (5) Finally, the threat to kill David in 59.1 is anticipated by his assurance that God will vindicate him and let him wash his feet in his enemy's blood (58.11-12).

52. Seybold, *Die Psalmen*, 237, thinks that the notion of God as sovereign in vv. 8-10 creates an affinity with 59.14 and 61.7-8, whilst that of the fortress in 60.11 comes close to 59.18 and 61.3-4. This shows the import of Ps. 60 at this juncture. Moreover, the cultic implications of the divine oracle of Ps. 60 can be linked to the call in Ps. 59 for God to arise.

supremacy but also stimulates action that can be taken in the strength of that image. However, the commanding image of God presented leaves David with a minimal role to play. It is the Lord himself who paves the way for the psalmist to face the encounter with Edom, no matter what the contours of that enmity might be. God goes before the psalmist (קדם 59.11) and leads him to the rival city (יבל + נחה, 60.11). The verb יבל ('to bear along') actually gives the impression that this warrior is going to be carried to his place of victory.[53]

In the strength of the oracle which had been preceded immediately by a request for God to answer his prayer, the psalmist poses three consecutive questions in vv. 11-12 (מי ×2; interrogative particle ה) which are then followed by a plea (v. 13) and a statement of assurance in God's salvation (v. 14).[54] Whilst the first two sections of the psalm open with the divine name אלהים, the third opens with the interrogative מי, suggesting that the answer to the question is God himself. The invasion of Edom can safely be said to be connected to the tragedy of the destruction of Jerusalem due to Edom's involvement in the event.[55] Concerning the related Isa. 63.1-6, J. Vermeylen opines: 'Édom y représente sans doute l'oppresseur de la communauté des «justes»'.[56] Yet, thanks to the title,

---

53. C. Süssenbach, *Der elohistische Psalter. Untersuchungen zu Komposition und Theologie von Ps 42–83* (Tübingen: Mohr Siebeck, 2005), 156, aptly notes how trust and petition in vv. 6-7 are inverted in vv. 13-14.

54. Relate this to the sense of confidence felt when an oracle of salvation was given, such that a sense of fulfilment was acknowledged in anticipation as suggested by J. Begrich, 'Das priesterliche Heilsorakel', *ZAW* 52 (1934): 84: '…nun der Beter, das Wort des Orakels aufnehmend, in der Gewißheit der Erhörung selbst im Perfekt sprechen kann'. Reading this psalm in relation to Ps. 108, the conclusion of Eaton, *Kingship and the Psalms*, 60 (i.e. it is the psalmist's personal recollection of the oracle) seems to suggest that even in Ps. 60 there is a particularly optimistic aura.

55. Cf. Ogden, 'Psalm 60', 91; E. Assis, 'Why Edom? On the Hostility Towards Jacob's Brother in Prophetic Sources', *VT* 56 (2006): 14–15, gives the theological background with which to interpret this conflict. According to M. Alshekh, *The Book of Psalms with Romemot El / Commentary by Rabbi Moshe ben Chayim Alshich (hakadosh); Translated and Condensed by Eliyahu Munk* (Jerusalem: n.p., 1992), 419, the sages saw this psalm as speaking of the Jews in exile, namely under the Edomites, Romans etc. Yet, the rabbi explains that when under the exile of the Medes, the Jews were *redeemed* from destruction at the hands of Haman in Shushan, to which על־שושן in v. 1 refers (cf. p. 421).

56. J. Vermeylen, *Du prophète Isaïe à l'apocalyptique : Isaïe, 1–35, miroir d'un demi-millénaire d'expérience religieuse en Israël, Vol. 2* (Paris: J. Gabalda, 1978), 489.

the king emerges as the one who renders witness to God's victory.⁵⁷ But the meaning of the entire composition is derived when one reads to the end, where one reaches the succinct statement in v. 13b שוא תשועת אדם ('the help of man is worthless'), which must be linked to the figure of Joab, as argued above.

Contrasting the use of בוס ('to trample') in v. 14 to its occurrence in 44.6 shows that in Psalm 60 it is meant to aggrandize the image of God.⁵⁸ In the national lament Psalm 44, it is the people who trample on their adversaries, whereas in Psalm 60 it is God who does so. This is confirmed by the image of God in Isaiah 63 where he himself takes vengeance on Edom. Here, the metaphorical reading of דרך ('to tread') that serves to show God's greatness in stature can be gleaned from the association of Edom with a winepress which is trodden by God (vv. 1-3). For God, the enemies are reduced to the size of grapes which burst under his feet.⁵⁹ It is in this light that we must read Susan Gillingham's observation about the oracle: 'God is now on the side of his own people, and a battle will soon be won'.⁶⁰ Susan makes this point in an article she penned on Ps. 60.10 in which she boldly challenges the imagery employed in the psalm. My intention here is not to single out the particular Moabite depiction detailed there, which Susan expounded very convincingly, but rather to gauge the impact of the ensemble of images furnished particularly by the oracle.

On Imagination

Brueggemann's insights on the role of imagination in creating an alternative world by using extraordinary images is the point of departure of an article penned by L. P. Maré in which he seeks to explicate the function of

---

57. Cf. S. Bazylinski, *1 Salmi 20–21* (Rome: Miscellanea Francescana, 1999), 141 and 212, who sees Ps. 20 as a prayer preceding a battle and Ps. 21 as hanging in the balance between a former victory and future ones. Ps. 20.10, הושיעה המלך יעננו, comes very close to 60.7, הושיעה ימינך וענני. The assurance of being restored in 20.9 (עוד in *hithpolel*, 'to be restored'; *qal*, 'to bear witness'), would lead to a testimony given by the king (עדות, 60.1).

58. Steinberg, *Ketuvim*, 243, has highlighted the similarities and differences between these two psalms, stating that Ps. 60 does not linger in lamentation as much as Ps. 44.

59. The propinquity of Ps. 60 and Isa. 63 can be surmised from the identical description of God who intoxicates with alcoholic drink (Ps. 60.5 and Isa. 63.6).

60. S. Gillingham, '"Moab Is My Washpot" (PS.60:8[MT10]): Another Look at the MLF (Moabite Liberation Front)', in *Interested Readers: Essays on the Hebrew Bible in Honor of David J. A. Clines*, ed. James K. Aitken, Jeremy M. S. Clines, and Christl M. Maier (Atlanta: SBL, 2013), 61–71 (here p. 64).

18.8-16.⁶¹ This theophany, he concludes, is not a mere report of historical facts, but a hope-generating imaginative text that offers new realities and possibilities beyond the present crisis of the psalmist. By the same token, the question is not whether Psalm 60 is a prayer of hope or a fulfilled prayer. Beyond David's efficacy or otherwise in prayer, the matter at stake is a theological truth regarding God's sovereignty. What constitutes both the kernel of the psalm and the heart of its message is, therefore, the community's resolve to bring to mind the words of God and to appropriate them for itself. This is similar to the resolve to affirm God's greatness in Psalm 45 after a communal lament. What is achieved in the first Korah group by means of the juxtaposition of psalms features here internally within this one single psalm.

It might be plausible to hold that the real gauge of one's faith is not the outcome of one's prayer, but one's ability to create a mental worldview that jars completely with any present moment of distress. In other words, great faith demands imagining the unimaginable. In this respect, though form-critical considerations of how former oracles were inserted into laments may be correct from a historical-critical perspective, they might not fully do justice to the high degree of faith that is transmitted when the oracle is read synchronically as a projection of the psalmist's own imagination.⁶² In fact, contrary to several modern translations, it may not be ideal to translate the phrase אלהים דבר in 60.8 as 'God has spoken', as though this had happened in the past, prior to the petition. Rather, it should be rendered as 'God spoke' and interpreted as having happened in answer to the prayer, in line with the request וענני in v. 7.⁶³ Interpreting

61. Cf. L. P. Maré, 'The Theophany Report in Psalm 18 as Expression of an Alternative Reality', *JSem* 19 (2010): 98–112 (98–9); W. Brueggemann, *Hopeful Imagination*, Prophetic Voices in Exile (London: SCM, 1986, 1992), 96–7.

62. Ps. 60.7-12 reappear as the second section of Ps. 108 (vv. 7-14), the first part of which (vv. 1-6) corresponds nearly perfectly to 57.7-11. Undoubtedly, such pieces may have been utilized by psalmists as parts of their picture puzzle, but the writers' potential for imagination can better be grasped when one reads the text as a narrative from beginning to end, without explaining things away by discourse on insertions. On the use of imagination in the oracle of Ps. 60, see Gillingham, 'Moab Is My Washpot', 67–8.

63. C. Westermann, *Lob und Klage in den Psalmen* (Göttingen: Vandenhoeck & Ruprecht, 1977), 48, speaks about the relation of oracles of salvation both with respect to psalms and to the Psalter at large. He avers: 'es ist kein Zufall, daß das Heilsorakel in den Psalmen selbst kaum je begegnet, häufig aber (fast regelmäßig) *als Antwort* auf Klagen des Volkes in den prophetischen Büchern' (italics added). His belief that the binding of an oracle with a lament produces a 'prophetic liturgy' more than a psalm throws light on the nature and purpose of this composition.

this otherwise would render וענני a mere rhetorical expression, with the psalmist already knowing what the answer would be. This is surely not what the community is intent on doing here in such a lament, since the lament would lose all its force. Reading the oracle as a product of the author's faith-inspired imagination rather than some kind of older literary form that fitted conveniently into this poem would safeguard the author's ability to transport himself to an alternative space from which he could look back at his own predicament. In his analysis of metaphor, P. Ricoeur asserts the following:

> Imagination does not merely *schematize* the predicative assimilation between terms by its synthetic insight into similarities nor does it merely *picture* the sense thanks to the display of images aroused and controlled by the cognitive process. Rather, it contributes concretely to the *epoché* of ordinary reference and to the *projection* of new possibilities of redescribing the world.[64]

One might wonder what relevance such an imagination would have had, especially if the creation of such metaphors for God were considered to be tantamount to daydreaming. In other words, what concrete reality could have instigated the genesis of the grandiose metaphors used in vv. 8-10? It was, undoubtedly, faith in the sovereignty of God over the land of Canaan, faith which came down to the poet through the age-old traditions of Israel. What is interesting is that bellicose metaphors were created to express this faith because this is what the present moment demanded, namely military engagement. These very same linguistic devices thus became a vehicle by which some kind of corresponding action could be taken by the believing community. Their performative function is twofold – they serve to praise God's sovereignty and they also change the psalmist's disposition towards the present impasse.[65] On the other hand, as far as God is concerned, the informative function of these metaphors limits itself to a juridical truth, namely that he is Lord of the entire land. And as far as the psalmist is concerned, the concepts utilized by these metaphors inform us about his faith, of which they are a graphic representation.

---

64. P. Ricoeur, 'The Metaphorical Process as Cognition, Imagination, and Feeling', *Critical Inquiry* 5 (1978): 154.

65. On the performative function, see K. Nielsen, *There is Hope for a Tree: The Tree as Metaphor in Isaiah*, JSOTSup 65 (Sheffield: Sheffield Academic), 56–60.

It has been rightly stated that repetitions of lexemes in a text involve a different nuance each time. This is related to what R. Alter, for instance, calls 'structures of intensification'.[66] One notes that the verb זנח ('to reject') appears twice with God as subject and the people as object, forming a frame around the psalm. The first instance is in v. 3 and it reflects a *present* feeling of despair. The second one appears in v. 12 after the divine words are pronounced, but this time its implication differs from that of the first one. I dare suggest that, contrary to what Alter observes in Psalm 13, here we have an intensification of hope, or rather a mitigation of despair. Though this may be subject to personal interpretation, in my view the second זנח evokes more of a past reality for, subsequent to the oracle, the hope of salvation is dawning. This can be confirmed from the questions asked in vv. 11-12. If the request וענני ('answer me') in v. 7 resulted in the divine oracle concerning God, the questions put to God in vv. 11-12 demand yet another answer, this time concerning David and the community. And the answer expected to the question הלא־אתה ('Is it not you...?') is clearly in the affirmative, rendering the reality of rejection a transitory phase.[67]

Concluding Remarks

The influence of the biographical title and the psalm proper goes in both directions – the psalm fuelled the imagination of the redactors for whom the text spoke of David and his dealings with Joab, and at the same time the title created the setting for a specific interpretation of the psalm.[68] The title effectively alters the meaning of the psalm such that, in line with other personages that appear prior to Psalm 60, wariness concerning the trustworthiness of others is advocated: Doeg (Ps. 52), the unnamed friend-turned-foe (Ps. 55), Saul (Pss. 57 and 59), and finally Joab (Ps. 60).

The pertinence of reading the title of Psalm 60 in line with the surrounding titles also transpires partly from the desire expressed in our psalm to conquer Edom, which links back to the first lament of this group of Davidic psalms where reference is made to Doeg the Edomite who

---

66. R. Alter, *The Art of Biblical Poetry* (New York: Basic Books, 1985), 62–84. In commenting on the fourfold question 'How long?' in Ps. 13, he notes on p. 65 that this anaphoric series 'reflects an ascent on a scale of intensity'.

67. The double use of מי, 'who?', in v. 11 may be related to the double use of אלהים at the beginning of each section, namely in v. 3 and v. 8.

68. An indication that the psalm titles were added after the actual composition of the psalms is the fact that the quasi-identical Pss. 14 and 53 do not bear identical titles.

harms David (52.2). That situation commenced a series of events in which David faced trouble at the hands of brethren (e.g. Saul) and foreigners (e.g. Philistines) alike.[69] That Joab, appearing between Saul and Absalom, denotes a precarious situation for David comes as no surprise given his appearance in this series, his notorious background vis-à-vis David, and the sense of nonfulfillment that exudes from Psalm 60. The psalmist's mental pictorializing of God as a mighty overlord and warrior is the real weapon employed to dare request victory. In this regard, the divine words reported should be read, not as some former discourse that was conveniently inserted at the centre of the psalm, but as an expression of faith that is generated by the psalmist's certainty concerning God's sovereignty. This oracle has the power to shift the believer's focus and to predispose him to receive that for which he pleads.

As regards the annotation ללמד ('for teaching'), this redactional insertion must be taken to refer to aspects found both in the title and the psalm.[70] It seems plausible to surmise that what is being taught has to do with the impact that can be had by proclaiming the divine words. Whilst the psalmist per se expects to make the gigantic leap from cracked land (v. 4) to fortified city (v. 11) by listening to the divine address, the reader makes an even bigger leap together with the redactionally inserted David, going from dependence on man's help to the shunning thereof in order to seek only God's help. This transpires from the frame of the psalm when its title is included.

Exegesis characteristically implies delving into the mind of the authors and redactors in order to discover the true meaning of the texts they produced. In this respect, it involves an immersion into their conceptual world that leads to a better understanding of how they envisaged it. Susan Gillingham's relatively recent interest in reception history has aptly led her to better grasp how the sacred author's literary world has ignited the imagination of various interpreters throughout history, hence completing the picture that can be construed thus far, since texts presuppose readers, and biblical accounts demand the contemporary reader's reaction to them.

---

69. The ability to imagine Elohim as being able to trample down the Edomites (60.14) is in line with the philippic of Ps. 52 which announces the removal of the (Edomite) adversary from his tent.

70. R. Alter, *The Writings*, vol. 3 of *The Hebrew Bible* (New York: W. W. Norton & Co., 2019), 149, suggests that the term might either refer to the song David wants to teach or to some moral lesson one should learn. I hold that the latter is the case, as there is no real reason why David would have wanted to teach *this* psalm, and not others.

Texts born of imagination become, in turn, generators of imagination, but these two forms of imagination are practically never identical, which is the reason why the sacred authors' mental creativity can be considered so fecund.

Bibliography

Alshekh, M. *The Book of Psalms with Romemot El / Commentary by Rabbi Moshe ben Chayim Alshich (hakadosh)*. Translated and condensed by Eliyahu Munk. Jerusalem: [publisher not given], 1992.
Assis, E. 'Why Edom? On the Hostility Towards Jacob's Brother in Prophetic Sources'. *VT* 56 (2006): 1–20.
Attard, S. M. *The Implications of Davidic Repentance: A Synchronic Analysis of Book 2 of the Psalter (Psalms 42–72)*. Rome: Gregorian & Biblical Press, 2016.
Attard, S. M. 'From Well-Fed Lions to Sitting Ducks: A Study of Complex Metaphors in Psalm 17'. Pages 173–91 in *Networks of Metaphors in the Hebrew Bible*. Edited by D. Verde and A. Labahn. BEThL 309. Leuven: Peeters, 2020.
Barbiero, G. 'Il secondo e il terzo libro dei Salmi (Sal 42–89): due libri paralleli'. *RivBib* 58 (2010): 145–75.
Barbiero, G. 'The Risks of a Fragmented Reading of the Psalms'. *ZAW* 120 (2008): 67–91.
Barton, J. *Oracles of God: Perceptions of Ancient Prophecy in Israel after the Exile*. London: Darton, Longman & Todd, 1986.
Bazylinski, S. *1 Salmi 20–21*. Rome: Miscellanea Francescana, 1999.
Briggs, C. A., and E. G. Briggs, *A Critical and Exegetical Commentary on the Book of Psalms*, Vol. 2. ICC. Edinburgh: T&T Clark, 1907.
Brueggemann, W. 'Response to James L. Mays, "The Question of Context"'. Pages 29–41 in *The Shape and Shaping of the Psalter*. Edited by J. Clinton McCann. JSOTSup 159. Sheffield: Sheffield Academic, 1993.
Brueggemann, W. *Texts Under Investigation: The Bible and Postmodern Imagination*. London, SCM, 1993.
Brueggemann, W. *Hopeful Imagination: Prophetic Voices in Exile*. London: SCM Press, 1986.
Childs, B. S. 'Psalm Titles and Midrashic Exegesis'. *JSS* 16 (1971): 146–7
Delitzsch, F. *Biblical Commentary on the Psalms, Vol. 2*. Edinburgh: T. & T. Clark, 1880.
Driver, G. R. 'Notes on the Text of Psalms'. *Harvard Theological Review* 29 (1936): 171–95
Eaton, J. H. *Kingship and the Psalms*, 2nd ed. Sheffield: JSOT, 1986.
Fabry, H.-J., and J. F. Sawyer, 'ישע *jš''*. *ThWAT* 3 (1982): 1035–59.
Gillingham, S. E. *A Journey of Two Psalms: The Reception of Psalms 1 and 2 in Jewish and Christian Tradition*. Oxford: Oxford University Press, 2013.
Gillingham, S. E. '"Moab Is My Washpot" (Ps.60:8 [MT10]): Another Look at the MLF (Moabite Liberation Front)'. Pages 61–71 in *Interested Readers: Essays on the Hebrew Bible in Honor of David J. A. Clines*. Edited by J. K. Aitken, J. M. S. Clines, and C. M. Maier. Atlanta: SBL, 2013.
Gunkel, H., and J. Begrich. *Einleitung in die Psalmen: Die Gattungen der religiösen Lyrik Israels*. 1933. Repr., Göttingen: Vandenhoeck & Ruprecht, 1985.

Hossfeld, F.-L. 'Das Prophetische in den Psalmen. Zur Gottesrede der Asafpsalmen im Vergleich mit der des ersten und zweiten Davidpsalters'. Pages 223–44 in *Ich Bewirke das Heil und Erschaffe das Unheil (Jesaja 45,7). Studien zur Botschaft der Propheten. Festschrift L. Ruppert*. Edited by F. Diedrich and B. Willmes. FzB 88. Würzburg: Echter Verlag, 1998.
Hossfeld, F.-L., and E. Zenger. *Psalms 2: A Commentary on Psalms 51–100*. Edited by Klaus Baltzer. Minneapolis: Fortress, 2005.
Johnson, V. L. *David in Distress: His Portrait Through the Historical Psalms*. New York: T&T Clark, 2009.
Kirkpatrick, A. F. *The Book of Psalms. Books II and III, Psalms XLII–LXXXIX*. 1895. Repr., Cambridge: Cambridge University Press, 1904.
Knauf, E. A. 'Psalm 60 und Psalm 108'. *VT* 50 (2000): 55–65.
Kraus, H. J. *Psalms 60–150: A Continental Commentary*. Translated by Hilton C. Oswald. Minneapolis: Fortress, 1993.
Kraus, H. J. *Psalmen, Vol. 2*. 5th ed., BK 15. Neukirchen: Neukirchen Kreis Moers, 1978.
Maré, L. P. 'The Theophany Report in Psalm 18 as Expression of an Alternative Reality'. *JSem* 19 (2010): 98–112.
May, H. G. '"AL...." in the Superscriptions of the Psalms'. *The American Journal of Semitic Languages and Literatures* 58 (1941): 70–83.
Ogden, G. S. 'Psalm 60: Its Rhetoric, Form, and Function'. *JSOT* 31 (1985): 83–94.
Ravasi, G. *Il libro dei Salmi. Commento e attualizzazzione, Vol. 2*. Bologna: Edizioni Dehoniane, 2002.
Rendtorff, R. 'The Psalms of David: David in the Psalms'. Pages 53–64 in *The Book of Psalms: Composition and Reception*. Edited by P. W. Flint and P. D. Miller. VTSup 99. Brill: Leiden, 2005.
Ricoeur, P. 'The Metaphorical Process as Cognition, Imagination, and Feeling'. *Critical Inquiry* 5 (1978): 143–59.
Romero-Girón Deleito, J. *Historia de la Cartografía, La Evolución de los Mapas: Primera Parte. El Mundo Antiguo de la Prehistoria a Roma*. Madrid Edición Personal, 2018.
Seybold, K. *Die Psalmen*. HAT 1/15. Tübingen: Mohr, 1996.
Steinberg, J. *Die Ketuvim: ihr Aufbau und ihre Botschaft*. BBB 152. Hamburg: Philo, 2006.
Süssenbach, C. *Der elohistische Psalter: Untersuchungen zu Komposition und Theologie von Ps 42–83*. Tübingen: Mohr Siebeck, 2005.
Uehlinger, C. 'Antiker Tell, lebendiges Stadtviertel: Das Psalmenbuch als Sammlung von Einzeldichtungen und als Großkomposition'. *BK* 56 (2001): 174–7.
Vermeylen, J. *Du prophète Isaïe à l'apocalyptique: Isaïe, 1–35, miroir d'un demi-millénaire d'expérience religieuse en Israël, Vol. 2*. Paris: J. Gabalda, 1978.
Weiser, A. *Die Psalmen, Vol. 1*. ATD 14. Göttingen: Vandenhoeck & Ruprecht, 1987.
Westermann, C. *Lob und Klage in den Psalmen*. Göttingen: Vandenhoeck & Ruprecht, 1977.
Willgren, D. '"May YHWH avenge me on you; but my hand shall not be against you" (1 Sam. 24.13): Mapping Land and Resistance in the "Biographical" Notes of the "Book" of Psalms'. *JSOT* 43 (2019): 417–35.
Wright, J. W. 'The Innocence of David in 1 Chronicles 21'. *JSOT* 60 (1993): 87–105.

The Two 'Solomon' Psalms:
Psalm 72 and 127 in the Light of the
Solomonic Attribution*

Katharine J. Dell

Whilst attributions to David dominate the Psalter, often accompanied by a description of the occasion for the psalm, Solomon only has a marginal place in the psalm superscriptions. His name occurs only twice, in the superscriptions to Psalms 72 and 127 (as לשלמה, 'of Solomon', i.e. 'pertaining to Solomon').[1] Whilst it is likely that the psalm superscriptions are a later aspect of the Psalter (possibly added in the Second Temple period[2]) some scholars have taken issue with that conclusion and see more significance in them in relation to individual psalms. Michael Goulder in particular puts forward the view that the headings are important.[3] He points out that 73 psalms out of 150 bear the לדוד ('to David')

---

* It is a great pleasure to contribute this piece to a volume honouring Sue Gillingham. I have known Sue over many years and always appreciated her work as well as her friendship. She has patiently chaired me at the Oxford Old Testament Seminar for a large chunk of the 15 or so papers I have presented there!

1. Brevard S. Childs, *Introduction to the Old Testament as Scripture* (Philadelphia: Fortress, 1979), 143–8, suggests translating 'for Solomon' with the inference 'and hence spoken by David'. Samuel L. Terrien, *The Psalms: Strophic Structure and Theological Commentary*, Eerdmans Critical Commentary (Grand Rapids: Eerdmans, 2003), 519, also suggests 'for Solomon' in the sense of 'composed for him'. There is early textual evidence of ascribing this psalm to David in the LXX (where it is Ps. 71) and in Syriac tradition.

2. This would also explain the headings of some psalms that are attributed to the Levitical singer, Asaph – i.e. Ps. 50 and Pss. 73–83.

3. Michael D. Goulder, *The Prayers of David (Psalms 51–72)*, Studies in the Psalter II, JSOTSup 102 (Sheffield: JSOT, 1990). He had already put forward this theory in reference to the psalms attributed to the sons of Korah in his *The Psalms of*

title and most of those are in Books 1 and 2 of the Psalter. He argues that the normal dismissal of the association of these psalms with David rests upon the 'flimsiest' basis. He posits that if occasional poems are plausibly attributed to David within narrative texts such as in Samuel, then why not the other way around.[4] Goulder writes, 'Somewhere in the Psalter there is a core of David psalms, and…the sons of Korah, Asaph and others have added to these and perhaps amended them'.[5] He makes three assumptions: (1) He accepts the association with David without thinking that David necessarily wrote them. They may have been composed in his court, however, in response to situations during his lifetime. (2) He accepts the order of the psalms as representing the chronological order of their writing and hence mirroring sequences of events in the king's life to which they are a response. (3) He accepts the idea behind the historical notes in the Headings, i.e. that a Psalm can be understood only in the light of the circumstances for which it was composed.[6] The actual historical notes could be late glosses or guesses, but not all are in that category. He extends the David conclusions to Solomon – Psalm 72, he argues, could well have been a psalm composed for the accession of King Solomon (and the details link up with the 1 Kgs 1–12 account), which happened before David's death.

In the canon there are three books attributed, either directly or indirectly, to Solomon – Song of Songs, Proverbs and Ecclesiastes – famously said by the Rabbis to align with three stages of Solomon's life in which he might have expressed the different sentiments of romantic love,

---

the Sons of Korah, Studies in the Psalter I, JSOTSup 20 (Sheffield: JSOT, 1982). His third volume (of four), *The Psalms of Asaph and the Pentateuch*, Studies in the Psalter 3, JSOTSup 233 (Sheffield: Sheffield Academic, 1996), was on the psalms attributed to the sons of Asaph.

4. Psalm 18 in particular has a special link with David in that it closely parallels his Song in 2 Sam. 22 and Davidic authorship (or at least court authorship) is still considered possible.

5. Goulder, *The Prayers of David*, 12.

6. It is surprising that these ideas from Goulder have not been taken up more widely. In a full article on the topic of the role of the Davidic superscriptions, David Willgren Davage does not even mention this work (David Willgren Davage, 'Why Davidic Superscriptions Do Not Demarcate Earlier Collections of Psalms', *JBL* 139 [2020]: 67–86), although similar conclusions are reached: i.e. 'the proper contexts of interpretation for these superscriptions are the individual psalms themselves' (p. 21), rather than looking to how they demarcate collections of psalms. Davage argues this, though, on the basis of the idea that sequences and superscriptions in the psalms were not fixed early on, as indicated by the fluidity of attribution in the Qumran scroll evidence that he cites.

sagacious ethics and pessimistic musings.[7] The ascriptions in these cases are also often seen as later additions, although I have argued elsewhere that there is likely to be more to them than just a later attempt to claim authority for each book[8]. The ascription in Ecclesiastes is more veiled ('son of David, king in Jerusalem', 1.1, 18), but the Solomonic 'guise' adopted in ch. 2 adds to the weight of the association with Solomon, even though no one nowadays would say that he actually wrote it.[9] My point is that there could be an early association of these books with Solomon, reflecting his reputation for wisdom in 1 Kgs 4.34 and linking up with it,[10] even if he did not literally write such books. The same could be true of the two psalms that I am considering today – Solomon may well have had an early association with these psalms even if he did not actually write them. Brueggemann, although he finds no historical link for the headings (following Childs), confirms the possibility of a link that derived from material within the psalm texts.[11] He writes, 'We may look within the psalms themselves to see what may have occurred in the traditioning process that evoked the superscription reference to Solomon and that in turn invited canonical readers to entertain the psalms in the horizon of the imagined Solomon of the canon'.[12] The question remains, though, whether there might be any kind of historical or literary link. What is it within these psalms in particular that, at any stage, suggested a link to Solomon

---

7. In *Cant. Rab.* 1.1 Rabbi Jonathan wrote of Solomon, 'When a man is young he composes songs; when he grows older he makes sententious remarks; and when he becomes an old man he speaks of the vanity of things'.

8. Katharine J. Dell, 'Ecclesiastes as Mainstream Wisdom (without Job)', in *Goochem in Mokum/Wisdom in Amsterdam: Papers on Biblical and Related Wisdom Read at the Fifteenth Joint Meeting of The Society of Old Testament Study and the Oudtestamentisch Werkgezelschap, Amsterdam July 2012*, ed. George J. Brooke and Pierre Van Hecke, OTS 68 (Leiden: Brill, 2016), 43–52.

9. For a lively discussion of the Solomonic attribution and its relation to authorship by Qoheleth, see Tomas Bolin, *Ecclesiastes and the Riddle of Authorship* (London: Routledge, 2017). He finds within its pages "a variety of partial, fragmentary authorial voices that often frustrate more than they clarify our attempts to read the text as a coherent unit" (p. 6) and this is as true of the history of 'reading' this text as it is about more diachronic questions of how the book came to be in its final form.

10. See Katharine J. Dell, *The Solomonic Corpus of wisdom and its Influence* (Oxford: Oxford University Press, 2020), Chapter 4: '"The Lord loved him": Solomon as Idealized Character and Paradigm for Character Ethics within the "Solomonic" Canon'.

11. Walter Brueggemann, *Solomon: Israel's Ironic Icon of Human Achievement* (Columbia: University of South Carolina Press, 2005).

12. Ibid., 215.

and gave him a canonical link to the book of Psalms as well as to the Solomonic canon of Song of Songs, Proverbs and Ecclesiastes? These are the questions to be addressed in this paper.

Following Gunkel's classification of the psalms into different 'genres',[13] Psalm 72 is a royal psalm with 'the king' as its subject and largely sounds a note of praise for the king as the giver of all good things. There is no overt indication however of a specific king. Psalm 127 is very different – it is one of Gunkel's 'psalms of ascent' in the series of Psalms 120–134, as indicated by 'A Song of Ascents' in the heading, and yet it has also been classified as a 'pilgrim song'[14] and as a 'wisdom psalm' by some scholars (see below) and this aspect is of interest as we explore the link with Solomon.

Solomonic Connections

Psalm 72.1 makes mention of 'a king's son', which might evoke Solomon, comparing both to the dynastic promise to David in 2 Samuel 7 (which explicitly mentions David's son) and to the attributions to the 'son of David' in Eccl. 1.1, 12. Verse 2 speaks of judging 'with righteousness... and justice' which may recall the tale of the judgement of Solomon in 1 Kgs 3.16-28 when he adjudicates between two women as to their claims to a baby. Verse 10 mentions both bringing 'tribute' and 'the kings of Sheba', possibly linking up with 1 Kgs 4.21 and 10.1-13 (on the Queen of Sheba) in the account of Solomon's reign. We also find 'gold of Sheba' described in v. 15. The psalm also concerns itself with economic issues with which, naturally, the king would be involved with reference to the poor and the oppressor (cf. Ps. 72.1-4, 12-14) and it has an international scope with foreign kings bringing tribute and gifts and kings and nations giving him 'service' (v. 11), which would certainly not have been true before Solomon's reign with its international outreach. As James Crenshaw writes, 'The association of Solomon with Psalm 72 seems natural, given its concern for royal justice, the reference to emissaries bringing gifts from distant Sheba, and the stress on the vast extent of the king's domain'.[15] Likewise, Brueggemann writes, 'Clearly the

---

13. Hermann Gunkel, *Einleitung in die Psalmen: Die Gattungen der religiösen Lyrik Israels* (Göttingen: Vandenhoeck & Ruprecht, 1933).

14. H. J. Kraus, *Psalmen* 1, BKAT 15 (Neukirchen-Vluyn: Neukirchener Verlag, 1961).

15. James L. Crenshaw, *The Psalms: An Introduction* (Grand Rapids: Eerdmans, 2001), 32. The comments immediately following this citation go too far in my view, however.

convergence of power, wealth, and honor is appropriate to Solomon as to no other king that was ever celebrated in ancient Israel'.[16] Brueggemann adds the point that Ps. 72.18-19 with its reference to God (sometimes seen as a later addition) forges a fresh emphasis on royal prosperity as a gift of God, a theme of 1 Kings 3–11 when wisdom and more is God's gift to Solomon. More subtly – and linking intertextually to wisdom concerns – as part of the description of the king as the giver of good things, which importantly involves language of the natural world, there are echoes of proverbial kingly wisdom. 'May he [the king] be like rain that falls on the mown grass, like showers that water the earth' (Ps. 72.6) echoes Prov. 16.15, a proverb about the king, that reads: 'In the light of a king's face there is life, and his favour is like the clouds that bring the spring rain'. Similarly, Prov. 19.12, 'A king's anger is like the growling of a lion, but his favour is like dew on the grass', links up with v. 6; and the mention of grass links up with the final part of v. 16: 'may the people blossom in the cities like the grass of the field'.

Psalm 127 links less closely to Solomon, but themes of 'house' (which could refer to dynasty), 'city' (which could denote Jerusalem) and 'sons' (as guarantors of the dynasty) might lend themselves to a royal setting, even to a Solomonic one. Indeed, Crenshaw sees the very attribution to Solomon as being because of the mention of building a house in v. 1. He writes, 'The association of Psalm 127 with the name Solomon in the inscription was an extrapolation from the topic of verse 1, building a house. The reference to Yahweh's guarding the city suggested to someone Solomon's construction of the temple over which Yahweh stood guard'.[17] The mention of 'in vain/vanity' (vv. 1, 2) might recall Ecclesiastes except that the word used is not הבל.[18] Mention of 'toil' too may offer a link – here toiling too hard with anxiety (cf. Eccl. 2.18-23; 6.7) is contrasted with the calm sleep offered by the Lord to 'his beloved'.[19] Brueggemann suggests that the reference to 'sons' in vv. 3-5 may echo the urgency for sons as guarantors of the Davidic dynasty (as found in 2 Sam. 7.12) – he reads these verses in the context of the 'unless' of v. 1 to reveal 'a profound either/or about all of life and…about royal life'.[20] Brueggemann

---

16. Brueggemann, *Solomon*, 216.

17. Crenshaw, *The Psalms: An Introduction*, 22.

18. Brueggemann, *Solomon*, argues that the word used (ישוא) is in the same semantic field as הבל. He thus concludes that the psalm offers a critique of Solomon, much as he believes Ecclesiastes does.

19. Echoing Nathan's term used in naming Solomon ('Jedediah' in 2 Sam. 12.25), or an overtone of Song of Songs (2.3, 16; 4.16).

20. Brueggemann, *Solomon*, 223.

then goes on to overread this as a critique of Solomon's attempts 'to raise a house without the Lord building it. Solomon tried to rule a city without the Lord guarding it. Solomon tried to produce a dynasty of sons without the Lord's blessing'.[21]

Wider Contextual Issues

In terms of context, Psalm 72 is usually seen as a cultic psalm, possibly recited at a festival involving the king[22] or a prayer for the king at his coronation.[23] Psalm 127 is often considered, as with other wisdom psalms, as non-cultic. I have elsewhere challenged this assumption, springing from Mowinckel,[24] that wisdom psalms are non-cultic[25] – but the question here is whether Psalm 127 is to be classified as a wisdom psalm at all and whether then there is a link to the Solomonic wisdom corpus.[26] Terrien argues that this psalm may have been conceived in the sapiential circles of Judahite kings, perhaps at the court of King Hezekiah whose name features in Prov. 25.1.[27]

Psalm 72 puts a particular emphasis on the poor which for some scholars (notably Brueggemann[28]) puts it outside the realm of Solomonic concern, indeed Brueggemann thinks that it is a critique of Solomon simply because of this emphasis which he does not see as characterizing his reign. He points out that in Ps. 72.2 the royal commitment to justice and righteousness (stated twice in the first 2 verses in chiastic fashion) has as its object 'your poor'. In v. 4 'the poor of the people' and 'the needy' are

---

21. Ibid.
22. Aubrey R. Johnson, *Sacral Kingship in Ancient Israel*, 2nd ed. (Cardiff: University of Wales Press, 1967).
23. Comparisons have been made with Ashurbanipal's coronation hymn in c. 669 BCE, see Susan E. Gillingham, *Psalms Through the Centuries: A Reception History Commentary on Psalms 1–72, Vol. 2*, Wiley Blackwell Bible Commentaries (Oxford: Wiley-Blackwell, 2018), 386.
24. Sigmund Mowinckel, 'Psalms and Wisdom', in *Wisdom in Israel and in the Ancient Near East*, ed. M. Noth and D. W. Thomas, VTSup 3 (Leiden: Brill, 1955), 205–44.
25. Katharine J. Dell, '"I will solve my riddle to the music of the lyre" (Psalm 44:4 [5]): A Cultic Setting for Wisdom Psalms?', *VT* 54 (2004): 445–58.
26. I prefer to use the terminology of the Solomonic wisdom corpus, rather than the traditional nomenclature of 'wisdom literature' (which includes Job). See Dell, *The Solomonic Corpus of Wisdom*.
27. Terrien, *The Psalms*, 830.
28. Brueggemann, *Solomon*.

specified. This emphasis also features in vv. 12-14.[29] Following Jobling he argues that 'the primary accent in this psalm is upon the condition of compassionate justice as a prerequisite for monarchal well-being'.[30] He thus argues that the psalm is a criticism of Solomon because, although he exercised justice, there is no mention of the poor and needy. Although the Queen of Sheba speaks of Solomon's 'justice and righteousness', Brueggemann dismisses this as 'standard royal hyperbole'[31] and he finds a general tone of self-aggrandizement in the 1 Kings text to suggest that 'the Solomonic enterprise practiced by the urban elites was completely lacking in the conditions stated in Psalm 72 for royal well-being'.[32] He sees Psalm 72 therefore as presenting an ideal of the just king and public critique of an unjust one, notably Solomon. I think Brueggemann overstates the case here and I am not convinced of Jobling's premise that the entire psalm revolves around the treatment of the poor. Brueggemann even sees a possibility of reading the neighbouring psalm, Psalm 73, as the words of a chastened Solomon, a king wishing to stress law and communion with God afresh after he was tempted away.

Psalm 72: Themes and Interpretation

Going back to Psalm 72, there is certainly an idealistic element here, but it is not clear that this is simply a critique of one king, rather in my view it is a more generic statement of the elevated hopes of the people for the God-given blessings that a king might bestow – right judgement, prosperity, defending causes, crushing oppressors and delivering the needy (vv. 1-4). A parallel is 1 Kgs 3.9, which has Solomon asking God for the ability to 'govern your people, able to discern between good and evil'. These qualities are linked in the psalm to the continuity of a dynasty, not simply to one king, although Solomon clearly stands as a model for the dynasty. I don't see vv. 5 and following as dependent upon the poverty sentiment in vv. 1-4. Rather the language about the king becomes even more elevated and ideological in the appeal to nature and to the cosmic – in v. 3 we already had 'the mountains', now sun and moon, rain and showers come into the picture, with all generations, abounding

29. See David Jobling, 'Deconstruction and the Political Analysis of Biblical Texts: A Jamesonian Reading of Psalm 72', *Semeia* 59 (1992): 95–127, who argues that the introductory כי ('for') in v. 12 affirms that making the case for the vulnerable in vv. 1-4 is the *cause* of dominion, longevity and prosperity for the king in vv. 5-11.
30. Brueggemann, *Solomon*, 217.
31. Ibid.
32. Ibid., 218.

peace, wide dominion, subjugation of enemies and the admiration of the nations being high on the royal agenda. By comparison, in 1 Kgs 5.4 Solomon says that 'The Lord my God has given me rest on every side; there is neither adversary nor misfortune' and so he has time to build the temple. Verses 12-14 return to the idea of the poor who have no helper, who are dependent upon the 'redemption' offered by the king – this does not immediately bring Solomon to mind, but his judgement on the two women and the baby might fit the bill, if we wanted to make such a specific association. In the next three verses the key motif is abundance, excess of gold, reflecting what the Queen of Sheba gave Solomon in 1 Kgs 10.10, and of blessing, fruitful blossoming and that highest of Hebrew honours – an enduring name. The final two verses read like a standard doxology and are often regarded as a later addition, also terminating the second book of the Psalter.

The psalm also has what Susan Gillingham calls 'an exaggerated ideology', notably in reference to the homage expected from other nations, in tension with 'a pragmatic realism' in its concern for social justice and care for the poor (this theme linking up with Pss. 51 and 69–71).[33] Scholarly interest in Psalm 72 has also centred on its placement at the end of Book 2 of the Psalter.[34] Paralleled by the placement of Psalm 89 at the end of Book 3, the placement of Psalm 72 might suggest a desire to bring prominence to the Davidic monarchy and line. It may enable a future slant, even suggesting a messianic hope, with the accompanying emphases on eternal peace and worldwide dominion (v. 17 suggesting this in particular). Within Book 2, Gillingham points to a relationship with Psalm 51 because of the heading that concerns Bathsheba and Solomon. She writes of Psalm 72: 'It comes almost at the mid-point of the Psalter: it is one of the most contested of the psalms, with Jews and Christians interpreting the prayers of the king – for justice and cosmic fertility (verses 1-7, 12-14, 16) and for world-wide dominion (verses 8-11, 17) – in entirely different ways'.[35] Gillingham also notes that messianic readings were given to the psalm in both Jewish and Christian circles from early times,[36] arguing that 'the ideology of world domination and the concern

---

33. Gillingham, *Psalms Through the Centuries*, 2:386.

34. Notably by R. N. Whybray, *Reading the Psalms as a Book*, JSOTSup 222 (Sheffield: Sheffield Academic, 1996), 92.

35. Gillingham, *Psalms Through the Centuries*, 2:386.

36. Jews read it messianically from Hellenistic times and Christians quickly adopted it as a prophecy of the Messiah – it is often read at the Feast of the Epiphany, 'applied to the visit of the royal wise men and their adoration of the infant Jesus (Matt. 2:9-12)', as noted by Terrien, *The Psalms*, 522.

for the poor are at the heart of the contentious and different "messianic" readings'.³⁷ She makes the point that the placement of Psalm 72 in the collection of Book 2 would have happened long after the monarchy had come to an end and so a messianic interpretation was in many ways inevitable as the future was anticipated. These points about placement also reinforce the Solomonic connection. Following on from Psalms 70–71 we have the prayer of David (when old and close to death), followed by a prayer for kingship to pass to his son, Solomon, by succession. Gillingham points to links between Psalms 71 and 72, including the emphasis on righteousness, reflections on later generations and use of תמיד 'continually' (Ps. 71.3, 6, 14; 72.15).³⁸

Psalm 127 and the 'Wisdom' Classification

The evidence for a wisdom connection for Psalm 127 is piecemeal, but the scholarly consensus seems to be in favour of its inclusion.³⁹ Daniel Estes uses it as his prime example of a wisdom psalm and writes, 'Ps 127 is included in virtually all the proposed lists of wisdom psalms. The psalm consists of two sayings that reflect some of the prominent emphases of the wisdom sayings'.⁴⁰ It was agreed by older scholars that this psalm was in some sense wisdom literature (Gunkel,⁴¹ Kraus⁴²), although there were and still are difficulties defining exactly what kind of discussion actually constituted the category.⁴³ Whilst some have divided it into two parts on thematic grounds (vv. 1-2; vv. 3-5),⁴⁴ most have treated it as a unified whole (e.g. Miller⁴⁵). The psalm contains little reference to God,

37. Gillingham, *Psalms Through the Centuries*, 2:386.
38. Ibid., 2:387.
39. Included by me too on a 'broader definition' of wisdom; see Dell, 'I will solve my riddle'.
40. Daniel J. Estes, *Handbook on the Wisdom Books and Psalms* (Grand Rapids: Baker, 2005).
41. Gunkel, *Einleitung in die Psalmen*.
42. Kraus, *Psalmen* I.
43. Whybray, *Reading the Psalms as a Book*, notes that this is a different kind of 'wisdom' to an 'intellectual or introspective' type. Problems of defining both 'wisdom' and 'wisdom literature' are common, aired most recently by Will Kynes, *An Obituary for Wisdom Literature: The Birth, Death, and Intertextual Reintegration of a Biblical Corpus* (Oxford: Oxford University Press, 2019).
44. E.g. Gunkel, *Einleitung in die Psalmen*.
45. Patrick D. Miller, Jr, 'Psalm 127: The House That Yahweh Builds', *JSOT* 22 (1982): 119–32.

which some have (mistakenly) used as a 'wisdom' criterion,[46] although mention of God being in the very first verse and then again in v. 3 does seem to contradict this point. As Whybray writes, 'There is also a thematic consistency within the psalm in that it expresses or implies the thought that nothing can be successfully accomplished without the help of Yahweh'.[47] Indeed, as Simon Stocks mentions when arguing that ambiguity is present in wisdom elements in the Psalter, 'The same sentiment is evident in Psalm 127, along with yet more ambiguity about exactly how Yhwh might build the house or guard the city. The clear blessings of progeny (vv. 3-5) typify those sources of security that cannot be laboured for but depend upon Yhwh'.[48] Indeed the two references to 'the Lord' seem to link the two halves of the psalm. The expression 'builds the house' was taken by Schmidt to mean 'founds a family' thus enabling an even stronger linkage with vv. 3-5 on the blessings of progeny.[49] Dahood found an inclusion between 'guarding the city' in v. 1 and 'speaking in the gate' in v. 5 thus linking the sections.[50] The theme of 'toil' is also a link between the two halves of the Psalm.[51] Estes summarizes the thematic links thus: 'The disorientation of human futility in toil apart from Yahweh is answered by the new orientation of the permanent effect possible through the nurture of children. The pain of vanity is assuaged by the prospect of lasting impact upon human society'.[52] Scholars often point to the use of אשרי 'happy is' in v. 5, a frequently used word in Proverbs, although this evidence would not, alone, be enough for a wisdom classification.

Kenneth Kuntz argues for 127 as a wisdom psalm and also includes 128 and 133 as 'sentence' wisdom psalms. [53]Leo Perdue sees Psalm 127,

---

46. Mistakenly, as wisdom material is full of references to Yahweh, see Katharine J. Dell, *The Book of Proverbs in Social and Theological Context* (Cambridge: Cambridge University Press, 2006).

47. Whybray, *Reading the Psalms as a Book*, 69–70.

48. S. P. Stocks, '"Children, listen to me": The Voicing of Wisdom in the Psalms', in *Exploring Old Testament Wisdom: Literature and Themes*, ed. D. Firth and L. Wilson (London: Apollos, 2016), 194–204 (quotation, p. 198).

49. Hans Schmidt, *Die Psalmen*, HAT (Tübingen: Mohr, 1934). Cf. Miller, 'Psalm 127: the house that Yahweh builds', who finds a word play between *bana* ('build') and *banim* ('sons') (pp. 123-4).

50. Mitchell Dahood, *Psalms, Vols. 1–3*, AB 16–17a (Garden City: Doubleday, 1966, 1968, 1970).

51. Leslie C. Allen, *Psalms 101–150*, WBC 21 (Waco: Word, 1983).

52. Estes, *Handbook on Wisdom Books and Psalms*, 196.

53. J. K. Kuntz, 'The Canonical Wisdom Psalms of Ancient Israel – Their Rhetorical, Thematic, and Formal Dimensions', in *Rhetorical Criticism: Essays in*

with Psalms 1, 19b, 34, 37, 73 and 112, as a proverb poem.[54] Whybray comments on, 'the proverb-like style' of the psalm and links it closely to its surrounding Psalms 126 and 128 which also 'reflect everyday domestic concerns'.[55] In his later, *The Good Life in the Old Testament*, Whybray stresses in particular the link of family concerns between Psalms 127 and 128.[56] He draws out the point, made in vv. 3-5, that sons and possibly also daughters ('the fruit of the womb') are an 'inheritance/heritage' (נחלה) and reward (שׂכר) from God. He notes that 'like arrows in the hand of a warrior' (v. 4) may be a reference to the father's virility and it is clear from v. 5 that a large family gives the head of the family high standing in the community and at the city gate. Whybray writes then of Psalm 128: 'closely related to the previous psalm, [Psalm 128] affirms that a man will enjoy a good life whose sons contribute to the productivity of his farm; he will be happy at home when he sees them assembled around his table'.[57] He enjoys a 'fruitful vine' of a wife and has the blessing of grandchildren to anticipate.

Certain verses may air similar themes to wisdom. Crenshaw writes, 'Occasionally psalms use expressions and images that can also be found in Wisdom literature. For example, Psalm 127 elaborates upon the sages' claim that human plans often go awry due to divine intentions (127:1-2). This psalm also has the image of children as arrows in a quiver (127:4)'.[58] In general, though, Crenshaw does not favour going outside a fairly narrow definition of 'wisdom literature' to find connections, although he does seem to acknowledge a category of wisdom psalms which appears to include this psalm. Perhaps the main argument is that the sum of the verses arguably read like sentence literature, as do other Psalms of Ascents.

Conclusion

It is clear that these two psalms are very different – Psalm 72 is more easily linked in literary and historical terms to Solomon by its classification as a royal psalm and its mention of aspects linked to the 1 Kings account of

Honor of James Muilenburg, ed. Jared J. Jackson and Martin Kessler (Pittsburgh: Pickwick, 1974), 186–222.

54. Leo G. Perdue, *Wisdom and Cult*, SBLDS 30 (Missoula, MT: Scholars Press, 1977).

55. Whybray, *Reading the Psalms as a Book*, 70.

56. R. N. Whybray, *The Good Life in the Old Testament* (London: T. & T. Clark, 2002).

57. Ibid., 143.

58. James L. Crenshaw, *Old Testament Wisdom: An Introduction*, 3rd ed. (Louisville: Westminster John Knox, 2010), 193.

Solomon's life. Psalm 127 is less clearly linked to Solomon but does come under discussion in relation to the 'wisdom psalms' genre and so may have had a looser connection with sages at the courts of kings. The pairing of the two psalms would certainly not have been a natural one, but for the mention of this kingly figurehead; their alignment is thus an enigma. Is this alignment an early association with this wisest of kings or is it, at the other extreme, a canonical conundrum from those who finalized the Psalter? Such questions remain to tantalize us, as readers and interpreters.

Bibliography

Allen, Leslie C. *Psalms 101–150*. WBC 21. Waco: Word, 1983.
Brueggemann, Walter. *Solomon: Israel's Ironic Icon of Human Achievement*. Columbia: University of South Carolina Press, 2005.
Childs, Brevard S. *Introduction to the Old Testament as Scripture*. Philadelphia: Fortress, 1979.
Crenshaw, James L. *Old Testament Wisdom: An Introduction*. 3rd ed. Louisville: Westminster John Knox, 2010.
Crenshaw, James L. *The Psalms: An Introduction*. Grand Rapids: Eerdmans. 2001.
Dahood, Mitchell. *Psalms*. 3 vols. AB 16–17a. Garden City: Doubleday, 1966–70.
Dell, Katharine J. *The Book of Proverbs in Social and Theological Context*. Cambridge: Cambridge University Press, 2006.
Dell, Katharine J. 'Ecclesiastes as Mainstream Wisdom (without Job)' Pages 43–52 in *Goochem in Mokum/Wisdom in Amsterdam: Papers on Biblical and Related Wisdom Read at the Fifteenth Joint Meeting of The Society of Old Testament Study and the Oudtestamentisch Werkgezelschap, Amsterdam July 2012*. Edited by George J. Brooke and Pierre Van Hecke. OTS 68. Leiden: Brill, 2016.
Dell, Katharine J. '"I will solve my riddle to the music of the lyre" (Psalm 44:4 [5]): A Cultic Setting for Wisdom Psalms?' *VT* 54 (2004): 445–58.
Dell, Katharine J. *The Solomonic Corpus of Wisdom and Its Influence*. Oxford: Oxford University Press, 2020.
Estes, Daniel J. *Handbook on the Wisdom Books and Psalms*. Grand Rapids: Baker, 2005.
Gillingham, Susan E. *Psalms Through the Centuries: A Reception History Commentary on Psalms 1–72, Vol. 2*. Wiley Blackwell Bible Commentaries. Oxford: Wiley-Blackwell, 2018.
Goulder, Michael D. *The Prayers of David (Psalms 51–72)*. Studies in the Psalter 2. JSOTSup 102. Sheffield: JSOT, 1990.
Goulder, Michael D. *The Psalms of Asaph and the Pentateuch* Studies in the Psalter 3. JSOTSup 233. Sheffield: Sheffield Academic, 1996.
Goulder, Michael D. *The Psalms of the Sons of Korah*. Studies in the Psalter 1. JSOTSup 20. Sheffield: JSOT, 1982.
Gunkel, Hermann. *Einleitung in die Psalmen: Die Gattungen der religiösen Lyrik Israels*. Göttingen: Vandenhoeck & Ruprecht, 1933.
Jobling, David. 'Deconstruction and the Political Analysis of Biblical Texts: A Jamesonian Reading of Psalm 72'. *Semeia* 59 (1992): 95–127.
Johnson, Aubrey R. *Sacral Kingship in Ancient Israel*. 2nd ed. Cardiff: University of Wales Press, 1967.

Kraus, H. J. *Psalmen* 1. BKAT 15. Neukirchen-Vluyn: Neukirchener Verlag, 1961.
Kuntz, J. K. 'The Canonical Wisdom Psalms of Ancient Israel – Their Rhetorical, Thematic, and Formal Dimensions'. Pages 186–222 in *Rhetorical Criticism: Essays in Honor of James Muilenburg*. Edited by Jared J. Jackson and Martin Kessler. Pittsburgh: Pickwick, 1974.
Kynes, Will. *An Obituary for Wisdom Literature: The Birth, Death, and Intertextual Reintegration of a Biblical Corpus*. Oxford: Oxford University Press, 2019.
Miller, Jr, Patrick D. 'Psalm 127: The House That Yahweh Builds'. *JSOT* 22 (1982): 119–32.
Mowinckel, Sigmund. 'Psalms and Wisdom'. Pages 205–44 in *Wisdom in Israel and in the Ancient Near East*. Edited by M. Noth and D. W. Thomas. VTSup 3. Leiden: Brill, 1955.
Perdue, Leo G. *Wisdom and Cult*. SBLDS 30. Missoula, MT: Scholars Press, 1977.
Schmidt, Hans. *Die Psalmen*. HAT. Tübingen: Mohr, 1934.
Stocks, Simon P. '"Children, listen to me": The Voicing of Wisdom in the Psalms'. Pages 194–204 in *Exploring Old Testament Wisdom: Literature and Themes*. Edited by D. Firth and L. Wilson. London: Apollos, 2016.
Terrien, Samuel L. *The Psalms: Strophic Structure and Theological Commentary*. Eerdmans Critical Commentary. Grand Rapids: Eerdmans, 2003.
Whybray, R. N. *The Good Life in the Old Testament*. London: T. & T. Clark, 2002.
Whybray, R. N. *Reading the Psalms as a Book*. JSOTSup 222. Sheffield: Sheffield Academic, 1996.

Imagining Prayer:
Deepening Awareness of Audiences
in the Psalms

M. I. J. Daffern

William P. Brown highlighted Sue Gillingham's passion that the Psalms should be both *understood* and *appreciated*.[1] In his seminal study of metaphor in the Psalms, the work of linguists and theologians coalesced with potency.[2] Highlighting the vast array of imagery in these poetic texts, he reflected on select metaphors – salient symbols of refuge, pathway, water, trees, and light – to bring a unified depth of meaning to the reader's appreciation of the Psalms as a whole and to invite further reflections on the Psalms' iconic metaphors.

Brown's concept of the poetic role of imagining[3] leads me to think of the 'Psalmist'[4] (as well as the later reader or pray-er of the Psalms) as *imaginer*. To consider in general what the Psalmist imagines himself doing in the composition, editing, transmission, and performing of psalm texts would be an attractive (indeed imaginative) project but too large for a study of this length. I therefore offer instead the more specific study of who the Psalmist imagines to be hearing (or reading) his texts. What audiences – addressees and other hearers – are imaged in the Psalter?

---

1. S. E. Gillingham, *The Poems and Psalms of the Hebrew Bible* (Oxford: Oxford University Press, 1994), 4.
2. W. P. Brown, *Seeing the Psalms: A Theology of Metaphor* (Louisville: Westminster John Knox, 2002).
3. Ibid., 9.
4. It would be impossible in a short paper to do justice to the identity the authorial and editorial influences in the Psalms. I therefore use the term 'Psalmist' to denote the collective 'author/editor' of the final form of the text, and the traditional masculine singular pronoun to represent that 'Psalmist'.

This connects with linguistics and psycholinguistics.[5] I therefore begin by considering select relevant contributions from these disciplines. I proceed to examine Psalm 31 as a text which represents a wide "audience participation" in the intratextual world of the Psalms. I conclude with insights gained through this use of the critical imagination in terms of how such texts function,[6] and how they might have been (and still might be) used.[7]

---

5. Performance criticism asks similar questions, developed from theatre studies. I concentrate specifically on my linguistics and psycholinguistics since they provide focused contributions which benefit the precise focus of the present study, rather than evaluating a third critical methodology. For further reading around performance critical methods, particularly with reference to the Hebrew Bible, see W. Doan and T. Giles, eds., *Prophets, Performance, and Power: Performance Criticism of the Hebrew Bible* (London: T&T Clark, 2005); W. Doan and T. Giles, 'Performance Criticism of the Hebrew Bible', *Religion Compass* 2, no. 3 (2008); T. Giles and W. Doan, *Twice Used Songs: Performance Criticism of the Songs of Ancient Israel* (Peabody: Hendrickson, 2009). More recent studies of performaetivity consider narratives or narrative frames within the Hebrew Bible: see T. M. West, 'The Art of Biblical Performance: Biblical Performance Criticism and the Genre of the Biblical Narratives' (Ph.D. diss., Vrije Universiteit Amsterdam, 2018); J. Vayntrub, *Beyond Orality: Biblical Poetry on Its Own Terms* (Abingdon: Taylor & Francis, 2019).

6. A number of scholars use literary methods to explore the function of prayer texts within the Bible, providing variously systematic surveys or analyses of various prayer texts, or detailed thought developed from textual difficulties within prayer texts. See Patrick D. Miller, *They Cried to the Lord: The Form and Theology of Biblical Prayer* (Minneapolis: Fortress, 1994); Walter Brueggemann, *Great Prayers of the Old Testament* (Louisville: Westminster John Knox, 2008); J. G. Janzen, B. A. Strawn, and P. D. Miller, *When Prayer Takes Place: Forays into a Biblical World* (Eugene, OR: Wipf & Stock, 2012). Samuel Balentine sees prayer texts as imaging the human response to God, balancing theocentric perspectives in the study of the Hebrew Bible with anthropocentric perspectives. This demonstrates the significance of the study of biblical prayer texts for the understanding and appreciation of the theology of the Hebrew Bible as a whole. See Samuel Balentine, *Prayer in the Hebrew Bible* (Minneapolis: Fortress, 1993), Chapter 9.

7. A research question based on function invites attention to form- or genre-critical methods. Selectivity therefore requires the present study to be less concerned with historical criticism than with form criticism, which is more closely related to the literary methods featured here. Sigmund Mowinckel, for instance, bases much of his work on the identifying of cultic acts and drama: this connects with the concerns of performance criticism and the (psycho)linguistic acts under scrutiny; Sigmund Mowinckel, *The Psalms in Israel's Worship*, trans. D. R. Ap-Thomas (Oxford: Blackwell, 1962).

*Imagining Addressees and Audiences in Prayer Events:
Method with Linguistics*

The linguistic pragmatics of Speech Act Theory and Discourse Analysis have been variously adapted and used by Biblical scholars.[3] Using the language of 'prayer event' to denote analysis on a discourse rather than illocutionary level, I begin with the work of Allan Bell. Bell's development of 'Audience Design' – incorporating elements of the illocutionary 'Informative Analysis' of Herbert H. Clark and Thomas B. Carlson[9] – invites the distinguishing of speaker, addressee, auditor, overhearer, and eavesdropper.[10]

Bell describes how

> [A]udience design informs all levels of a speaker's linguistic choices... The audience is, at one level, simply the people who hear the speaker's utterances. Yet...in a theatre, the audience is the responsible, critical forum before whom the utterances are performed... [S]peakers 'have an audience with' their hearers. They are in a real sense subject to their audience, dependent on its goodwill, responsive to audience response. It is that responsiveness which informs a speaker's style design.[11]

---

8. For a bibliography on pragmatic linguistics and how they may inform hermeneutics see my 'Prayers for Remembering in the Psalms' (D.Phil. thesis, University of Oxford, 2014).

9. Herbert H. Clark and Thomas B. Carlson, 'Hearers and Speech Acts', *Language* (1982): 332–73; Allan Bell, 'Language Style as Audience Design', *Language in Society* 13, no. 2 (1984): 145–204.

10. K. M. Hartvigsen uses Clark and Carlson's Informative Analysis powerfully in her analysis of St. Mark's Gospel as she considers *how the audience members regard themselves* (cf. K. M. Hartvigsen, *Prepare the Way of the Lord: Towards a Cognitive Poetic Analysis of Audience Involvement with Characters and Events in the Markan World* [Berlin: de Gruyter, 2012]). This allows her to avoid Allan's criticism that Clark and Carlson confused 'perlocutionary effects of utterances or cooperative expectations from participants...with speakers' illocutionary intentions' (cf. Keith Allan, 'Hearers, Overhearers, and Clark & Carlson's Informative Analysis', *Language* 62, no. 3 [1986]: 509–17). However, it seems to me that the detailed examination of the speaker's language register that Bell employs in 'Language Style as Audience Design' goes well beyond the critique that Allan makes specifically of the Informative Analysis. Note that I simply employ the 'Audience Design' of Bell's analysis, as opposed to his 'Referee Design', since the essence of prayer is that when composed and performed it is only felicitous when performed in faith, i.e. with the divine in some way regarded as a presence (addressee or audience) rather than a non-present influence (referee). Even the complete desolation of the text of Ps. 88 depends on the Psalmist having the possibility, however remote, of a divine hearing.

11. Bell, 'Language Style as Audience Design', 161.

Analysing the effects of addressees and auditors in conversation, he goes on to state: 'How a person speaks *before* a given auditor reflects how that person speaks *to* the same individual as addressee'.[12]

For these reasons I use the term 'prayer event' to describe the collections of speech acts within texts which represent the act of praying. Even the simplest of prayers, such as those Aejmelaeus termed 'traditional prayers', include the three elements of address, imperative petition and expression of complaint or confidence in Yahweh which would act as a motivation.[13] This could be described in speech act terms as a combination of directive illocution (petition clause) with a variety of conjoined expressive, declarative, commissive, and assertive illocutions stated as address and motivation clauses. As a series of illocutions, then, sometimes embedded within each other, even the simplest prayer text is better described as discourse rather than just a speech act. Insofar as the language of prayer texts – particularly as we receive them in the Psalms – clearly vacillates between addressees (divine, human, and non-human), any analysis of such a prayer text requires sensitivity to the range of different illocutions it contains.

Bell's work further presents a framework which may deepen the reader's appreciation of the Psalms. Where a psalm addresses God, the reader may expect the divine-addressee-oriented text to demonstrate something of the Psalmist's response to God and their relationship, through style and register. Where a psalm addresses the human congregation, the reader may expect the human-addressee-oriented text to demonstrate something of the Psalmist's response to the community of which he is a part. Where a psalm is largely addressed to God but with asides addressed to the congregation, the reader may expect the text to demonstrate something of how the Psalmist is responsive to both the divine and human spheres simultaneously, with a corresponding variety of illocutions.[14] The picture of how a text is functioning – and what it tells the reader about how the prayer event works – becomes richer and more complex the more the varying audiences are taken into account. Such prayer texts thus express a great deal: Audience Design reveals much about how the Psalmist is responding to both God and the world around him.

---

12. Ibid., 174.
13. Anneli Aejmelaeus, *The Traditional Prayer in the Psalms* (Berlin: de Gruyter, 1986), 109.
14. For an examination of different voices interacting in Psalm texts, see Carleen Mandolfo, *God in the Dock: Dialogic Tension in the Psalms of Lament*, JSOTSup 357 (Sheffield: Sheffield Academic, 2002).

Bell's analysis leads to the hypothesis that the author of a prayer text would have created that text with an audience (embracing that range of addressees, auditors, overhearers, and eavesdroppers) in his mind's eye.[15] Seeing Audience Design as a means of using critical imagination in studying these texts brings a vivid array of images of the audience to bear. This in turn connects with the use in criticism of insights borne of psycholinguistics.

Insights from Psycholinguistics

B. A. Strawn[16] reflects on developments in psychology since Freud and focuses in particular on the work of the British Object Relations school. Strawn summarizes how scholars such as W. R. D. Fairbairn and D. W. Winnicott have argued that, instead of basic instincts of sex and aggression motivating human beings (as in Freud's view), it is actually relational needs that are primary and shaped during infancy.

Strawn connects this psychological perspective with the image of the parent in the Psalms, looking at Pss. 22.9-10, 139.13-16, 27.10, seeing the parent image as a metaphor for God. Analysing through the metaphor of Parent how the Psalms explore the God attachment as primary for human beings, he relates this to Brueggemann's orientation-disorientation-reorientation movement.[17] Strawn further connects the relationality expressed in the lament psalms with the therapeutic process of expressing and mourning negative feelings in order to enable new, more positive feelings. He sees such language in prayers of lament as a kind of 're-parenting'. He views imprecations through Object Relations theory, linking them with an infant's (or analysand's) feeling of 'subjective omnipotence'. The psalmist – like the infant – develops by realising that divine Parent does

---

15. What the later reader or speaker of such a prayer text would imagine they were doing – if in some way they were appropriating that text for their own performance of their faith – could be influenced by both the reader's imagination of their addressee/audience as well as their imagination of how the original author imagined his addressee/audience. Considering such a further meta-level for examination would be fascinating, in order to explore how the Psalms have been and are received; but it necessarily lies beyond the scope of the present study.

16. B. A. Strawn, 'Poetic Attachment: Psychology, Psycholinguistics, and the Psalms', in *The Oxford Handbook of the Psalms*, ed. William P. Brown (New York: Oxford University Press, 2014), 404–23.

17. Walter Brueggemann, 'The Psalms and the Life of Faith: A Suggested Typology of Function', *JSOT* 17 (1980): 3–32; W. Brueggemann, *Spirituality of the Psalms* (Minneapolis: Fortress, 2002).

not simply exist to satisfy the psalmist's needs, but as a real Other existing beyond the psalmist's demand.

Strawn suggests such transformational – or therapeutic – possibilities within the Psalms are in fact 'the intended goal of the psalmic process', offered to other pray-ers and readers.[18] In terms of Audience Design, this indicates that the psalmist imagines his audience to include others who would receive, re-use, re-read, re-pray the texts he is composing. Strawn supports this thesis with close attention to two anthropological essays by P. D. Miller.[19]

It is fitting that texts where relationality is so central should resonate with contemporary 'Psychological Attachment' theory; that relationality may be primarily about the divine–human attachment, but it is readily extended to include the attachments of a praying community through generations. That the psalms were prayer texts which were remembered (and therefore formed the identity of members within the community which prayed them) suggests that any composer of a prayer (that imaginably could thus become 'canonical') would also envisage the text's future audience(s). If the psalms in their reception history could be reimagined as 'poetic attachment: *attachment to God by means of poetry*',[20] then it is possible to conceive of the Psalmist imagining how these prayer texts could help develop auditors–*cum*–re-prayers of the Psalms in their relationship(s) with God.

William Downes also explores the pray-er's relationship with God, using cognitive pragmatics.[21] Downes uses the concept of 'cognitive register' as something learned that enables access into a cultural complex – such as religion, which has 'an especially normative, ethical-educative, ideological function'.[22] He argues that prayer is one of the most effective ways in which religious norms can be shaped and shared. He therefore examines the language of petitionary prayer as a 'cognitive register', in which each act of praying is a 'cognitive procedure'. He describes contrasting cognitive procedures with respect to petitionary prayer.[23] His

18. Strawn, 'Poetic Attachment', 415.
19. P. D. Miller, *The Way of the Lord: Essays in Old Testament Theology* (Tübingen: Mohr Siebeck, 2004), 226–49.
20. Strawn, 'Poetic Attachment', 418.
21. William Downes, 'Linguistics and the Scientific Study of Religion: Prayer as a Cognitive Register', in *Religion, Language, and the Human Mind*, ed. Paul Chilton and Monika Kopytowska (New York: Oxford University Press, 2018), 89–114.
22. Ibid., 90.
23. Ibid., 100. His delineation of petitionary prayer is akin to Aejmelaeus' 'traditional prayer' in terms of form, albeit with a contrasting method of diagramming informed by pragmatics.

'folk directive interpretation' regards the imperative grammar as *necessarily* enacting some sort of illocutionary directive, while his 'deep believers' desire interpretation' regards the petitionary clause as an assertive which is rather about the believer telling God of their desire for something.

Exploring in linguistic terms the varying interpretations of the one cognitive register, Downes engages with the problems of taking prayer as an actual attempt to change God's mind (which assumes that the divine addressee is a pragmatic person). He argues rather that 'prayer is a device for conforming the speaker's will to God's will'[24] – but with the caveat that 'believers must unconditionally SEEK a supernatural entity that… reciprocally SEEKS them'.[25] Relevant here then is how the speaker is imagining the divine audience – insofar as he is seeking God, and insofar as God is seeking him.[26] Further relevant here are Downes' concluding comments on how prayer also functions to integrate the individual within the religious community. For Downes, prayer not only conforms the speaker's will to God's will, but also integrates the speaker with the wider community.[27]

Downes is perhaps unwise to dismiss the potency of the 'folk directive' in the minds of praying believers, and to consider 'folk directive' and 'deep believers' desire' interpretations as mutually exclusive. Nevertheless, he enables a development from the folk-directive to a more nuanced SEEKING (or spiritual intention in prayer). This is crucial first in the

---

24. Ibid., 106.

25. Ibid., 113. Downes is referring to Panksepp's SEEKING system. J. Panksepp, *Affective Neuroscience: The Foundations of Human and Animal Emotions* (New York: Oxford University Press, 2004).

26. Note how the 'deep believers' desire' interpretation comes close to Balentine's suggestion that prayer is a literary vehicle characterizing God (as well as the believer) – so the activity of prayer is also a way to get to know God better. Balentine, *Prayer in the Hebrew Bible*, Chapters 4 and 5.

27. Similar observations are made in the field of performance criticism: 'As applied to the Hebrew Bible, performance criticism is most closely aligned with those theorists of social drama, such as Victor Turner and Richard Schechner, who focus on "what performance does in a culture to promote social cohesion and to resolve conflict"' (Doan and Giles, 'Performance Criticism', 276; see also M. T. Crane, 'What Was Performance?', *Criticism* 43, no. 2 [2001]: 169–87, esp. 170). Although in Doan and Giles' context this citation of Crane serves to defend Downes' notion of the conforming power of prayer, Crane was originally contrasting the 'social drama' theorists' approach focusing on what performance *does* as opposed to the Foucauldian 'symbolic action' critics who focused on what a performance *means* or *represents* as the key to understanding what it *does*.

conforming of speaker to God's will, and second in the integrating of individual speakers within a congregation. Thus reflecting on the SEEKER and the object of SEEKING, Downes like Strawn arrives at the imagining of the relationship between human and divine – between speaker, addressee, and audience of prayer.

Imagined Addressees and Audiences

Letting these insights inform my reading of Psalm texts,[28] I now offer a close focused reading of one Davidic 'individual lament', Psalm 31,[29] which in the first person singular closely resembles Aejmelaeus' model of 'traditional prayer'. I then broaden my focus to end with further reflections taken from across the Psalter.

Psalm 31

Described as a Davidic *mizmor* or melody, for the 'Director (of Music)', the superscription immediately creates a sense of public performance with more participants present than just the speaker and divine addressee. A text and melody that names not only an 'author' but also a 'performer' further imagines those before whom the performance is given.[30]

The first words of the psalm text itself, 'In you, O LORD, have I sought refuge', demand God's hearing as divine addressee. The second person preposition 'in you' is in emphatic position, before the covenantal name of the LORD – the name itself conveying relationship through its revealed place in the salvation history of God's people (Exod. 3.14). The honorific address of God is clarified with the language of refuge (חסה). This root

---

28. The Hebrew numbering is used throughout.

29. Notably, Ps. 31 has been regarded as demonstrative of 'the psychology and logic of the life of prayer', underlining the relevance of psycholinguistics to this text. Artur Weiser, *The Psalms: A Commentary*, trans. Herbert Hartwell (London: SCM, 1962), 275.

30. Indeed, considered as a whole, the psalm – complete with sudden transition between prayer and lament to thanksgiving and praise – is read by form critics as evidence of a liturgical act within a cultic context, thus again indicating some kind of public performance context: Peter C. Craigie, *Psalms 1–50*, WBC 19 (Waco: Word, 1983), 262. The same conclusion arises from looking ahead to the final verses: Hans-Joachim Kraus, *Psalms 1–59: A Commentary* (Minneapolis: Augsburg, 1988), 361. Further, the 'confessional ring' of the declarations of trust suggests 'that the audience of cult members is to witness the creedal statement' of v. 6: cf. Erhard Gerstenberger, *Psalms, Part 1, with an Introduction to Cultic Poetry*, FOTL 14 (Eerdmans: Grand Rapids, 1988), 138, 139.

occurs either in thanksgiving psalms or parts of psalms which express trust in God: such vocabulary reflects Strawn's poetic attachment theory and is a primary metaphor for Brown.[31] The directive cohortative follows: 'let me not be ashamed'. This root בוש occurs frequently in the Psalms, predominantly in lament texts, largely representing either a plea not to be shamed in the eyes of an enemy, or an imprecation that the enemy be shamed. The verb itself images the persona of the enemy contrasting with the faithful speaker(s) addressing God.

Thus within the first two verses a number of hearing participants are imagined. In terms of Bell's concentric circles of audience design, at the centre is the speaker, who is either David, or the Director of Music, which then entails the image of performers who have already received the prayer and are now performing it afresh. In the next concentric circle comes the divine addressee capable of both hearing and fulfilling this prayer. The third concentric ring includes auditors listening to the performance of the prayer. They in turn receive the prayer text, and may re-perform the text with other potential audiences in mind as participants in the future.

As yet unidentified but already implicit in the 'prayer event' of this Psalm event, the enemy persona is present. The Psalmist might wish 'the enemy' be overhearing his plea to God to uphold *him*, rather than those (enemies) amongst whom he might 'be ashamed'. This enemy persona throughout the psalm moves between the fifth concentric circle of Bell's – the eavesdropper; the fourth – the overhearer; and even (as I shall later explore), the third – the auditor who is a known presence.

There is strength in this design. God is immediately enlisted as a friend to the speaker – effectively a commissive illocution, the Psalmist committing himself to God thereby binds God to himself, a safe and secure place as well as a helper. A crowd of witnesses is imaged on the Psalmist's side: the performer(s) introduced in the superscription as receiver(s) of the text, as well as those present at this performance. All this support provides a powerful bulwark against the as yet variously darkly imagined menacing presence of those who would wish to do the speaker ill.

Thus, in both the envisaged concentric circles of performer(s), addressee, and audience, and in the reality of the text, supporters are immediately on hand before the enemy gets close. A self-protective resilience is effectively encoded in the Psalmist's words, echoing Strawn's therapeutic interpretation of the function of the Psalms. The power of Downes' 'folk directive' is harnessed – but to commit the divine addressee to conform his will to that of the Psalmist, rather than *vice versa*. Put

---

31. Brown, *Seeing the Psalms*, Chapter 1.

another way, the Psalmist is seeking to be conformed to the divine will *by arming himself with God*, rather than *surrendering himself to God's will*. A series of phrases playing on God as refuge heaps up this metaphor in the following verses (Ps. 31.2-5). These images seem to highlight Strawn's strengthening therapeutic function and delineate it from Downes' more submissive cognitive function.

Does the more passive imagery that follows (v. 6), 'Into your hand I entrust my soul', reverse this?[32] In one sense, it is a reminder that for all the Psalmist's best efforts at making himself strong through enlisting his divine ally, it is nevertheless the LORD who has power to redeem, not the Psalmist. If so, Downes' 'deep believers' desire' notion finds more support. Taking seriously the self-committal of the Psalmist in 31.6a supports the reading of the *qal* of פדה as precative in the balancing parallelism.[33] Conversely, reading the *qal* as an anticipatory perfect resolutely – rather than submissively – declares the Psalmist's certitude in this deliverance.[34]

The strength of conviction in this reading matches the opening verses, which show the Psalmist rather as a challenging adversary for the enemy on the literary and concentric-circles horizon of Audience Design. This powerful tone connects seamlessly with the emphatic 'I hate' in v. 7. Again the enemies are brought closer to the scene with the denunciation of 'those who look to worthless idols'.[35] It is easy to imagine someone uttering a threat with the hope that – although the one threatened is not immediately present – the threat might be overheard and taken to heart by those overhearers. This implicit declarative denunciation draws the enemy closer to the speaker, moving in Bell's Audience Design terms

---

32. The various changes of tone in Ps. 31 are examined in form critical readings with differing amounts of detail. Despite a not wholly accurate representation of the distinction between the level of speech acts and speech event in discourse criticism, Wendland offers here a fair compromise on arguably the most helpful amount of specificity. Compare Robert G. Bratcher and William David Reyburn, *A Translator's Handbook on the Book of Psalms*, Helps for Translators (New York: United Bible Societies, 1991), 399; Gerstenberger, *Psalms I*, 136–7; Ernst R. Wendland, 'Genre Criticism in the Psalms', in *Biblical Hebrew and Discourse Linguistics*, ed. Robert D. Bergen (Winona Lake: Eisenbrauns, 1994), 374–414, esp. 400–402.

33. Translating v. 6b as imperative: Craigie, *Psalms 1–50*, 256, 260.

34. With John Goldingay, *Psalms, Vol. 1*, Baker Commentary on the Old Testament Wisdom and Psalms (Grand Rapids: Baker Academic, 2006), 439–40; Kraus, *Psalms 1–59*, 361.

35. The idols of the enemies are themselves envisaged – but in a way which notes *their* imaging as pointless and misleading. See Goldingay, *Psalms*, 440.

from eaves-dropper to overhearer. This also increases the appearance of strength of the speaker – he is afraid of no one, but rather those enemies should be warned![36]

Verses 8-9 continue this tone both confident in the Psalmist's self and in his God. Phrased in cohortative language vowing gladness and rejoicing in God's loving-kindness to the Psalmist, it depicts God's salvation as already having taken place in the past (like the anticipatory perfect of v. 6). This is presented to the Psalmist's auditors as good reason for confidence, and to the enemy overhearer as good reason to be wary. It also serves to bolster the Psalmist's continuing confidence, as he reminds himself of the salvific stories he has known in his own life.

The more assertively vv. 1-9 are read, the more surprising is the abrupt change of tone in v. 10. Suddenly more inward-looking, vv. 10ff. seem more private. The straitened circumstances of צר־לי, 'I am in distress', literally diminish the imagined performance space (contrasted particularly with the expansive מרחב, 'broad place', of v. 9) to something more intimate. Quieter, less confident words are spoken with a new hesitance. The 'wasting away' עשש of the Psalmist's נפש ('soul') and בטן ('body') depicts a shrinking of physical size, particularly with respect to the latter, which could be more specifically translated as 'belly'. But this is not all. The phrase evokes a subduing of the voice, insofar as the נפש is literally the 'throat': the part of the body where the breath of life enters is also where the voice comes from. Focusing on his own body, the Psalmist's introversion further shrinks the performance arena. This creates the sense that the admission of vv. 12-14 – that the Psalmist is shunned by friends to the extent that friends and enemies are as one – could even be whispered.

Gone is the tone of loud confidence. Here is the painful confession of one who has been undermined so far by enemies that his friends have denied him too. There is no one to shout to with assertions of the righteousness of his God. Instead of his friends and the faithful congregation, now disembodied slander surrounds the Psalmist (v. 15). The text expresses the isolation and grief of the speaker. Apart from v. 10, even the divine addressee remains unnamed. These verses are a wholehearted performance of the isolated, individual lament. The enemy – one-time eavesdropper, later overhearer – now has supplanted the Psalmist's friends as auditors. The speaker, it would seem, has very good reason to lower his tone. Could the enemy even have displaced the divine addressee?

---

36. Resonating with Strawn's attachment theory: the 'child' who believes himself omnipotent, until he sees the 'parent' as the Other whom he does not control. Strawn, 'Poetic Attachment', 410.

It is as if this question plagues the Psalmist when he makes the massive effort to reverse this in the pivotal v. 15. These verses remind the faithful auditor – which now includes the speaker's own self – of the context of the performance made so plain in vv. 1-9. First and foremost, God *is* there to be addressed, and even trusted in, in v. 15. Quoting his own direct speech, the Psalmist declares to any who might hear, 'You are my God!' The most important audience in this perlocution is the Psalmist's *very own self*: practically repeating his words of v. 7b, he reminds himself of his confidence in God.

The Psalmist in his lowest moment even perhaps doubted God's hearing in the most tentative vv. 12-14, when he sought to understand how he could have become someone shunned, even like one literally obliterated, slandered and vulnerable. Yet while *they* in v. 14 have conspired to take the Psalmist's נפש, through trusting in God the Psalmist can declare once again his 'I-ness' at the start of v. 15. His own breath, enabling him to assert his relationship with God, gives him spirit and life. Introducing himself as auditor seems to bring distance and therefore perspective into his words of prayer, to create space to build up both himself and his faithful audience.

The Psalmist's confidence continues to increase. Verse 16 returns to the image of the Psalmist committing his life to God as he calls upon God for deliverance. The protecting hands of God are contrasted to the dangerous hands of the enemies. Blurring the boundaries of the metaphor and physical reality, the repetition of the bodily יד evokes the enemy receding from the immediate presence of the speaker. God once more takes up that space beside the Psalmist, who in v. 17 now images God's face shining on him: the prayer is effectively fulfilled before the human audience as the Psalmist is restored.[37]

The enemy *per se* is banished. They are no longer named as such: later verses refer instead to the wicked or the proud, or those who commit wrongs. The plea the Psalmist makes to his divine addressee in v. 18 is for the 'wicked' now to be ashamed, even silenced in Sheol. This contrasts with the motivational clause adducing the Psalmist's own addressing of God as evidence of his faithfulness to the divine. The slander of vv. 10-14 has been silenced, and with it the enemy. In v. 19, the Psalmist's newly rediscovered voice to address God overwhelms any word uttered to the contrary, with the jussive 'may they be struck dumb!'

---

37. On the 'visualization' of YHWH, see Kraus, *Psalms 1–59*, 364.

The challenge in v. 19 is to auditors – if they should truly hear it and take it on board – to consider who are the members of the group (identified simply now by the participle) 'speaking against the righteous'. Could this apply even to them? The earlier treacherous act of the friends siding with the enemy (vv. 12-14) is overturned: some of the human audience, on reflection, could awkwardly find themselves situated among this otherwise unspecified wicked people.

In the presence of this newly increased and potentially varied audience, the final verses are a climactic act of praise of the God who shelters the righteous from the slanderous wicked. Verses 20-21 continue to be addressed to this divine 'you', while v. 22 switches to speaking of God in the third person: the ברוך יהוה who has demonstrated his loving-kindness. Now the human audience hearing this praise is explicit: they learn and join in worshipping this saving God. Verse 23 summarizes the story, now again addressed to God in the second person, emphatically depicting the Psalmist in his isolated first person singular state. This continues the sense that an immediate human audience is attending to these words, as much as the reader today might be.

It is, then, hardly surprising that the final vv. 24-25 unambiguously address the human congregation, as the Psalmist gives them words of instruction (using plural imperatives and plural suffixes). Speaking in peaceful language to those amongst whom he numbers himself – *if* they are people of integrity who love the LORD – he simultaneously motivates them to ensure they do not act out of pride. Whereas the divine addressee of the directive petitions earlier was offered motivation for fulfilling the Psalmist's request, now the human audience of the directive commands are offered motivation for doing as he guides them by word and example. If they do show themselves to be people who wait upon the LORD, then they too could be in a position to be strong despite afflictions, and to grow in confidence – just as they have heard and seen the Psalmist.

The text thus effectively enables the speaker to act out the experience of being slandered and restored. The performance markings – including the dynamic range in musical terms – are evident in the text itself. The text involves a dramatic audience to witness to the Psalmist's faithful relationship with God and how that plays out in prayer and in life. The Psalmist is finally shown as an exemplar, a faithful man of prayer whose responses to distressing circumstances can be seen, heard, and copied. Not only is the text being handed down to the audience who hears it, but the moral drama of the pray-er invites such audience participation that they should copy the acts it portrays.

Prayer (Re-)Performed, Prayer (Re-)Imagined

So what *do* the Psalmist and the performer of Psalm texts imagine they are doing when they use these texts as prayer? My study of Psalm 31 has suggested that the function of texts as prayer is closely linked with the addressee and audience. The text itself shows the Psalmist's imagined construction of his audience. Considering how the Psalmist imagines his audience opens up a vista of function that centrally embraces – but is not confined to – Strawn's psychotherapeutic intention, as well as *both* the 'folk-directive' and 'deep believers' desire' interpretations of Downes' construction of prayer.[38] Space prevents consideration of other audiences (as imagined in other Psalm texts)[39] or how imagined audiences of biblical texts beyond the Psalms might impact a theology of the Hebrew Bible more broadly,[40] but this short foray into the imaginative application of Audience Design principles has opened up a vast range of further observations and questions.[41]

Close application of simple Audience Design principles to this traditional prayer text has thus enabled a reading of Psalm 31 that, first, enriches an understanding of its function opening out beyond traditional form-critical methods and, second, resonates with psycholinguistic considerations. This has shown the value of imagining audiences to a deeper appreciation of the text with the result that it broadens the concept

---

38. Further to the work of both Strawn and Downes, it could be suggested that the very transmission of prayer texts handed down either individually or within a wider Biblical narrative offers a vehicle for the faithful to insert themselves imaginatively into the narrative of salvation history, and to connect their experiences with the Scriptural story.

39. Such as non-human addressees of creation (e.g. Pss. 19, 148) or the city of Zion (e.g. Ps. 24).

40. For instance, how does the imagined audience of a prayer *narrative* compare to the audience of prayer *per se*, and how does that affect the reading of the text? Balentine, *Prayer in the Hebrew Bible*, 134.

41. It is worth reflecting, for instance, on the observation that the first person plural forms in the Psalmist's voice never represent a 'God-and-I/we' partnership, but solely a creaturely partnership such as 'Congregation-and-I', or 'Creation-and-I/we'. The closest any psalm text gets to the 'God-and-I/we' partnership is the 'With God, we…' identical statements of Pss. 60.14 and 108.14. Similarly, consider the semantic constraints dependent on who is addressee or auditor: God, for instance, cannot be the addressee of the active imperatives 'Praise!' or 'Fear!' but in the Psalms he must be the auditor of such directives. Janzen's writing also leads his reader to ask what the difference is between an audience *for* and an audience *to* in a text; Janzen, Strawn, and Miller, *Prayer*, 132.

of what an 'individual lament' might be or do, at least with respect to Psalm 31.[42] It has also given a further instance of how methods informed by linguistics – and indeed the critical imagination – bring colour to texts performed both in ancient times and ever since. As such, I hope it is closely aligned to Sue Gillingham's aspiration for Psalms study, and a small gift to honour her encouragement for a serious seeking after a deeper appreciation of the Psalms, in the reading and practice of both student and believer.

Bibliography

Aejmelaeus, Anneli. *The Traditional Prayer in the Psalms.* Berlin: de Gruyter, 1986.
Allan, Keith. 'Hearers, Overhearers, and Clark & Carlson's Informative Analysis'. *Language* 62, no. 3 (1986): 509–17.
Balentine, Samuel. *Prayer in the Hebrew Bible.* Minneapolis: Fortress, 1993.
Bell, Allan. 'Language Style as Audience Design'. *Language in Society* 13, no. 2 (1984): 145–204.
Bratcher, Robert G., and William David Reyburn. *A Translator's Handbook on the Book of Psalms.* Helps for Translators. New York: United Bible Societies, 1991.
Brown, W. P. *Seeing the Psalms. A Theology of Metaphor.* Louisville: Westminster John Knox, 2002.
Brueggemann, Walter. *Great Prayers of the Old Testament.* Louisville: Westminster John Knox, 2008.
Brueggemann, Walter. 'The Psalms and the Life of Faith: A Suggested Typology of Function'. *JSOT* 17 (1980): 3–32.
Brueggemann, Walter. *Spirituality of the Psalms.* Minneapolis: Fortress, 2002.
Clark, Herbert H., and Thomas B. Carlson. 'Hearers and Speech Acts'. *Language* (1982): 332–73.
Craigie, Peter C. *Psalms 1–50.* Word Biblical Commentary 19. Waco: Word, 1983.
Crane, M. T. 'What Was Performance?' *Criticism* 43, no. 2 (2001): 169–87.
Daffern, Megan I. J. 'Prayers for Remembering in the Psalms'. D.Phil. thesis, Oxford, 2014.
Doan, W., and T. Giles, 'Performance Criticism of the Hebrew Bible'. *Religion Compass* 2, no. 3 (2008): 273–86.
Doan, W., and T. Giles, eds. *Prophets, Performance, and Power: Performance Criticism of the Hebrew Bible.* London: T&T Clark, 2005.
Downes, William. 'Linguistics and the Scientific Study of Religion: Prayer as a Cognitive Register'. Pages 89–114 in *Religion, Language, and the Human Mind.* Edited by Paul Chilton and Monika Kopytowska. New York: Oxford University Press, 2018.
Gerstenberger, Erhard. *Psalms: Part 1, with an Introduction to Cultic Poetry.* FOTL 14. Grand Rapids: Eerdmans, 1988.

---

42. Further study could broaden this particular observation to all those psalms previously regarded as 'individual' – tying in with other responses to form criticism stretching back for over fifty years, e.g. James Muilenburg, 'Form Criticism and Beyond', *JBL* 88 (1969): 1–18.

Giles, T., and W. Doan. *Twice Used Songs: Performance Criticism of the Songs of Ancient Israel*. Peabody: Hendrickson, 2009.

Gillingham, S. E. *The Poems and Psalms of the Hebrew Bible*. Oxford: Oxford University Press, 1994.

Goldingay, John. *Psalms*. Baker Commentary on the Old Testament Wisdom and Psalms 1. Grand Rapids: Baker Academic, 2006.

Hartvigsen, K. M. *Prepare the Way of the Lord: Towards a Cognitive Poetic Analysis of Audience Involvement with Characters and Events in the Markan World*. Berlin: de Gruyter, 2012.

Janzen, J. G., B. A. Strawn, and P. D. Miller. *When Prayer Takes Place: Forays into a Biblical World*. Eugene, OR: Wipf & Stock, 2012.

Kraus, Hans-Joachim. *Psalms 1–59: A Commentary*. Minneapolis: Augsburg, 1988.

Mandolfo, Carleen. *God in the Dock: Dialogic Tension in the Psalms of Lament*. JSOTSup 357. Sheffield: Sheffield Academic, 2002.

Miller, Patrick D. *They Cried to the Lord: The Form and Theology of Biblical Prayer*. Minneapolis: Fortress, 1994.

Miller, Patrick D. *The Way of the Lord: Essays in Old Testament Theology*. Tübingen: Mohr Siebeck, 2004.

Mowinckel, Sigmund. *The Psalms in Israel's Worship*. Translated by D. R. Ap-Thomas. Oxford: Blackwell, 1962.

Muilenburg, James. 'Form Criticism and Beyond'. *Journal of Biblical Literature* 88 (1969): 1–18.

Panksepp, J. *Affective Neuroscience: The Foundations of Human and Animal Emotions*. New York: Oxford University Press, 2004.

Strawn, B. A. 'Poetic Attachment: Psychology, Psycholinguistics, and the Psalms'. Pages 404–23 in *The Oxford Handbook of the Psalms*. Edited by William P. Brown. New York: Oxford University Press, 2014.

Vayntrub, J. *Beyond Orality: Biblical Poetry on Its Own Terms*. Abingdon: Taylor & Francis, 2019.

Weiser, Artur. *The Psalms: A Commentary*. Translated by Herbert Hartwell. London: SCM, 1962. Translation of *Die Psalmen*. 5th ed. Das Alte Testament Deutsch 14/15. Göttingen: Vandenhoeck & Ruprecht, 1959.

Wendland, Ernst R. 'Genre Criticism in the Psalms'. Pages 374–414 in *Biblical Hebrew and Discourse Linguistics*. Edited by Robert D. Bergen. Winona Lake: Eisenbrauns, 1994.

West, T. M. 'The Art of Biblical Performance: Biblical Performance Criticism and the Genre of the Biblical Narratives'. Ph.D. diss., Vrije Universiteit Amsterdam, 2018.

Part II

THE PSALMS AND THEOLOGICAL IMAGINATION

Psalms and Performance: On the Differences of Rehearsed and Literary Old Testament Prayers*

Erhard S. Gerstenberger

Ancient Lyrics

No doubt, ancient lyrics have come down to us only in written documents. There are no soundtracks or video clips of performed songs or rituals nor any other audible recordings. Is it a valid enterprise to search for peculiarities of texts which without doubt have been put to various performative tasks – granted that in most early literary cultures antedating, let's say, the Hellenistic age the art of writing and reading was very much limited to a small percentage of the population? In the light of more than thirty years of recent psalm research, ever since Gerald Wilson published his dissertation on 'The Editing of the Hebrew Psalter' in 1935, we well may answer in the affirmative. There has been, in my opinion, a highly overestimated emphasis on literary, redactional, intellectual influence on the shape and shaping of the 'Book' of Psalms. One of the outstanding defenders of a purely literary, final evaluation of the *tehillim* of old has been Erich Zenger, esteemed friend and colleague.[1] Fortunately, the tide

---

* This is an overdue gift of gratitude for scholarly openness and help to my esteemed colleague Susan Gillingham, who is very much in line with considerations of life-settings and performance; cf., e.g., her most recent essay on 'postexilic poetry' (Susan Gillingham, 'Postexilic Poetic Traditions in the Writings', in *The Oxford Handbook of the Writings of the Hebrew Bible*, ed. Donn F. Morgan [New York: Oxford University Press, 2019], 132–48) in which 'performance' and 'performative' are important key words. For my part, I am trying to bundle up and test reflections on long-term research as well as more recent deliberations.

1. Erhard S. Gerstenberger, 'Der Psalter als Buch und als Sammlung', in *Neue Wege der Psalmenforschung*, ed. Klaus Seybold and Erich Zenger, HBS 1 (Freiburg: Herder, 1994), 3–13.

has turned in more recent years, especially since David Willgren[2] came up with a thorough scrutiny of the ways and methods the phalanx of canonical interpreters of the Old Testament psalms employed in their arguments favouring purely literary activities at the final assemblage of a varied crop of poems and songs of Ancient Israel. Willgren, after all, found the arguments in favour of a literary production of the Psalter not convincing. This may be the point to reflect anew on the secrets of Hebrew Psalm poetry. Perhaps we may come to the conclusion that literary shape and functional performance are not so mutually exclusive as we have been thinking, with the end result being the heated discussions about the pros and cons of 'holistic' interpretations of the Psalter. In all of these deliberations we have to keep in mind that present-day conceptions of a literate, reading society may well be at some odds with ancient social realities wherein writing, schools, books (or scrolls) did play a rather marginal role. After examining a few arguments in favour of an inherent performative nature of Hebrew psalm poetry we shall turn to texts composed to be put on the stage instead of being read in private enclosures.

Poetry and Public Presentation

There are numerous indications within the Old Testament psalm literature itself points to its consistent use in group communication. In fact, all these phenomena have been treated extensively ever since the particular language of Hebrew poetry caught scholarly attention. Therefore it may be sufficient here to just briefly remind ourselves of some features of poetic language in contradistinction to narrative style. The psalmists employ peculiar grammatical expressions (e.g. verbal tempora), syntactic features, metaphors and images, forms of speech, line-arrangements (*parallelismus membrorum*), metre, and so on. All these linguistic features imply an inherent quality of poetry to arouse human emotions, to reach the ear of some listeners and not the eyes of potential readers. (A self-critical question may be permitted: What about acrostic poems?) The most extensive summary of linguistic features in Psalm poetry certainly is Gunkel and Begrich,[3] though we should also mention Gillingham,[4]

---

2. David Willgren, *The Formation of the 'Book' of Psalms* (Tübingen: Mohr Siebeck, 2016).

3. Hermann Gunkel and Joachim Begrich, *Introduction to Psalms: The Genres of the Religious Lyric of Israel*, trans. James D. Nogalski, Mercer Library of Biblical Studies (Macon: Mercer University Press, 1998).

4. Susan E. Gillingham, *The Poems and Psalms of the Hebrew Bible* (Oxford: Oxford University Press, 1994), 23–8, 51–8.

Seybold[5] and many others. Gunkel includes in his array of notable characteristics of diverse Psalm genres the overall structure of a given text. Peculiar passages or formal units and their sequence, in his analysis, demonstrate public performance of the texts. And he is eager to identify life-settings for the different genres, mainly hymns, complaints, thanksgivings, and (to a lesser extent) wisdom texts, where the specimens have been recited and the ends for which they have been generated discussed. The linguistic and literary forms of Hebrew Psalm poetry, then, in themselves do betray a predisposition towards public presentation.

Interestingly enough, the very first studies on record of Hebrew poetry already laid the ground for such recognition. Two fathers of this branch of Old Testament research, Robert Lowth[6] and Johann Gottfried Herder,[7] keenly observed the extraordinary (in distinction to literary prose styles) emotional and expressive ways those ancient poets used to articulate their concerns. Thus, Robert Lowth in his famous treatises on the Sacred Poetry of the Hebrews, after classifying the purpose of poetry in general as 'to instruct while it gives pleasure'[8] continues to eulogize poets over against philosophers in that the former are capable to 'to adduce at once all the decorations of elegance, and all the attractions of amusement: who display, as in a picture, the actions, the manners, the pursuits and passions of men; and by the force of imitation and fancy, by the harmony of numbers, by the taste and variety of imagery, captivate the affections of the reader, and imperceptibly, or perhaps reluctantly, impel him to the pursuit of virtue'.[9] Although Lowth visualized 'readers' of poetry, he very much grasps its power over human sentiments activating enormous expressive outbursts of (moral) energy. This very gift poetic language has received becomes paramount when it is 'employed on sacred subjects, and in subservience to Religion. This indeed appears to have been the original office and destination of Poetry; and this it still so happily performs, that in all other cases it seems out of character, as if intended for this purpose alone.'[10] The prime example of inspiring religious usage of poetic language for

---

5. Klaus Seybold, *Studien zu Sprache und Stil der Psalmen*, BZAW 415 (Berlin: de Gruyter, 2010).

6. Robert Lowth, *De Sacra Poesia Hebraeorum*, trans. G. Gregory, 2 vols., 1969 facsimile ed. (Hildesheim: Georg Olms, 1787).

7. Johann Gottfried Herder, *Vom Geist der ebräischen Poesie* (Leipzig: Johann Ambrosius Barth 1787; repr., Norderstedt: Hansebooks, 2016).

8. Lowth, *De Sacra Poesia Hebraeorum*, 1:3.

9. Ibid., 11.

10. Ibid., 36.

Lowth, of course, is Hebrew poetry,[11] because the Bible in his times still was considered the oldest literary work of humankind. It is worthwhile to offer an extended quote from Lowth:

> [T]he human mind can conceive nothing more elevated, more beautiful, or more elegant; in which the almost ineffable sublimity of the subject is fully equaled by the energy of the language, and the dignity of the style... [S]ome of these writings exceed in antiquity the fabulous ages of Greece, in sublimity they are superior to the most finished productions of that polished people. Thus if the actual origin of Poetry be inquired after, it must of necessity be referred to Religion; and since it appears to be an art derived from nature alone, peculiar to no age or nation...it must be wholly attributed to the more violent affections of the heart, the nature of which is to express themselves in an animated and lofty tone, with a vehemence of expression far remote from vulgar use... [T]hese affections break and interrupt the enunciation by their impetuosity; they burst forth in sentences pointed, earnest, rapid, and tremulous; and in some degree the style as well as the modulation is adapted to the emotions and habits of the mind. This is particularly the case in admiration and delight; and what passions are so likely to be excited by religious contemplations as these? What ideas could so powerfully affect a new-created mind (undepraved by habit or opinion) as the goodness, the wisdom, and the greatness of the Almighty? Is it not probable, that the first effort of rude and unpolished verse would display itself in the praise of the Creator, and flow almost involuntarily from the enraptured mind? Thus far at least is certain, that Poetry has been nurtured in those sacred places where she seems to have been first called into existence; and that her original occupation was in the temple and at the altar.[12]

Lowth in this fashion implies a dynamic of poetical language which is close to the performative visions of contemporary linguists, putting higher emphasis, however, on moods and sentiments of people in contrast to solely rational deliberations.[13] He unfolds his theory in subtle observations on meter, verse, metaphor, comparisons and so on, of psalm poetry, but also analyses prophetic and sapiential language as related to the cultic idiom.[14] Elegies and odes attract his special interest.[15] Song of Songs and Job are close to dramatic (dialogical) poetry[16] and lyrics, widely used

---

11. Ibid., 37.
12. Ibid.
13. Cf. ibid., lectures XIV–XVII.
14. Cf. ibid., lectures XVIII–XXI; XXIV.
15. Cf. ibid., lectures XXIIXXIII; XXV–XXVIII.
16. Cf. ibid., lectures XXX–XXXIV.

in the Old Testament, are sung by the accompaniment of the lyre.[17] The genres of poetry identified by Lowth all fall into the categories of public presentation. They did not lose their living dynamics one bit by having been put into writing.

Ritual and Ceremonial Usage of the Psalms

In the same vain we may ask for traces of ceremonial or ritual use of the texts themselves. Of course, they may be literary imitations only and not indicate real inclusion in a line of action. But the frequency of such references and their apparent spontaneity rather lead to the conclusion that such references are genuine echoes of real performance. They do occur most of all in communal hymns and prayers. Processions of singing groups are mentioned (cf. Ps. 48.13), question and responses appear within a feasting crowd (cf. Pss. 15; 24), summons to worship are issued (cf. Pss. 118.1-4; 135.1-4), admonitions to prepare the altar are given (cf. Ps. 118.27), musical instruments accompany songs (cf. Pss. 57.9; 92.4; 98.4-6; 150.3-5), choirs intoned the praise, people responding with 'halleluyah' or 'amen' (cf. Pss. 66.1-12; 67; 95.1-17), sacrifices, dancing, shouting took place (cf. Pss. 45.16; 65.13; 66.15; 85.7; 95.1; 106.5; 116.17; Exod. 32.18-19), and, last but not least, the number of songs which use the first person plural is astonishingly high; it very probably betrays active participation of a congregation in sacred feasting (cf. Pss. 8.2–3.10; 46; 48.9-15; 50.3; 95.1-7; 100; 103.10-14). The examples may be augmented and supplemented by testimonies from outside the Psalter. Furthermore, indications of ceremonial use are not limited to congregational songs and prayers, but also occur in individual psalms, in particular of thanksgiving. This means that these prayers of a healed or saved person were, indeed, ritual affairs, including not necessarily a whole assembly of believers but probably a smaller group of friends and neighbors (cf. Ps. 22.23). Psalm 107.4-32 gives advice on when and how people who cried to the Lord and were saved had to fulfil their vows: 'Let them thank Yahweh for his steadfast love, for his wonderful works to humankind. And let them offer thanksgiving sacrifices and tell of his deeds with songs of joy' (vv. 21-22; cf. 2 Sam. 15.7-8). 'To offer thanks' (Hebrew: *ydh*), especially the nominal form *todah*, implies ritual action. To reconstruct ritual backgrounds of individual complaints and petitions is more difficult. The prayers themselves may hint to certain standard acts like 'preparing an offering' and 'watching out for a divine oracle' (cf. Ps. 5.4),

---

17. Cf. ibid., lectures XXV–XXVI.

pleading for an audible divine assurance (cf. Ps. 35.5), vying for a 'cup of salvation' (cf. Ps. 116.13). And there are, indeed, oracles of salvation preserved in some texts (cf. Ps. 91). Still, we do not get a complete picture of how individual complaints were enacted in the Psalter (cf. sporadic and ephemeral evidence in 2 Kgs 4.18-25; 5.8-14; Num. 5.11-28), because it is lacking all practical prescriptions of how to enact prayer. Narratives like 1 Sam. 1.12-18 do not portray a prayer session, either.

Babylonian Ritual and Ceremonial Incantations

Under these circumstances, the vast material on individual prayer rituals available on Babylonian cuneiform tablets in my opinion should be consulted. Since I first broached the subject,[18] there has been little acceptance of this proposal. But should it not be a valid argument? Babylonian collections of formalized prayer for individual patients do exhibit a remarkable affinity with Old Testament complaints and petitions, the largest group of psalms in the Psalter. Therefore, may we assume that the Old Testament specimens are of the same ceremonial background, namely incantation rituals for warding off evil viz. healing misfortune and illness? We have Babylonian collections of texts that offer patients' prayers as centre pieces of more or less extensive ritual actions, described and prescribed step by step, under the auspices of a trained conjurer or priest. Furthermore, there are similar ceremonial setups in other contemporary cultures.[19]

To give but one striking example of Babylonian ritual involving extensive ceremonial prescriptions and, in the very centre of the incantation expert's performance, a prayer of the patient quite akin to the individual complaints of the Hebrew Psalter, Stefan M. Maul describes carefully and in great detail the ritual of the Babylonian series *namburbi*.[20] This incantation series is dedicated to the 'dispersion of ills, which are threatening by bad omens' (*namburbi* = 'its dispersion'). An extensive Sumerian and Akkadian literature of evil portents and deep-seated anxieties looms in

---

18. Erhard S. Gerstenberger, *Der bittende Mensch: Bittritual und Klagelied des Einzelnen im Alten Testament*, WMANT 51 (Neukirchen-Vluyn: Neukirchener Verlag, 1980; repr., Eugene, OR: Wipf & Stock, 2009).

19. Cf. Erhard S. Gerstenberger, *Theologie des Lobens in sumerischen Hymnen*, ORA 28 (Tübingen: Mohr Siebeck, 2018).

20. Stefan M. Maul, *Zukunftsbewältigung: eine Untersuchung altorientalischen Denkens anhand der babylonisch-assyrischen Löserituale (Namburbi)*, Baghdader Forschungen 18 (Mainz am Rhein: Philipp von Zabern, 1994), 37–113.

the background of such incantations. After a thorough diagnosis of the patient's afflictions and the expert's suggestion of a relevant cure,[21] the incantation expert (*āšipu*) as well as the sufferer had to undergo a period of purification and 'sanctification' by taking ablutions and obeying dietary rules forbidding determined dishes.[22] During the night before the ritual was staged, the *āšipu* prepared the 'holy water' (*agubbû*) for ablutions using intricate ingredients.[23] A prayer for its effectiveness was in order.[24] A specialty of the *namburbi*-ritual was the formation of an image (a figurine) being able to substitute for that object which had shown the evil portent to the patient.[25] The healing ceremony itself started with a sacrifice to three highest gods (Ea, Šamaš, and Asalluḫi) who were to be entreated to undo the bad omen;[26] a very complicated procedure involving a small altar (*paṭiru*), a choice of incenses on a special stand (*nignakku*), and sacrificial materials, prayers and magic formulas. Interestingly, this sacrifice at the home of the patient, consisting of vegetables and drinks, 'always occurred at early dawn'.[27] The offering-site was fenced off and imagined evil persons were admonished: 'Wicked tongues shall turn away'.[28] After the sacrifice had been accepted, according to Maul's interpretation, and the high deities had assembled (perhaps represented by statues), the decisive part of the ritual began, a 'juridical fight' before Šamaš, sun-god and judge.[29] In Maul's understanding, the conjurer (*āšipu*) and the patient fight against the object which carried the evil portent, pleading for a reversal or dispersion of its destructive power. The patient had to approach the sacred sacrificial site, stepping on to a carpet of garden-herbs (*šammū kirî*) with their purifying capacities.[30] They, so to speak, sucked in the evil powers threatening the patient. But an essential part of the 'law-case' was the verbal petition for liberation from bad portents spoken by patient and

21. Nils Heeßel, *Babylonisch-assyrische Diagnostik*, AOAT 43 (Münster: Ugarit Verlag, 2000).
22. Maul, *Zukunftsbewältigung*, 39–41.
23. Ibid., 41–6.
24. Ibid., 45.
25. Ibid., 46–7.
26. Ibid., 48–57.
27. Ibid., 48. Cf. Ps. 5.4: 'O Lord, in the morning hear my voice, in the morning I sacrifice to you [אֶעֱרָךְ־לְךָ = I arrange for you] and watch out for you'. Small altars have been found in many old Israelite homes.
28. Ibid., 55; a direct address of potential enemies, also found in Pss. 4.3-5; 6.9; 52.3-7; 58.2-3; 62.4, 11.
29. Ibid., 60–71.
30. Ibid., 61–6.

conjurer.³¹ This liturgical, fixed prayer 'in many rituals first was spoken by the conjurer for the patient. The latter, then, had to recite it after the conjurer'.³² Those fixed 'sacred' words (which were thought to be the gift of the gods) 'were then repeated three, sometimes seven times. But in addition, the affected person had the opportunity [according the ritual instructions] to articulate his or her personal affliction, pleas and wishes before the divine judge... Such a "free prayer" certainly did have a liberating effect just like the oral confession in the catholic church.'³³ An elaborate discussion of the 'transfer of evil to the substitute figure',³⁴ the 'removal of the substitute', which now is the carrier of the evil (cf. Lev. 16.5-22),³⁵ and final purifications of patient and his environment (Pss. 94–100) as well as re-integration of the saved one into his social group and further prophylactic measures (Pss. 101–113) constitute the rest of Maul's treatise.

The supplication, spoken by conjurer and patient, held a central place in all the concomitant rites and words. It was part and parcel of the ceremony. One example of a *namburbi*-prayer must suffice:

1) Incantation: Šamaš, king of heaven and earth,
2) lord over right and justice,
3) lord over the Anunna-gods, lord over the spirit of the dead,
4) whose 'Yes' no other god
5) can change and whose decree
6) cannot be altered.
7) Šamaš, to revive the deadly ill,
8) to free the bound one,
9) is in your power! Šamaš,
10) I, your servant
11) N.N. son of N.N. whose
12) gods are Marduk (and)
13) Zarpanitum,
14) am standing before you now, yes, you.
15) I hold on to your seam.
16) Because of that evil which came out of the snake appearing in my house.
17) It did catch a prey.
18) I did see it.
19) Therefore I am afraid, terrified

31. Ibid., 67–9.
32. Ibid., 67.
33. Ibid., 69.
34. Ibid., 72–84.
35. Ibid., 85–93.

20) and constantly put into panic. Let me pass
21) this evil, then
22) I shall always praise your great deeds,
23) and extol you!
24) People who shall see me
25–26) shall eternally praise you! Text of the incantation.[36]

The structural elements of the prayer are clearly visible: praise of Šamaš (lines 1-9), self-presentation (10-14), affirmation of confidence (15), complaint (16-20a), petition (20b-21), vow to praise (22-23), witness to others (24-26a), scribal note (26b). With some particularities standing out (denomination as 'incantation'; praising invocation; insertion of personal name; scribal note; lack of imprecations), the elements and their arrangement correspond to the ones found in Hebrew complaint psalms. Other Babylonian petitionary rituals, like *šuilla*, *eršaḫunga*, *eršemma*, and so on, show very similar prayers of the afflicted supplicant.[37]

The ritual setting, position, and importance of the patient's prayer (which is formulaic, not biographical, and totally dependent on the acting expert) in Babylonian incantations make these specimens perfect analogies of Hebrew individual complaints.[38] The heart of the matter really is this: the supplications have been made to fit into the ritual. Their language and structure complies with the ultimate goal of the whole enactment, to procure salvation and rehabilitations for a determined sufferer. We have here a symbiosis of formulated words and concomitant ceremonial actions. The prayers are not meant to be read separately nor used outside their proper ritual setting. Language and action are deeply intertwined. What matters is not only a possible variant vocabulary of psalm discourses, but the whole range of grammatical, stylistic, structural specialties involved, and, at the bottom of all this, the emotional ingredients of this kind of poetry. As Robert Lowth recognized long ago,[39] the

---

36. Ibid., 297: my translation from the German edition.

37. The bracketed section is taken from Erhard S. Gerstenberger, 'Navajo Chants, Babylonian Incantations, Old Testament Psalms: A Comparative Study of Healing Rituals', *INTEGRITÉ* 17 (2018): 16–35 (24–5).

38. Some scholars stress ephemeral differences to caution against a close relationeship (cf. Anna Zernecke's introduction in: Alan Lenzi, ed., *Reading Akkadian Prayers and Hymns: An Introduction* [Atlanta: SBL, 2011], 61–8). On the other hand, this important introduction to prayers and hymns acknowledges ceremonial settings: 'it is advisable to think about most prayers as "ritual-prayers", comprising *dromena*, that which is done, and *legomena*, that which is spoken' (ibid., 37).

39. See above.

sentiments and passions, also the urgency and force expressed in Hebrew poetry, particularly in its sacred branches, are a decisive mark of poetry which is destined to be enacted or performed.

Contemporary Performances of Poetry

A legitimate question arises at this point: has the type of performable and to-be-performed-poetry been limited to ancient times in more or less illiterate societies or do we find similar phenomena in our highly literate cultures of the West in which individual reading is the most common way of dealing with the written (printed, digitalized etc.) word? Language, in fact, sometimes seems to be reduced to its visible forms in our own environments. The audible word recedes into the background, it seems. And if we discover comparable artifices in our vicinity, are they useful in a discussion of Hebrew Psalm poetry?

First, let us take a look at real, contemporary articulations of texts destined to be performed, ones not only read aloud before an audience (as happens with individual artists presenting their literate poetry) but enacted with great ado sometimes in mass rehearsals together with solo or band music, often accompanied by such things as dancing, lighting, and stage decoration. Ever since modern media like radio and TV came on the scene, the merger of texts with the audio-visual media has become a huge enterprise encompassing all kinds of rock, pop, soul, jazz, rap and many other styles of performances. We do not need to preoccupy ourselves with the different variations of poetry or music style entering the scene. They all share the intricate melding together of articulated texts and the rest of performative ingredients. No doubt, all these genres of music together spell and create the emotive force which takes hold of the audience, making it resound with the performed cocktail of word and tone, rhythm, light, dance, emotion. The symbiosis of all of these elements is such that one can hardly single out one particular aspect: the idea is to remember the power of the event in itself. Clearly enough, text and music versions of songs are available in print, and it may be the case that somebody wants to verify textual or musical details of a given performance. Yet, in all probability these cases are rare and are often enough propelled by a desire to delve again into the performative whole, that is, the presentation of the integral piece of art. Text and music have been composed as inseparable units, as most performers would testify.

But do the texts in themselves reveal characteristics of belonging to a special type of poetry, let us call it 'performative discourse' in distinction to 'literary poetry'? I assume they do. As pointed out with the Old Testament Psalms, we do find indications of performative language, structure, even sometimes grammar in those ancient compositions. Furthermore, outright references to enactment at the accompaniment of instruments, vocal expressions, bodily motion, and strongly emotive articulations abound. The same is true for modern 'performative poetry', as we shall see shortly. Of course, such specific poetry can be imitated by merely 'literate poets'. But as a rule, it seems to me, countless publications of poetry to be read individually lack vital signs of the 'performative poetry' in question, even if entitled as ballads, songs, hymns or the like. The performative kind, however, surely exposes vestiges of concomitant action.

In order to make the case clearer we need to study some examples of modern performative poetry. Duke Ellington (1899–1974), Louis Armstrong (1901–71); Elvis Presley (1935–77); Joan Baez (b. 1941), Bob Dylan (b. 1941), Elton John (b. 1947), Madonna (b. 1958), Michael Jackson (1958–2009), Prince (1958–2016); The Beatles, The Rolling Stones, Whitney Houston (1963–2012); Pink Floyd; Megan thee Stallion (b. 1995), to name but very few famous artists do witness to this merger of words and sounds. The list of English-speaking singers alone seems endless. A website – https://www.lyrics.com – lists about 80,000 names of mostly Anglo-Saxon singers/composers/song-writers. And other cultural regions have their own icons of popular artists in this area. Although some of them may use existing texts and wrap them into their live performance, the overwhelming majority of modern musicians prefer to have their own texts created just for their special ends, the musical performance of this – and no other – visionary project. They either turn out to be poets personally or else engage a gifted person of their confidence to compose appropriate texts. Whatever the case may be, the creation of a new piece of performable song is an intricate and intertwined affair. Texts and sounds practically grow into one piece. The text mostly takes on an important position in this process. Many times, it will be remembered as giving name and meaning to the gamut of emotions, sound, and aesthetic effects. People will quote the songs by their words, but they certainly remember the music and the special circumstances of great concerts with huge crowds in loaded sport arenas. The text gives rational and emotional meaning to the performed entity presented on stage by singers and orchestras. The poetic words do not dominate the scene, but they certainly do characterize it in tight conjunction with all the audible and visual elements given to it by the author or authors. As to the contents of popular music in our day, the range of topics is immense. Many musical works deal with the individual person's anxieties and jubilations, self-scrutinies and ardent hopes. And the problems of personal identity and purpose in life almost invariably extend to human relations in the spheres of intimacy as well as of social and political life. The 'other', 'counterpart' or simply the 'you' has a great stake in song-texts. A myriad of examples could be cited. They have passed mostly unnoticed in theological discussion for a long time. Only within the last two decades have some practical-theological investigations taken place.[40] Yet, the idea of looking for analogies to psalm-texts in modern pop-song discourse, it seems to me, has not been heeded very much. A few more or less random examples must suffice at this point.

Before we probe this subject further we may quote one representative of recent positive evaluation of pop music demonstrating the keen interest in its exact significance for theologians. Tom Beaudoin focuses mainly on the revealing contents of this down to earth poetry:

> pop music becomes popular because it so well characterizes a social group's values, behaviors, or identity. The music seems to 'fit' or 'depict' what people are like, and that is what makes it 'popular'. For example, there is music that seems to speak particularly to teenage life, to racial-ethnic realities, to religious affiliation, to local or regional tastes, to gender dynamics, or to specific levels of formal education or status or social privilege. Insofar as a musical artist, lyric, song, album, video, concert, or the like symbolizes a quality of a social group, popular music is the music or culture 'of the people'. Popular music is frequently experienced by fans as 'my music' or 'our music' precisely for these reasons… [H]ow we make theological sense of it, it would look something like this: We might begin by asking who wrote this song, what we know about their life, and what were they trying to communicate. Who paid for this music to be recorded and marketed, and what are their motivations to have it sell, and to whom? What are the deep social dynamics of the society in which this music is made and sold, and how are those social dynamics being legitimated or interrupted in the sound, the words, the images of this music? We would also want to know what this song tells us about the people who like it, and about the culture in which it came to be – how and why it speaks to these people in this moment. And we should be curious about how this song fits into larger patterns of life on the ground for its fans: when they listen to it, how important the lyrics are and what they mean to people, how the song informs their thoughts, dreams, conversations, perceptions, and self-perceptions, and how it opens or closes people to other music, feelings, relationships, and politics. That is admittedly a lot to find out, and few scholars can tackle all of that.[41]

---

40. Cf. Tom Beaudoin, ed., *Secular Music and Sacred Theology* (Collegeville: Liturgical, 2013). The fact that especially pietistic and charismatic Christian communities long have used rhythms and music of beat and rock art, underlying it with missionary texts is a different matter.

41. Beaudoin, *Secular Music and Sacred Theology*, XIV–XV.

And now a few examples of the enormously wide-spread and deeply influential musical culture of our days and its texts:

Tanita Tikaram (b. 1969), with Indian and Malaysian background, lives and works in Great Britain. Her world-wide hit in 1988 was the album 'Ancient Heart' with the key song 'Twist in my sobriety' (1988). She still gives concerts abroad; her self-composed songs reach a large international audience. In 'Twist in my sobriety', the poet/singer takes into account that her poetry remains ambiguous and mysterious. But together with her melancholic voice and music the entire song creates a deep impression of longing, self-reflection, and reaching out to the anonymous 'you'.

'Your Song', which came out in 1970, is one of the most famous songs of Elton John (b. 1947). The texts for his music largely come from his friend and lyricist Bernie Taupin. John himself was and is involved in social matters, promoting research against aids and recognition of LGBT minorities as urgent concerns in his work. The lyrics of 'Your Song' suggest that the singer interprets the world by way of acknowledging the other as equally important as oneself, and may well be a central Christian concern. Emmanuel Levinas (1905–95), the Jewish thinker, is an outstanding witness of this philosophy.[42]

Madonna (b. 1958) did cause some irritations along her career because of her unusual language and exhibitive performances. It should be recognized also, however, that the renowned singer can make real life in all its shades transparent to spiritual meanings. For example, in 'Like a Prayer' (1989), Madonna describes being called by name, while feeling drawn to another in the way the song expresses may be a heavenly experience. 'Like a Prayer' appeared in Madonna's fourth album in 1989; it is only one example of her own brand of (Roman Catholic) spirituality.

The Beatles (founded 1960) started a whole new movement of popular music with inspiring sounds and words. 'Rooted in skiffle, beat and 1950s rock and roll, their sound incorporated elements of classical music and traditional pop in innovative ways; the band later explored music styles ranging from ballads and Indian music to psychedelia and hard rock. As pioneers in recording, songwriting and artistic presentation, the group revolutionized many aspects of the music industry and were often publicized as leaders of the era's youth and sociocultural movements.'[43]

---

42. Cf. Emmanuel Levinas, *Alterity and Transcendence*, trans. Michael B. Smith (New York: Columbia University Press, 1999); Emmanuel Levinas, *Entre Nous: On Thinking-of-the-Other*, trans. Barbara Harshav and Michael B. Smith (New York: Columbia University Press, 2000).

43. 'The Beatles', https://en.wikipedia.org/wiki/The_Beatles (accessed 13 February 2020).

Free exposition of inner feelings is apparent in their song 'Help!' (1965) in a straightforward, uninhibited way. Emotions to be communicated to the audience are present. The generalized 'I' of this song implores the 'you' that the song is directed towards. Fervent plea is there. Some irony, too? ('when I was younger...', and smiling faces at the performance). The texts of the band to a great extent go back to John Lennon (1940–80) and Paul McCartney (b. 1942).

Bob Dylan (b. 1941) has become the paragon of an accomplished musician and an outstanding lyricist, at least since he received the Nobel Prize for Literature in 2016. He wrote many love-songs but kept a keen interest in social affairs and spirituality, for example in songs such as 'Ain't No Man Righteous, No Not One' (1979)[44] and 'The Times They Are A-Changin'' (1963).[45] Furthermore, Bob Dylan himself has been musing about the relationship of songs to written literature. In his Nobel banquet speech 2016, read by Azita Raji, he states: 'I've made dozens of records and played thousands of concerts all around the world. But it's my songs that are at the vital centre of almost everything I do... Not once have I ever had the time to ask myself, "Are my songs *literature*?"'[46] He concludes:

> If a song moves you, that's all that's important. I don't have to know what a song means. I've written all kinds of things into my songs. And I'm not going to worry about it – what it all means... [R]eading [Dylan in particular refers to 'Moby Dick', 'All Quiet on the Western Front' and 'The Odyssey']...gave you a way of looking at life, an understanding of human nature, and a standard to measure things by. I took all that with me when I started composing lyrics. And the themes from those books worked their way into many of my songs, either knowingly or unintentionally. I wanted to write songs unlike anything anybody ever heard, and these themes were fundamental... Our songs are alive in the land of the living. But songs are unlike literature. They're meant to be sung, not read... [L]yrics in songs are meant to be sung, not read on a page. And I hope some of you get the chance to listen to these lyrics the way they were intended to be heard: in concert or on record or however people are listening to songs these days.[47]

---

44. 'Ain't No Man Righteous, No Not One', https://www.bobdylan.com/songs/aint-no-man-righteous-no-not-one/ (accessed 11 January 2021)

45. 'The Times They Are A-Changin'', https://www.bobdylan.com/songs/times-they-are-changin/ (accessed 11 January 2021).

46. The banquet speech as well as Dylan's Nobel Prize (2016) address can be found here https://www.nobelprize.org/prizes/literature/2016/dylan/speech/?TB_iframe=true&width=921.6&height=921.6 (accessed 11 November 2020).

47. Ibid.

The laureate obviously clings to the popular prejudice that 'literature', according to our own reading culture, only comprises lengthy written novels and reports, perhaps with the marginal inclusion of some literary lyrics. He fails to admit performative, *ad hoc* written wordings into the wider realm of literature. But he acknowledges, and this is very important, the difference between all types of written literature for reading purposes and the song-texts he composed himself for his music: 'They're meant to be sung, not read'.[48] Maybe he somewhat underestimates the words in his music: 'I don't have to know what a song means'.[49]

What Can We Learn from Popular Songs in Regard to Psalm Studies?

If we accept for a moment, even hypothetically, a certain affinity between text production in pop music and of some ancient prayers, in that, in both cases, texts are composed precisely for upcoming performances, we get an inestimable insight into the mechanics of these proceedings. The generation of pop-song compositions we can observe first-hand, in our own reality and environment. We can attend personally communal events in which these texts are being performed. We can ask the authors, singers and poets, how they feel about their compositions, how they work into them own experiences and those of the generalized 'I' and 'You'. This is certainly a unique chance of being able to grasp first-hand the whole range of emotions, actions, impressions of authors and participants in such word-music happenings, or text-ritual life-settings. We may find, in my opinion, some good reasons for placing Old Testament Psalms into the category of 'performative texts' just as we did with pop-poetries of today.

Continuing along this lane, a closer look at present-day texts should be warranted. Aside from certain existential moods in pop songs, including the outcries of sorrow, joy, and longing for the other, the simple linguistic forms and structures betray the performative ends of said poetry. Redundancy and repetition, word-plays and metaphors, periodicity and rhythm, approaches to the vernacular: so many features point to the intended performance. Performative poetry, in antiquity and today, is not really meant 'to be read' but 'to be heard', 'to be enjoyed live', 'to embrace and enthuse' the participant and to make him sensitive to the needs of others. The anonymous 'you' advances to an alter-ego being helper, friend, or opponent. He or she is addressed in imperatives,

48. Ibid.
49. Ibid.

admonitions, inquiries, reproaches. God, in fact, is rarely mentioned, but the 'other' sometimes assumes the role of the divine. Language of performative poetry in all its facets is destined to serve in ritualized action or presentation before audiences who actively participate in the event.

Consequences for the Understanding and Interpretation of Psalm-texts

Preserved poems did for the most part – as should be clear from the above short investigation of Psalm language, structure, style, reference to rituals, and so on – originate as performative poems to be part of diverse sorts of public ceremony, be they individual complaints, thanksgivings, hymnic feasts, communal mourning, popular instruction and the like.[50] Many Babylonian prayers and some supplications found in other cultures do support this theory. When the Hebrew Psalms were committed to scrolls they lost their ritual instructions, probably because these were considered to be apostate practices. But the psalms certainly have not been put into writing to serve private reading purposes. Presumably, they still in their canonical form served communal practices of adoration and petition. In this case, the coexistence of written and spoken word can be postulated. Possibly, together with Torah reading (Neh. 8; Jer. 36), casual prayer, and praise (thanksgiving) rituals, they were used as performative elements. Lowth already recognized the special character of this kind of poetry. He pointed to its emotional and spiritual quality, so did Johann Gottfried Herder (1744–1803)[51] who also took note of its oriental origins. Are we justified to postulate a quality *sui generis* of psalm-poetry? Should we presume that all poetic language inherently is somehow bound to be articulated live, or performed within groups? Even writers do public readings. Poets stage declamatory shows. Be that as it may, for practical purposes, too, it would be advisable to acknowledge the extraordinary essence of poetic performative speech which cannot be lost whenever such articulation is being put into writing. And this is decisive for our present investigation. Obviously, even if the psalm literature of the Hebrew Bible when jotted down on scrolls may have unwittingly suffered some 'literary' adaptation, on the whole, the texts retained their performative character. In the process of canonization they were not made 'readable' in the sense of holistic interpretation.[52]

50. Cf. Gillingham, 'Postexilic Poetic Traditions in the Writings', 136–44.
51. Cf. Herder, *Vom Geist der ebräischen Poesie*.
52. There is a marked difference in the Hebrew Bible between 'narrated, literary' prayers (cf. Gen. 24.12-14; 1 Sam. 1.10-15) and inserted or quoted psalms (cf. 1 Sam.

Modern theories of performativity ('Performativität')[53] tie in with all those observations of a particular character of psalm poetry. Language in itself encompasses a, so to speak, DNA-like disposition to incite action and create new realities. When language is put into poetic forms, and employed in ritual action, then this capacity is brought into full swing. Words are formed and arranged in a way other than colloquial; they are 'elevated'[54] to the express performative level of articulation.[55] Usually, some kind of ritual or ceremonial envelope receives the words. They merge with sound and action, playing an important part in the unified ensemble, the performed presentation.

I hope my musings on poetry and psalms strike a chord in Susan's musical being. 'A good deal of poetry is for performative purposes':[56] yes, it sure is. Hebrew Psalm poetry has been powerful through the ages.[57]

Bibliography

Alter, Robert. *The Art of Biblical Poetry*. New York: Basic Books, 1985.
Austin, John L. *How to Do Things with Words*. Cambridge, MA: Harvard University Press, 1962.
Barnstone, Aliki, and Willis Barnstone, eds. *A Book of Women Poets from Antiquity to Now*. New York: Schocken, 1992.
Beaudoin, Tom, ed. *Secular Music and Sacred Theology*. Collegeville: Liturgical, 2013.
Bellenberg, Karl. *Else Lasker Schüler. Ihre Lyrik und ihre Komponisten*. Berlin: Wissenschaftlicher, 2019.
Carr, David M. *'Writing on the Tablets of the Heart'. Origins of Scripture and Literature*. Oxford: Oxford University Press, 2005.
Chamness, Nancy O. *The Libretto as Literature, 'Doktor Faust' by Ferrucio Busoni*. Frankfurt: Peter Lang, 2001.
Dylan, Bob. *Lyrics. Sämtliche Song-Texte 1962–2012*. Hamburg: Hoffmann & Campe, 2016.
Eder, Sigrid. *Identifikationspotenziale in den Psalmen. Emotionen, Metaphern und Textdynamik in den Psalmen 30, 64, 90 und 147*. BBB 183, Göttingen: V&R Unipress, 2018.
Erbele-Küster, Dorothea. *Lesen als Akt des Beten*. Eugene, OR: Wipf & Stock, 2013.

2.2-10; Isa. 38; Jon. 2).

53. Cf. Erika Fischer-Lichte, *Performativität. Eine Einführung*, 3rd ed. (Bielefeld: Transcript Verlag, 2016).

54. Cf. Lowth, *De Sacra Poesia Hebraeorum*.

55. Rappers consciously break this rule, taking a defiant stand: they employ plain narrational language to tell their stories.

56. Gillingham, 'Postexilic Poetic Traditions in the Writings', 133.

57. Cf. Susan E. Gillingham *Psalms Through the Centuries*, vols. 1 and 2, Wiley Blackwell Bible Commentaries (Chichester: Wiley-Blackwell, 2008/2018).

Fischer-Lichte, Erika. *Performativität. Eine Einführung*. 3rd ed. Bielefeld: Transcript Verlag, 2016.
FitzGerald, William. *Spiritual Modalities: Prayer as Rhetoric and Performance*. University Park, PA: Pennsylvania State University Press, 2012.
Gerstenberger, Erhard S. *Der bittende Mensch: Bittritual und Klagelied des Einzelnen im Alten Testament*. WMANT 51. Neukirchen-Vluyn: Neukirchener Verlag, 1980. Repr., Eugene, OR: Wipf & Stock 2009.
Gerstenberger, Erhard S. 'Navajo Chants, Babylonian Incantations, Old Testament Psalms: A Comparative Study of Healing Rituals'. *INTEGRITÉ* 17 (2018): 16–35.
Gerstenberger, Erhard S. *Psalms Part I*. FOTL XIV. Grand Rapids: Eerdmans, 1988.
Gerstenberger, Erhard S. *Psalms Part II*. FOTL XV. Grand Rapids: Eerdmans, 2001.
Gerstenberger, Erhard S. 'Der Psalter als Buch und als Sammlung'. Pages 3–13 in *Neue Wege der Psalmenforschung*. Edited by Klaus Seybold and Erich Zenger. HBS 1. Freiburg: Herder, 1994.
Gerstenberger, Erhard S. *Theologie des Lobens in sumerischen Hymnen*. ORA 28. Tübingen: Mohr Siebeck, 2018.
Gillingham, Susan E. *The Poems and Psalms of the Hebrew Bible*. Oxford: Oxford University Press, 1994.
Gillingham, Susan E. 'Postexilic Poetic Traditions in the Writings'. Pages 132–48 in *The Oxford Handbook of the Writings of the Hebrew Bible*. Edited by Donn F. Morgan. New York: Oxford University Press, 2019.
Gillingham, Susan E. *Psalms Through the Centuries*, vols. 1 and 2. Wiley Blackwell Bible Commentaries. Chichester: Wiley-Blackwell, 2008/2018.
Gunkel, Hermann, and Joachim Begrich. *Introduction to Psalms: The Genres of the Religious Lyric of Israel*. Translated by James D. Nogalski. Mercer Library of Biblical Studies. Macon: Mercer University Press, 1998.
Heeßel, Nils. *Babylonisch-assyrische Diagnostik*. AOAT 43. Münster: Ugarit Verlag, 2000.
Hempfer, Klaus W., and Jörg Volbers, eds. *Theorien des Performativen: Sprache – Wissen – Praxis. Eine Kritische Bestandsaufnahme*. Bielefeld: Transcript Verlag, 2011.
Herder, Johann Gottfried. *Vom Geist der ebräischen Poesie*. Leipzig: Johann Ambrosius Barth 1787. Repr., Norderstedt: Hansebooks, 2016.
König, Ekkehard. 'Bausteine einer allgemeinen Theorie des Performativen aus linguistischer Perspektive'. Pages 43–68 in *Theorien des Performativen: Sprache – Wissen – Praxis. Eine Kritische Bestandsaufnahme*. Edited by Kaus W. Hempfer and Jörg Volbers. Bielefeld: Transcript Verlag, 2011.
Lenzi, Alan, ed. *Reading Akkadian Prayers and Hymns: An Introduction*. Atlanta: SBL, 2011.
Levinas, Emmanuel. *Alterity and Transcendence*. Translated by Michael B. Smith. New York: Columbia University Press, 1999.
Levinas, Emmanuel. *Entre Nous: On Thinking-of-the-Other*. Translated by Barbara Harshav and Michael B. Smith. New York: Columbia University Press, 2000.
Lowth, Robert. *De Sacra Poesia Hebraeorum*. Translated by G. Gregory. 1969 facsimile ed. Hildesheim: Georg Olms, 1787.
Maul, Stefan M. *Zukunftsbewältigung: Eine Untersuchung altorientalischen Denkens anhand der babylonisch-assyrischen Löserituale (Namburbi)*. Baghdader Forschungen 18. Mainz am Rhein: Philipp von Zabern, 1994.
Mowinckel, Sigmund. *Religion und Kultus*. Göttingen: Vandenhoeck & Ruprecht, 1953.

Rhoads, David. 'Performance Criticism: An Emerging Methodology in Second Testament Studies – Part I', *BTB* 36 (2006): 118–33, Part II, *BTB* 36 (2006): 164–84.

Rothenberg, Jerome, and Pierre Joris, eds. *Poems for the Millennium: The University of California Book of Modern and Postmodern Poetry*. 2 vols. Berkeley: University of California Press, 1998.

Schiffer, Gundula. 'Die Beredtheit der Form. Die (graphische) Deutung biblisch-hebräischer Poesie'. Ph.D. diss., Munich, 2010.

Seybold, Klaus. *Introducing the Psalms*. Edinburgh: T. & T. Clark 1990.

Seybold, Klaus. *Studien zu Sprache und Stil der Psalmen*. BZAW 415. Berlin: de Gruyter 2010.

Utzschneider, Helmut. 'Drama (AT)', www.bibelwissenschaft.de/wibilex, 2016.

Willgren, David. *The Formation of the 'Book' of Psalms*. Tübingen: Mohr Siebeck 2016.

'Until the Moon is no More':
Psalm 72 as Political Imaginary

Marcel V. Măcelaru

I am delighted to contribute to this celebratory volume in honour of Professor Susan E. Gillingham, who was the advisor for my doctoral studies at the University of Oxford. Below I explore an issue related to Dr. Gillingham's scholarship and the interpretive logic that singularizes her work on the reception of the Psalter. I offer a discussion on Psalm 72 (LXX 71) spurred by the honouree's observation that reception history reveals a 'trajectory of interpretation from a mainly theological reading of this psalm to include a more social and political interpretation over the last three hundred years'.[1] Particularly, I am noting the hyperbolic portrayal of king and kingdom available in Psalm 72 and the place this language has received in interpretations of this text. Needless to say, my indebtedness to Professor Gillingham's work goes deeper than the quote above. In addition to her reception commentary, where this remark is made, I also interact with several other publications in which she refers to Psalm 72 and related interpretive issues. Therefore, no one is better qualified than the honouree to weigh the value the following thoughts may have, for whatever insights I provide, they are due in great measure to her example. And no one deserves more than Professor Gillingham to receive this token of my esteem and gratitude, for the guidance she has provided on my journey as a student of the Hebrew Bible has been both vital and unique.

The Portrayal of the King

The Bible is a book that more often than not surprises its readers with startling images, bold promises and unusual claims. The text in view

---

1. Susan E. Gillingham, *Psalms Through the Centuries*. Vol. 2, *A Reception History Commentary on Psalms 1–72* (Chichester: Wiley Blackwell, 2018), 394.

here – Psalm 72 – fits well within this characterization, for the king and kingdom it envisions would undoubtedly qualify it for a leading place were a list of such passages to be compiled. The language of the poem is clearly hyperbolic – common experience teaches as much, for rulers and realms, back in the biblical times and nowadays, have never resembled the blessed dominion the Psalmist imagines. It is therefore no surprise that the prevailing trend in the reception of this text has been to interpret it in reference to a future (ideal) kingship, albeit one envisioned differently within Jewish and Christian communities. The Peshitta, the Targums, the Talmud and the Midrashim, as well as several medieval Jewish commentators, have seen in the king of Psalm 72 a messianic figure.[2] Within Christianity, although not cited directly in the New Testament, Psalm 72 has been interpreted consistently in reference to Christ and his reign – exclusively so in the pre-critical period,[3] and partially so in modern times.[4]

---

2. E.g. Rashi, Ibn Ezra, and Kimḥi. For references and discussions, see Yaakov Jaffe, 'Psalm 72 and Micah 5:1: The Primordial Messiah', *JBQ* 48 (2020): 90–8; Marcel Poorthuis, 'King Solomon and Psalms 72 and 24 in the Debate between Jews and Christians', in *Jewish and Christian Liturgy and Worship: New Insights into its History and Interaction*, ed. A. Gerhards and C. Leonhard, Jewish and Christian Perspectives 15 (Leiden: Brill, 2007), 257–78; Susan E. Gillingham, *Psalms Through the Centuries*, vol. 1 (Oxford: Blackwell, 2008), 85–7; and Gillingham, *Psalms Through the Centuries*, 2:387–8.

3. The available evidence attests the presence of a solid trend of christological interpretations in the pre-critical period: during the early Christian centuries (e.g. Justin Martyr, Tertullian, Origen, Eusebius of Caesarea, Hilary of Poitiers, Athanasius, Ambrose of Milan, John Chrysostom, Jerome, Theodore of Mopsuestia, Augustine of Hippo, Theodoret of Cyrrhus, Maximus of Turin), during the Middle Ages (e.g. Fulgentius of Ruspe, Cassiodorus, Braulio of Saragossa) and during the Reformation (e.g. commentaries on Psalms by Martin Luther and Jean Calvin). For references and discussions, see D. C. Mitchell, *The Message of the Psalter: An Eschatological Programme in the Book of Psalms*, JSOTSup 252 (Sheffield: Sheffield Academic, 1997), 250–3; Gillingham, *Psalms Through the Centuries*, 1:26–39, 145; Quentin F. Wesselschmidt, ed., *Psalms 51–150*, ACCS 8 (Downers Grove: InterVarsity, 2014), 93–100; and Gillingham, *Psalms Through the Centuries*, 2:388–9.

4. E.g. F. Delitzsch, *Psalms*, K&D 5 (Grand Rapids: Eerdmans, 1988), 297–307; George Dahl, 'The Messianic Expectation in the Psalter', *JBL* 57 (1938): 1–12; Roland E. Murphy, *A Study of Psalm 72 (71)* (Washington: Catholic University of America Press, 1948); Jean-Marie Carrière, 'Le Ps 72 est-il un psaume messianique?', *Biblica* 72 (1991): 49–69; Walter C. Kaiser, *The Messiah in the Old Testament* (Grand Rapids: Zondervan, 1995), 133–5; Craig C. Broyles, 'The Redeeming King: Psalm 72's Contribution to the Messianic Ideal', in *Eschatology, Messianism, and the Dead Sea Scrolls*, ed. C. A. Evans and P. W. Flint, Studies in the Dead Sea Scrolls and Related

Admittedly, it is unlikely that the messianic expectations interpreters have observed reflect theological concerns arising from the early stages of writing, editing and collating the psalms. As Professor Gillingham has demonstrated, neither in the pre-exilic compositional stage of the Psalter, nor in its post-exilic editorial and compilation processes would a mature eschatological consciousness have been available.[5] In fact, the predominant interpretive direction in contemporary scholarship is that Psalm 72 is a pre-exilic[6] *Königspsalm*,[7] in its initial setting a coronation song akin to ancient Near Eastern literature of the same kind,[8] which, at some point in its early compositional history, became associated with the Israelite monarchy in general and with Solomon in particular.[9] Given its *Sitz im Leben* in the Israelite monarchy, the focus in the psalm's pre-exilic

---

Literature 1 (Grand Rapids: Eerdmans, 1997), 23–40; Walter C. Kaiser, 'Psalm 72: An Historical and Messianic Current Example of Antiochene Hermeneutical *Theoria*', *JETS* 52 (2009): 257–70.

5. Susan E. Gillingham, 'The Messiah in the Psalms: A Question of Reception History and the Psalter', in *King and Messiah in Israel and the Ancient Near East: Proceedings of the Oxford Old Testament Seminar*, ed. John Day, JSOTSup 270 (Sheffield: Sheffield Academic, 1998), 209–37.

6. Suggestions of a post-exilic origin have also been made. For arguments and bibliography, see J. M. Auwers, 'Les Psaumes 70–72: Essai de Lecture canonique', *RB* 101 (1994): 242–57. However, this seems to remain a minority position, primarily due to the influence comparative-literature studies have had in establishing a pre-exilic *Sitz im Leben* for this psalm. For more on these, see section 2 below.

7. The 'royal psalms' genre is a classification first introduced by W. M. L. de Wette for Pss. 2, 20, 21, 45, 72, 110 (see W. L. M. de Wette and J. C. W. Augusti, *Commentar über Die Psalmen* [Heidelberg: Mohr & Zimmer, 1811], 4). Subsequently, Gunkel (see Hermann Gunkel, *Einleitung in die Psalmen: Die Gattungen der religiösen Lyrik Israels*, 4th ed. [Göttingen: Vandenhoeck & Ruprecht, 1985], 140) added to this list Pss. 18, 101, 132, and 144.1-11. For a history of research on the 'royal psalms' as genre, see Markus Saur, *Die Königspsalmen: Studien zur Entstehung und Theologie*, BZAW 340 (Berlin: de Gruyter, 2004), 3–9. See also Gillingham, *Psalms Through the Centuries*, 1:194–203, who helpfully places the discussion about 'royal psalms' within the larger context of the critical reception of the Psalter in the eighteenth and nineteenth centuries.

8. See the discussion in the second section below, especially the bibliography in n. 17.

9. E.g., J. L. McKenzie, *Myths and Realities: Studies in Biblical Theology* (Milwaukee: Bruce Publishing, 1963), 214–16. Also G. T. Sheppard, 'The Relation of Solomon's Wisdom to Biblical Prayer', *TJT* 8 (1992): 7–27, who discusses literary and thematic connections between Ps. 72 and the narrative of Solomon's kingship (1 Kgs 3–11).

use must have been 'present, immediate, literal and royal'.[10] Moreover, the same would have been true in the early post-exilic period, for although the Davidic monarchy was no longer a historical reality, God's promises to David in the psalm would have reminded of provided the Jerusalem Temple community with a distinct sense of identity, one that connected them to their past in order to help them make sense of the present.[11]

Still, the hyperbolic portrayal of the king's reach and power available in this psalm can hardly be explained unless allowing that at some stage during its compositional history 'some merging of a present political reality with an idealized future hope'[12] occurred. Initially, the resulting poem would have still been used in reference to a Davidic monarch and his descendants. However, the superlative language employed must have provided the basis for a shift toward a future-oriented reading of the psalm later on, in the non-royal cultus of the third century BCE post-exilic era.[13] This included the reinterpretation of the generic term 'messiah', and its novel use as 'a title of status, the "Messiah", referring to the one coming once and for all time from the house of David'.[14] According to Gillingham, such 'prophetic' logic was part of the theological rationale used in the compilation of the Psalter and would have provided for the 'incorporation' of the royal psalms into the larger collection 'with an increasingly eschatological awareness of their importance'.[15] Thus, messianic overtones, in Gillingham's view, are features that belong to the reception of the Psalter rather than its composition. In this sense, then, the Messiah some have 'recognized' in the hyperbolic language of Psalm 72 should not be regarded 'as a theological agenda arising out of the psalms themselves, but as one which has been imposed upon them'.[16]

---

10. Gillingham, 'The Messiah in the Psalms', 237.

11. Ibid. On the connection between biblical texts and community identity, see M. V. Măcelaru, 'From Divine Speech to National/Ethnic Self-Definition in the Hebrew Bible: Representation(s) of Identity and the Motif of Divine–Human Distancing in Israel's Story' (D.Phil. diss. Oxford University, 2008); published in Romanian, in two volumes: *Identitatea între povară și privilegiu: Reprezentări ale poporului sfânt în literatura deuteronomistă* (Cluj-Napoca: Editura Risoprint, 2012); and *Discursul etno-național în Biblia Ebraică: Repere metodologice în analiza narațiunilor istoriografice veterotestamentare*, Religie și Filosofie (Bucharest: Editura Universitară, 2012).

12. Gillingham, 'The Messiah in the Psalms', 222.

13. See Susan E. Gillingham, 'From Liturgy to Prophecy: The Use of Psalmody in Second Temple Judaism', *CBQ* 64 (2002): 470–89.

14. Ibid., 477.

15. Ibid.

16. Gillingham, 'The Messiah in the Psalms', 237.

The argument summarized above helpfully separates the messianic/Christological interpretive trajectory from the compositional history of the psalm and clarifies its relation to the canonical shape of the Psalter. However, it leaves Psalm 72's idealized portrayal of the king and his reign unaddressed. If the eschatological consciousness that led to messianic interpretations of the Psalter is as late an occurrence as argued by Gillingham, then the hyperbolic language of Psalm 72 cannot be a projection of eschatological hope; its origin predates the final stages of the compilation of the Psalter and therefore it predates the 'prophetic' logic that played a part in that process. Consequently, assessing the purpose of Psalm 72's hyperbolic language becomes a question inextricably connected to the early compositional history of the psalm.

Origins of Psalm 72

The issues of origins and the ideological milieu that gave birth to Psalm 72 are addressed in two interrelated lines of inquiry. Firstly, these concerns feature prominently in studies written in the wake of the history of religions scholarship, which challenged messianic/Christological interpretations of the text and explained its hyperbolical language as courtly exaggerations introduced in Israel following the example of court poetry (*Hofstil*) produced by the surrounding empires. After the pioneering explorations of such connections published by Gunkel, Gressmann and Mowinkel,[17] the search for parallels between ancient Near Eastern literature and biblical texts flourished beyond the initial *Hofstil* theory, to the point that Psalm 72 is now associated in various ways with: Babylonian texts,[18] Mesopotamian literature,[19] the Canaanite royal tradition,[20] Ugaritic

---

17. See H. Gunkel, 'Die Königspsalmen', *Preussische Jahrbücher* 158 (1914): 42–68; H. Gunkel and J. Begrich, *Einleitung in die Psalmen: Die Gattungen der religiösen Lyrik Israels* (Göttingen: Vandenhoeck & Ruprecht, 1933), 166; H. Gressmann, *Der Messias*, FRLANT 43 (Göttingen: Vandenhoeck & Ruprecht, 1929), 15–19; and S. Mowinkel, *He That Cometh: The Messiah Concept in the Old Testament and Later Judaism*, trans. G. W. Anderson (Oxford: Abingdon, 1956), 21–95. For discussion and further bibliography, see Susan E. Gillingham, 'Studies of the Psalms: Retrospect and Prospect', *ExpTim* 119 (2008): 209–10.

18. P. Grelot, 'Un Parallèle babylonien d'Isäie LX et du Psaume LXII', *VT* 7 (1957): 319–21.

19. S. M. Paul, 'Psalm 72:5: A Traditional Blessing for the Long Life of the King', *JNES* 31 (1972): 351–5.

20. O. Loretz, *Die Königspsalmen: Die altorientalisch-kanaanäische Königstradition in jüdischer Sicht, Teil 1: Ps 20, 21, 72, 101 und 144*, UBL 6 (Münster: Ugarit-Verlag, 1988), 125–7.

texts,[21] Assyrian royal literature,[22] particularly Assurbanipal's coronation hymn,[23] neo-Assyrian Šamaš theology,[24] ancient Syrian traditions,[25] and Sumerian temple hymns.[26] Since the issues involved, including arguments against the reliability of this approach, have been thoroughly researched and presented,[27] we are relieved of the necessity to cover this ground again, here. It suffices to note the influence this kind of research has had over

21. M. Dietrich and O. Loretz, 'Von hebräisch '*m/lpny* (Ps 72:5) zu ugaritisch '*m* "vor"', in *Ascribe to the Lord: Biblical and Other Studies in Memory of Peter C. Craigie*, ed. L. Eslinger and G. Taylor, JSOTSup 67 (Sheffield: JSOT, 1988), 109–16.

22. M. Arneth, *'Sonne der Gerechtigkeit': Studien zur Solarisierung der Jahwe-Religion im Lichte von Psalm 72*, BZABR 1 (Wiesbaden: Harrassowitz, 2000); Arneth, 'Psalm 72 in seinen altorientalischen Kontexten', in *'Mein Sohn bist du' (Ps 2,7): Studien zu den Königspsalmen*, ed. E. Otto and E. Zenger, SBS 192 (Stuttgart: Katholisches Bibelwerk, 2002), 135–72.

23. S. R. A. Starbuck, *Court Oracles in the Psalms: The So-Called Royal Psalms in their Ancient Near Eastern Context*, SBLDS 172 (Atlanta: SBL, 1999), 116–17; E. Otto, 'Political Theology in Judah and Assyria: The Beginning of the Hebrew Bible as Literature', *SEÅ* 65 (2000): 65–71; D. J. Human 'An Ideal for Leadership – Psalm 72: The (Wise) King – Royal Mediation of God's Universal Reign', *Verb. et Eccl.* 23 (2002): 669–73.

24. R. S. Salo, *Die judäische Königsideologie im Kontext der Nachbarkulturen: Untersuchungen zu den Königspsalmen 2, 18, 20, 21, 45 und 72*, ORA 25 (Tübingen: Mohr Siebeck, 2017), 273.

25. J. Dietrich, 'Psalm 72 in its Ancient Syrian Context', in *Mediating Between Heaven and Earth: Communication with the Divine in the Ancient Near East*, ed. A. Zernecke, J. Stökl and C. L. Crouch, LHBOTS 566 (London: Bloomsbury 2012), 144–60.

26. D. Willgren, 'Psalm 72:20: A Frozen Colophon?', *JBL* 135 (2016): 49–60.

27. The first thorough, and probably the strongest, refutation of the *Hofstil* theory has been provided by Roland Murphy, *Study*, 45–78. His conclusion is that it is 'an assumption without sufficient basis' (ibid., 78). For discussions of comparative approaches and further bibliography, see H.-J. Kraus, *Psalmen 60–150*, 5th ed., BKAT 15/2 (Neukirchen-Vluyn: Neukirchener Verlag, 1978), 657–9 = idem, *Psalms 60–150*, trans. H. C. Oswald, CC (Minneapolis: Fortress, 1993), 78–9; idem, *Theologie der Psalmen*, 2nd ed. (Neukirchen-Vluyn: Neukirchener Verlag, 1989), 134–9 = idem, *Theology of the Psalms*, trans. K. Crim (Minneapolis: Fortress, 1992), 107–11; Arneth, *'Sonne der Gerechtigkeit'*; B. Janowski, 'Die Frucht der Gerechtigkeit: Psalm 72 und die judäische Königsideologie', in Otto and Zenger, eds., *'Mein Sohn bist du' (Ps 2,7)*, 114–20; F.-L. Hossfeld and E. Zenger, *Psalms 2: A Commentary on Psalms 51–100*, trans. L. M. Maloney, Hermeneia (Minneapolis: Augsburg Fortress, 2005), 210–13; and Áron Németh, *'Királyok zsoltára, zsoltárok királya : a 72. zsoltár előállása és teológiája a Zsoltárok könyve redakciójának tükrében* ['*Psalm of Kings, King of Psalms': The Formation and Theology of Psalm 72 in Light of the Redaction of the Psalter*] (Cluj-Napoca: Exit, 2018), 30–7.

the years, evidenced by the widespread rehearsal of some of its conclusions, particularly the idea that Psalm 72 is a typical ancient Near Eastern coronation hymn that originated in the pre-exilic Israelite monarchy;[28] and that, in spite of dissenting voices that have criticized the method of comparison for its 'tenuous assertions of genetic intertextuality that do not hold up under scrutiny'.[29] Methodological fallacies notwithstanding, the value of this line of inquiry is in the fact that it incidentally brings to the fore the psalm's original political concerns. However, the hyperbolic language of the psalm is not examined beyond the comparison with ANE parallels; its independent function as conveyor of meaning, political, eschatological or otherwise, is not a concern comparative studies have.

In the second line of inquiry that addresses the origin of Psalm 72, complex compositional scenarios have been put forward and the hyperbolic elements of Psalm 72 have been explained as post-exilic additions that postdate biblical texts addressing similar themes (e.g. Gen. 12.3; 15.18; Isa. 49.7, 23; 60.6, 14; Zech. 9.9-10). To my knowledge, Áron Németh has made the most recent comprehensive proposal of this kind in his 2015 doctoral thesis.[30] He argues that the growth of Psalm 72 took place gradually, in a 'three-centuries-long multi-stage' compositional process, within which an initial pre-exilic literary stratum (*Grundschicht* – Ps. 72.1aβ-8, 12-14, 16-17aαβ), updated during the second half of the sixth century BCE (*Fortschreibung* – Ps. 72.9-11), was further expanded in response to historical and political realities that played a part in the literary and theological growth of the Psalter itself. Moreover, Németh argues that the fourth and fifth phases of expansion consist of bits of proto-Messianic interpretation added to the sixth-century BCE text.[31] Thus, in the fourth phase[32] a reinterpretation of Ps. 72.9-11 resulted in the addition of vv. 15 and 17aγ.b. This was a (political) actualization of

---

28. Several significant commentaries have picked up this idea: M. Dahood, *Psalms II: 51–100*, AB 17 (New York: Doubleday, 1968), 179; M. E. Tate, *Psalms 51–100*, WBC 20 (Dallas: Word, 1990), 222; Kraus, *Psalms 60–150*, 76; idem, *Theology*, 108; J. L. Mays, *Psalms*, IBC (Louisville: Westminster John Knox, 1994), 236; Gillingham, *Psalms 2*, 386.

29. D. M. Carr, *The Formation of the Hebrew Bible: A New Reconstruction* (Oxford: Oxford University Press, 2011), 393.

30. Németh, *'Királyok zsoltára, zsoltárok királya'*. For an alternative, recent compositional scenario, still arguing for three phases of textual development but dividing the text differently, see Salo, *Die judäische Königsideologie im Kontext der Nachbarkulturen*, 205–73.

31. Ibid., 213–39.

32. Ibid., 213–31.

the text to fit the more positive attitude toward other nations that characterized the Jerusalem Temple community during the fifth-century BCE Persian period. In it, the daily prayer for the king (which one may see as 'political duty' to the empire) is transformed into a 'spiritual program', in an incipient phase, that recasts the king, from being the one who receives the service of nations to one who *is* a blessing for the nations. Németh sees here an indication that a restoration of the Israelite kingship, under a ruler of Davidic descent, in the near future, was expected. As the time went by, however, and the hoped-for reestablishment of kingship did not happen, the prayer for blessing and prosperity becomes less centred on the king as an earthly figure and turns directly to God as the source of all that is good and desirable. According to Németh, this is evident in adjustments done to vv. 3* and 7* – the fifth phase of expansion, which retains the hope for the restoration of the house of David but relegates its fulfilment to an undetermined future.[33]

Evidently, as textual reconstructions of this kind usually go, the compositional history of Psalm 72 offered is unavoidably conjectural. The central hypothesis of Németh's study, namely that the three-centuries literary growth of Psalm 72 reflects the conceptional history of the entire Psalter, is just that – a hypothesis. Undoubtedly, Németh follows in the footsteps of a respectable tradition of redaction-critical studies.[34] However, since none of the textual layers he identifies are actually available in the manuscript evidence, the redactional history he proposes cannot be objectively verified. Consequently, nor can we reach a sure conclusion in regard to the compositional history of the psalm's hyperbolic language.

33. Ibid., 231–9.
34. On the compositional history of Ps. 72, see Loretz, *Die Königspsalmen*, 125–7; B. Renaud, 'De la bénédiction du roi à la bénédiction de Dieu (Ps 72)', *Bib* 70 (1989): 305–26; Arneth, *'Sonne der Gerechtigkeit'*, 29–39; idem, 'Psalm 72'; B. Janowski, *Stellvertretung: Alttestamentliche Studien zu einem theologischen Begriff*, SBS 165 (Stuttgart: Katholisches Bibelwerk, 1997), 41–66; idem, 'Die Frucht', 102–9; E. Zenger, '"So betete David für seinen Sohn Salomo und für den König Messias": Überlegungen zur holistischen und kanonischen Lektüre des 72. Psalms', *JBTh* 8 (1993): 57–72; idem, *Dein Angesicht suche ich: Neue Psalmenauslegungen* (Freiburg: Herder, 1998), 154–67; idem, '"Es sollen sich niederwerfen vor ihm alle Könige" (Ps 72,11): Redaktionsgeschichtliche Beobachtungen zu Psalm 72 und zum Programm des messianischen Psalters Ps 2–89', in Otto and Zenger, eds., *'Mein Sohn bist du' (Ps 2,7)*, 66–93; Salo, *Die judäische Königsideologie im Kontext der Nachbarkulturen*, 205–73.

The compositional argument aside, it should be noted that Németh does make an important point regarding Psalm 72's portrayal of kingship and consequently of Psalm 72's political overtones.[35] Borrowing from Jan Assmann's categorization of ancient Near Eastern theocracies, he observes that two visions of kingship are blended within the psalm. In the first (Assmann's *Repräsentative Theokratie*[36]), YHWH exercises his royal power and authority through a human proxy. In the second (Assmann's *Identitäre Theokratie*[37]), YHWH's kingship over Israel is exclusive and unmediated. Expectably, in tune with the diachronic argument he builds, Németh looks at these visions of kingship as proof of redactional development. The 'representative theocracy' model, he argues, is prevalent in the basic, pre-exilic literary layer of the psalm, which would have been composed at the height of the Israelite monarchy, and in its subsequent sixth- and fifth-century BCE expansions that resulted in Ps. 72.1-17, the section of the text which includes the hyperbolic language of the psalm. The 'identitary theocracy', on the other hand, is most evident in the final doxology (vv. 18-19), which in Németh's analysis is also the last textual layer added to the psalm.

Németh's 'fragmentary' reading, however, is problematic. It weakens the meaning-making power of the canonical text. If different textual layers were added in response to different contextual realities, what are the chances that the 'composite' text we now read conveys a coherent message? In fact, unless we assume that the process of textual expansion included a concern for consistency, the interpretation of the psalm as a cohesive whole is not entirely justified. However, if we assume such consistency, this ought to reduce the preoccupation of the interpreter with the compositional history of the poem and serve to refocus the analysis on the received canonical text.

---

35. In the ancient Near Eastern world, divine kingship was considered to be the source of human political power. On the close connection between the political and the religious in the ANE world, see H. Frankfort, *Kingship and the Gods: A Study of Ancient Near Eastern Religion as the Integration of Society and Nature* (Chicago: University of Chicago Press, 1948).

36. See J. Assmann, 'Monotheism and Its Political Consequences', in *Religion and Politics: Cultural Perspectives*, ed. B. Giesen and D. Šuber, ISRS 3 (Leiden: Brill, 2005), 141–59; idem, 'Theokratie im Alten Ägypten', in *Theokratie und theokratischer Diskurs: Die Rede von der Gottesherrschaft und ihre politisch-sozialen Auswirkungen im interkulturellen Vergleich*, ed. K. Trampedach and A. Pečar, CHT 1 (Tübingen: Mohr Siebeck, 2013), 22–7.

37. See Assmann, 'Theokratie im Alten Ägypten', 20–2.

Gianni Barbiero makes a similar point when he argues that the editor(s) of Psalm 72 employed a redactional logic that united the various parts of the text 'in harmony or counterpoint'.[38] No doubt, he explains, the existence of a multi-stage compositional history behind the canonical version of the text cannot. and should not, be denied. However, as it stands, Psalm 72 has 'internal unity', it is 'perfectly coherent', and its interpretation should be done in the light of this fact.[39] The advantage of such an approach here is that the two visions of kingship Németh interprets diachronically would be examined as elements of the imaginative world the psalm constructs rhetorically, the world into which it invites its readers to enter. So would be the case with its poetic and literary features, including the hyperbolic description of king and kingdom. I argue that this adjustment of interpretive focus, from solely 'explaining the world that created the Psalms' to 'understanding the world that the Psalms create',[40] in the case in view is emphatically necessary if the full effect of the psalm's hyperbolic language is to be reaped.

Political and Social Realities Concerning Psalm 72

The methodological point made above has been previously explained by Professor Gillingham in terms of an interpretive dialogue between 'understanding' and 'appreciation'. In her words:

> Understanding is necessary for academic study of and critical engagement with any poetic text. It involves discerning the structure, the form, and the conventions of language, and also (where possible) evaluating the setting of the poem in the life of the poet and the poet's culture. In this process, we, as readers, become the subjects of the exercise, and the poem and the poet are the objects. By contrast, an appreciation of poetry is a reversal of this process: the poem becomes the subject, so that as we allow ourselves to be addressed, the poetry is the active element and we are the recipients.
>
> This twofold approach might also be described as *looking at* a poem and *looking through* it. The difference is more one of degree than of kind; to look

---

38. Gianni Barbiero, 'The Risk of a Fragmented Reading of the Psalms: Psalm 72 as a Case in Point', *ZAW* 120 (2008): 90; cf. Carmen Diller, 'Er soll leben, solange die Sonne bleibt' (Ps 72,5): Die räumlichen und zeitlichen Dimensionen der Königsherrschaft in Psalm 72', in *Studien zu Psalmen und Propheten: Festschrift für Hubert Irsigler*, ed. C. Diller et al., HBS 64 (Freiburg: Herder, 2010), 1–26.

39. Barbiero, 'Risk', 90.

40. D. Bland and D. Fleer, 'Introduction: Performing the Psalms and the World Imagined in the Psalter', in *Performing the Psalms*, ed. D. Bland and D. Fleer (St Louis, MO: Chalice, 2005), 2.

at a poem has more to do with a process of detachment and analysis, whilst to look through it concerns more an attitude of engagement and receptivity. We need both in order to gain a more profound discernment of any poetry.[41]

The summary of approaches given above reveals that both 'understanding' and 'appreciation' have played a part in the interpretation of Psalm 72, although not always as concerns blended harmoniously into one interpretive model, as Gillingham's methodology of 'critical imagination' seems to suggest. The orientation in comparative and redactional studies is toward elucidating issues pertaining to the composition of the psalm – clearly a concern with 'understanding' the text. The messianic/Christological readings on the other hand have focused on the theological meaning of the text after its literary development ended. As such, here we may speak about the 'appreciation' of Psalm 72 in the communities of faith that have received it.

An approach that seems to provide a *via media* between historical and theological concerns is available in studies that read the psalm as a text that speaks of, and therefore speaks to, political and social realities. I propose that methodologically such readings come closest to incorporating 'understanding' and 'appreciation' in the process of interpretation. The premise is that, as a royal/coronation song, Psalm 72 is inherently political, since it reflects an underlying royal ideology, and therefore the 'ethical' approach to ascertaining its message is to account for what it says about the role and service of the king within the community where the psalm originated (understanding), as a means to restoring justice and righteousness in the community where the psalm is received (appreciation).[42]

Gillingham traces the beginnings of a steady political interpretive trend in the reception of the Psalter in England and Scotland, where, from the sixteenth century onwards, psalms are increasingly used as a resource for political discourse.[43] However, regarding Psalm 72, she observes that interpretations alluding to political rule and/or social justice were available much earlier. From the tenth-century connection with Byzantium imperial power in the *Paris Psalter*, through several hymns that refocus the application of the psalm to Britain,[44] to two scholarly renditions of political

---

41. Susan E. Gillingham, *The Poems and Psalms of the Hebrew Bible*, Oxford Bible (Oxford: Oxford University Press, 1994), 4.
42. See Gillingham, *Psalms Through the Centuries 2*, 394–5.
43. Gillingham, *Psalms Through the Centuries 1*, 131–312.
44. It was interesting to discover that political concerns permeate the reception of Psalm 72 also in my own context, in Romania. An early example comes from Metropolitan Dosoftei (1624–1693), a poet and scholar whose translation and

interpretation in more recent years, the history of the reception of Psalm 72 summarized by Gillingham reveals a growing tendency to apply this text to social realities while downplaying the superlative casting of the king it portrays.[45] Thus, while in hymns such as Isaac Watts' Christ's Kingdom among the Gentiles' and Brian Wren's 'With Humble Justice Clad and Crowned' the concern is with social justice, still seen as a result of Christ's reign, in the two contemporary scholarly examples Gillingham offers the psalm is read 'in a temporal and literal way', that is, in reference to political and social realities the ancient Judahite community would have faced.[46]

The first scholarly example given by Gillingham is a study of Psalm 72 authored by David Jobling,[47] who offers an analysis of 'contradictions' present in the text as reflections of ideological contradictions in the world that produced the text. Particularly, Jobling argues that the portrayal of the royal system in vv. 1-7, where the king's just rule is unconditional, reflects the ideology of the centralized monarchic power, while in the second half of the Psalm (vv. 12-14), the rule is contingent upon caring for the poor and the needy. As for the hyperbolic language of the psalm, in Jobling's view, its purpose is to support the royal ideology by evoking the idea of monarchic 'permanence' (vv. 5, 7, 17a), for instance, the idea of monarchy as enduring as the sun and the moon.

Differently than Jobling, Walter Houston[48] finds that the main contradiction in the psalm is of a moral nature. This is evident in the fact that

---

versification of the Psalter stands at the very cradle of modern Romanian language. In Dosoftei's rendition of Ps. 72, the kings of Tarshish (Ps. 72 10) are replaced by kings coming from the White Sea (north-west Russia) to pay homage to the ruler of the land. Although further research is necessary in order to ascertain Dosoftei's political position, it is significant to note that he writes during the seventeenth-century Russian expansion and the rise of the Romanovs as Russia's rulers. It would not be too big of a leap to imagine that homage paid by 'the kings from the White Sea', that is, by the ones who would have represented a real threat to surrounding hegemonies, would have been perceived as the best proof that the ruler portrayed in Ps. 72 has great power and authority.

45. Gillingham, *Psalms Through the Centuries 2*, 390–4.
46. Ibid., 393.
47. D. Jobling, 'Deconstruction and the Political Analysis of Biblical Texts: A Jamesonian Reading of Psalm 72', *Semeia* 59 (1992): 95–127.
48. For Houston's approach to Ps. 72, see: W. J. Houston, '"You shall open your hand to your needy brother": Ideology and Moral Formation in Deut. 15.1-18', in *The Bible in Ethics: The Second Sheffield Colloquium*, ed. J. W. Rogerson, M. Davies and M. Daniel Carroll R., JSOTSup 207 (Sheffield: Sheffield Academic, 1995), 298;

the prayers for the king to provide justice and righteousness on behalf of the poor and the needy are in stark contrast with the collection of tribute, which is inherently an oppressive action. The royal ideology promoted in the psalm portrays the monarchy as a divinely ordained system that sustains the fertility, peace and order of the land. However, there is an ethical angle to this, for the psalm also alludes to the fact that the right to rule in Israel is dependent upon the resolve of the king to act on behalf of the disadvantaged members of the society while also curbing the power of the oppressor.[49] As such, the psalm is both validation and warning – validation of the king's rule and warning against this rule becoming anything other than the blessing for the needy it is supposed to be.

The second study mentioned by Gillingham, authored by Andrew Mein,[50] builds on Houston's work. Mein speaks in a similar fashion about the ethics of kingship, which shows support for, but is also critical of, the monarchic system. The foundation of this contrast is found in the very idea that doing justice is the main business of the king. Mein argues that the king in Psalm 72 stands at the centre of a divinely ordained arrangement of the world, which encompasses harmoniously the cosmic, the moral and the social. As such, on the surface the psalm appears to be propagandistic – it presents a pro-monarchy ideological stance. Yet, in the midst of a seemingly all-encompassing royal ideology, moral contradictions inherent to kingship are also found. These can be used to undermine, criticise and correct kings and kingdoms; that is, to 'domesticate' the ancient Near Eastern monarchic *tendenz* of the psalm, and in doing so, to eventually reorient the accaparating social ideologies of the psalm's receivers centuries later. The sermon examples Mein gives[51] seem to support this point, for in both cases the language of Psalm 72 is recast

---

idem, 'The King's Preferential Option for the Poor: Rhetoric, Ideology and Ethics in Psalm 72', *BibInt* 7 (1999): 341–67; idem, *Contending for Justice: Ideologies and Theologies of Social Justice in the Old Testament*, LHBOTS 642 (London: T&T Clark, 2006), 139–50.

49. On the social ethics evoked by Ps. 72, see also E. Tamez, *Bible of the Oppressed*, trans. M. J. O'Connell (Maryknoll: Orbis, 1983), 21–7; Human, 'Ideal'; and M. J. Obiorah, 'Prayer for Good Governance: A Study of Psalm 72 in the Nigeria Context', *Open Journal of Philosophy* 3.1A (2013): 192–9.

50. A. Mein, 'The King's Justice? Early Modern Perspectives on the Ethics of Psalm 72', in *Psalmody and Poetry in Old Testament Ethics*, ed. Dirk J. Human, LHBOTS 572 (London: T&T Clark, 2012), 93–111. See Gillingham, *Psalms Through the Centuries 2*, 393, n. 1581.

51. These are: William Laud's sermon on Ps. 72.1, delivered on March 1631, and Parliamentarian Joseph Caryl's paraphrase of Ps. 72, delivered on March 1643.

in a manner that promotes a remedial view on the British monarchy. This proves that the 'political' potential of the psalm goes beyond its *Sitz im Leben*; it may, in fact, be contingent on a distinct 'appreciation' of its unique language as 'political imaginary'.

Political imaginary in Psalm 72

The notion of 'imaginary' introduced here refers to how people intuitively understand the world in the light of cultural, social, political, religious, etc information that belongs to their context, and should be distinguished from 'imagination', which is the faculty individuals possess to form new ideas. The use of 'imaginary' as a feature of socio-cultural perception can be traced back to Benedict Anderson's claim that awareness of one's national identity is instilled through (instinctive) social practice rather than through taught social theory and intentional choice.[52] The consistent socio-political application of the concept, however, is the merit of Charles Taylor,[53] who speaks of 'social imaginary' as a group's mind-set, the criteria by which we judge socio-political arrangements as legitimate or not. Building on Taylor's theory, theologian James K. A. Smith has explained that

> ...'social imaginary' is an affective, non-cognitive understanding of the world. It is described as an *imaginary* (rather than a *theory*) because it is fuelled by the stuff of imagination rather than the intellect: it is made up of, and embedded in, stories, narratives, myths and icons. These visions capture our hearts and imaginations by 'lining' our imagination, as it were – providing us with frameworks of 'meaning' by which we make sense of our world and our calling in it. An irreducible understanding of the world resides in our intuitive, pre-cognitive grasp of these stories.[54]

I propose that the millennia-long reception of biblical texts within Europe has provided European culture with such frameworks of meaning. In the case of the Psalter this is aptly demonstrated by Gillingham's reception history commentaries; within these, Psalm 72's messianic interpretive trajectory provides a particularly good example of the potential biblical

---

52. Benedict Anderson, *Imagined Communities: Reflections on the Origin and Spread of Nationalism* (London: Verso, 1983).

53. C. Taylor, *Modern Social Imaginaries* (Durham: Duke University Press, 2004), 23–30; idem, *A Secular Age* (Cambridge: Belknap Press of Harvard University Press, 2007), 159–211.

54. James K. A. Smith, *Desiring the Kingdom: Worship, Worldview and Cultural Formation*, Cultural Liturgies 1 (Grand Rapids: Baker Academic, 2009), 68.

texts have as imaginaries that socialize their receivers into particular mind-sets. To explain, the messianic/Christological interpretation of the psalm has wrought an imaginary, which we may describe as 'eschatological', that has informed, and continues to inform, Christian expectations regarding a 'messianic' age within which the universal lordship of Christ is made manifest. The main feature of such eschatological imaginary is the fact that it relegates the consequences of the kingship portrayed hyperbolically in Psalm 72 to an undetermined future; and this is, of course, its Achille's heel as well, for an interpretation exclusively referring to the future overshadows any application the psalm may have in the life of its receivers.

Alternatively, I propose that the development of social/political directions in the reception of Psalm 72 shape up a 'political imaginary' that organizes the language of the psalm in political categories and therefore may also organize the instituting process of the political in the world of the psalm's receivers by addressing and amending its congruent social realities. As such, the most important aspect of a political imaginary is its potential to sponsor theological ideas that speak to concerns in the contemporary public arena. This connects methodologically to the 'life-centred' interpretation of the psalms advocated by Gillingham[55] – an approach that has the advantage of offering present-day readers 'the most scope and flexibility in a fuller appreciation of Hebrew poetry in its broadest sense', and therefore of allowing for 'innumerable performances' of the psalms 'beyond one ancient cultic setting'.[56] Seen in this way, the potential of Psalm 72 as 'political imaginary' resides exactly in the fact that the non-limitative character of its hyperbolic language translates into non-limitative applications of this language within each interpretive context where the psalm is read. As such, the image of a blessed (messianic) existence evoked by the psalm is no longer an exclusive reference to a future unavailable to the reader. Rather, it becomes 'the horizon of possible experience in which the (literary) work displaces its readers'.[57]

---

55. The 'life-centred' reading of the Psalter testifies to the preoccupation with the performance of the psalms in the life of the psalmists themselves central to Gillingham's doctoral research (see S. E. Gillingham, 'Personal Piety in the Study of the Psalms: A Reassessment' [D.Phil. diss., University of Oxford, 1987]), and consequently with the effect of the psalms in the life of their receivers evident in Gillingham's subsequent work. Specifically, on this approach, see Gillingham, *Poems and Psalms of the Hebrew Bible*, 186–9.

56. Gillingham, *Poems and Psalms of the Hebrew Bible*, 189.

57. P. Ricoeur, 'The Text as Dynamic Identity', in *Identity of the Literary Text*, ed. M. J. Valdés and O. Miller (Toronto: University of Toronto Press, 1985), 183.

Regarding the operation of such interpretive logic in the case of Psalm 72, Robert Alter writes:

> A poem of this sort is surely not an effort at serious historical explanation, and like any utopian statement it is accountable to history only as a projection, from the scant historical grounds for hope, of how history might be transformed. What would the world look like, the psalmist implicitly asks, if we imagine a ruler governing not by coercion but by compassion and unswerving equity, who did not exploit the weak but championed them? The biblical writers may well have understood intuitively that such projections might be as spiritually indispensable as the most unblinking reports of the savagery that occurs in history, and with which the biblical record abounds. Although points of real geography are invoked, everything comes together not in the intersection of Sheba and Tarshish at Jerusalem but in the poetic structure where a king's defense of the helpless becomes rain over the land, the land itself burgeons with beauty, all the earth takes his name for a blessing, in a lovely verbal intimation of social and political harmony denied us by ordinary experience but which, in the momentum of the poem, goes on till the moon's no more.[58]

Admittedly, as Alter observes, the world evoked by the psalm does not conform to the reality experienced by the interpreter. However, I suggest in conclusion that it is exactly the hyperbolic portrayal of this utopic world that provides the psalm with the necessary persuasive 'power' to operate as political imaginary. To explain, the use of hyperbolic language 'forces' the reader to participate in the process of meaning-making by formulating the possible out of the impossible.[59] As such, the resulting political imaginary is further conscientized as a constituent element in the interpreter's worldview; in other words, the images evoked by Psalm 72 inform the present. Consequently, the appreciation of Psalm 72 as political imaginary 'forces' the reader to also engage in a process of world-making, for such rekindling of one's imagination prompts them to effect changes in their lived reality so as to resemble the world thus far available only in rhetorical representation. In this way, the very reception of Psalm 72 becomes an act of imaginative freedom that serves to activate and transform reality.

---

58. R. Alter, *The Art of Biblical Poetry* (New York: Basic, 1985), 133.
59. On the operation of hyperbolic language, see R. Carston and C. Wearing, 'Metaphor, Hyperbole and Simile: A Pragmatic Approach', *Language and Cognition* 3 (2011): 283–312; idem, 'Hyperbolic Language and Its Relation to Metaphor and Irony', *Journal of Pragmatics* 79 (2015): 79–92.

Bibliography

Alter, Robert. *The Art of Biblical Poetry*. New York: Basic Books, 1985.
Anderson, Benedict. *Imagined Communities: Reflections on the Origin and Spread of Nationalism*. London: Verso, 1983.
Arneth, Martin. 'Psalm 72 in seinen altorientalischen Kontexten'. Pages 135–72 in *'Mein Sohn bist du' (Ps 2,7): Studien zu den Königspsalmen*. SBS 192. Stuttgart: Katholisches Bibelwerk, 2002.
Arneth, Martin. *'Sonne der Gerechtigkeit': Studien zur Solarisierung der Jahwe-Religion im Lichte von Psalm 72*. BZABR 1. Wiesbaden: Harrassowitz, 2000.
Assmann, Jan. 'Monotheism and Its Political Consequences'. Pages 141–59 in *Religion and Politics: Cultural Perspectives*. Edited by Bernhard Giesen and Daniel Šuber. ISRS 3. Leiden: Brill, 2005.
Assmann, Jan. 'Theokratie im Alten Ägypten'. Pages 19–38 in *Theokratie und theokratischer Diskurs: Die Rede von der Gottesherrschaft und ihre politisch-sozialen Auswirkungen im interkulturellen Vergleich*. Edited by Kai Trampedach and Andreas Pečar. CHT 1. Tübingen: Mohr Siebeck, 2013.
Auwers, J. M. 'Les Psaumes 70–72: Essai de Lecture canonique'. *RB* 101 (1994): 242–57.
Barbiero, Gianni. 'The Risk of a Fragmented Reading of the Psalms: Psalm 72 as a Case in Point'. *ZAW* 120 (2008): 67–91.
Bland, Dave, and David Fleer. 'Introduction: Performing the Psalms and the World Imagined in the Psalter'. Pages 1–6 in *Performing the Psalms*. Edited by D. Bland and D. Fleer. St Louis, MO: Chalice, 2005.
Broyles, Craig C. 'The Redeeming King: Psalm 72's Contribution to the Messianic Ideal'. Pages 23–40 in *Eschatology, Messianism, and the Dead Sea Scrolls*. Edited by C. A. Evans and P. W. Flint. Studies in the Dead Sea Scrolls and Related Literature 1. Grand Rapids: Eerdmans, 1997.
Carr, David M. *The Formation of the Hebrew Bible: A New Reconstruction*. Oxford: Oxford University Press, 2011.
Carrière, Jean-Marie. 'Le Ps 72 est-il un psaume messianique?' *Biblica* 72 (1991): 49–69.
Carston, Robyn, and Catherine Wearing, 'Hyperbolic Language and Its Relation to Metaphor and Irony'. *Journal of Pragmatics* 79 (2015): 79–92.
Carston, Robyn, and Catherine Wearing, 'Metaphor, Hyperbole and Simile: A Pragmatic Approach'. *Language and Cognition* 3 (2011): 283–312.
Dahl, George. 'The Messianic Expectation in the Psalter'. *JBL* 57 (1938): 1–12.
Dahood, Mitchell. *Psalms II: 51–100*. AB 17. New York: Doubleday, 1968.
Delitzsch, F. *Psalms*. K&D 5. Grand Rapids: Eerdmans, 1988.
Dewey, John. *Intelligence in the Modern World: John Dewey's Philosophy*. Edited by Joseph Ratner. New York: Random House, 1939.
Dietrich, Jan. 'Psalm 72 in its Ancient Syrian Context'. Pages 144–60 in *Mediating Between Heaven and Earth: Communication with the Divine in the Ancient Near East*. Edited by A. Zernecke, J. Stökl and C. L. Crouch. LHBOTS 566. London: Bloomsbury 2012.
Dietrich, Manfried, and Oswald Loretz. 'Von hebräisch *'m/lpny* (Ps 72:5) zu ugaritisch *'m* "vor"'. Pages 109–16 in *Ascribe to the Lord: Biblical and Other Studies in Memory of Peter C. Craigie*. Edited by Lyle Eslinger and Glen Taylor. JSOTSup 67. Sheffield: JSOT, 1988.
Frankfort, Henri. *Kingship and the Gods: A Study of Ancient Near Eastern Religion as the Integration of Society and Nature*. Chicago: University of Chicago Press, 1948.

Gillingham, Susan E. 'From Liturgy to Prophecy: The Use of Psalmody in Second Temple Judaism'. *CBQ* 64 (2002): 476–8.
Gillingham, Susan E. 'The Messiah in the Psalms: A Question of Reception History and the Psalter'. Pages 209–37 in *King and Messiah in Israel and the Ancient Near East: Proceedings of the Oxford Old Testament Seminar*. Edited by John Day. JSOTSup 270. Sheffield: Sheffield Academic, 1998.
Gillingham, Susan E. 'Personal Piety in the Study of the Psalms: A Reassessment'. D.Phil. diss., University of Oxford, 1987.
Gillingham, Susan E. *The Poems and Psalms of the Hebrew Bible*. Oxford Bible. Oxford: Oxford University Press, 1994.
Gillingham, Susan E. *Psalms Through the Centuries: Volume 1* Oxford: Blackwell, 2008.
Gillingham, Susan E. *Psalms Through the Centuries: Volume Two: A Reception History Commentary on Psalms 1–72*. Chichester: Wiley Blackwell, 2018.
Gillingham, Susan E. 'Studies of the Psalms: Retrospect and Prospect'. *ExpTim* 119 (2008): 209–10.
Grelot, Pierre. 'Un Parallèle babylonien d'Isäie LX et du Psaume LXII'. *VT* 7 (1957): 319–21.
Gressmann, Hugo. *Der Messias*. FRLANT 43. Göttingen: Vandenhoeck & Ruprecht, 1929.
Gunkel, Hermann. 'Die Königspsalmen'. *Preussische Jahrbücher* 158 (1914): 42–68.
Gunkel, Hermann. *Einleitung in die Psalmen: Die Gattungen der religiösen Lyrik Israels*. 4th ed. Göttingen: Vandenhoeck & Ruprecht, 1985.
Gunkel, Hermann, and J. Begrich. *Einleitung in die Psalmen: Die Gattungen der religiösen Lyrik Israels*. Göttingen: Vandenhoeck & Ruprecht, 1933.
Hossfeld, Frank-Lothar, and Erich Zenger. *Psalms 2: A Commentary on Psalms 51–100*. Translated by L. M. Maloney. Hermeneia. Minneapolis: Augsburg Fortress, 2005.
Houston, Walter J. *Contending for Justice: Ideologies and Theologies of Social Justice in the Old Testament*. LHBOTS 542. London: T&T Clark, 2006.
Houston, Walter J. 'The King's Preferential Option for the Poor: Rhetoric, Ideology and Ethics in Psalm 72'. *BibInt* 7 (1999): 341–67.
Houston, Walter J. '"You shall open your hand to your needy brother": Ideology and Moral Formation in Deut. 15.1-18'. Pages 296–314 in *The Bible in Ethics: The Second Sheffield Colloquium*. Edited by J. W. Rogerson, M. Davies and M. Daniel Carroll R. JSOTSup 207. Sheffield: Sheffield Academic, 1995.
Human, D. J. 'An Ideal for Leadership – Psalm 72: The (Wise) King – Royal Mediation of God's Universal Reign'. *Verb. et Eccl.* 23 (2002): 658–77.
Jaffe, Yaakov. 'Psalm 72 and Micah 5:1: The Primordial Messiah'. *JBQ* 48 (2020): 90–8.
Janowski, Bernd. 'Die Frucht der Gerechtigkeit: Psalm 72 und die judäische Königsideologie'. Pages 94–134 in *'Mein Sohn bist du' (Ps 2,7): Studien zu den Königspsalmen*. SBS 192. Stuttgart: Verlag Katholisches Bibelwerk, 2002.
Janowski, Bernd. *Stellvertretung: Alttestamentliche Studien zu einem theologischen Begriff*. SBS 165. Stuttgart: Katholisches Bibelwerk, 1997.
Jobling, David. 'Deconstruction and the Political Analysis of Biblical Texts: A Jamesonian Reading of Psalm 72'. *Semeia* 59 (1992): 95–127.
Kaiser, Walter C. *The Messiah in the Old Testament*. Grand Rapids: Zondervan, 1995.
Kaiser, Walter C. 'Psalm 72: An Historical and Messianic Current Example of Antiochene Hermeneutical *Theoria*'. *JETS* 52 (2009): 257–70.
Kraus, Hans-Joachim. *Psalmen 60–150*. 5th ed. BKAT 15/2. Neukirchen-Vluyn: Neukirchener Verlag, 1978.

Kraus, Hans-Joachim. *Psalms 60–150.* Translated by H. C. Oswald. CC. Minneapolis: Fortress, 1993.
Kraus, Hans-Joachim. *Theologie der Psalmen.* 2nd ed. Neukirchen-Vluyn: Neukirchener Verlag, 1989.
Kraus, Hans-Joachim. *Theology of the Psalms.* Translated by Keith Crim. Minneapolis: Fortress, 1992.
Loretz, Oswald. *Die Königspsalmen: Die altorientalisch-kanaanäische Königstradition in jüdischer Sicht. Teil 1: Ps 20, 21, 72, 101 und 144.* UBL 6. Münster: Ugarit-Verlag, 1988.
Măcelaru, Marcel V. *Discursul etno-național în Biblia Ebraică: Repere metodologice în analiza narațiunilor istoriografice veterotestamentare.* Religie și Filosofie. Bucharest: Editura Universitară, 2012.
Măcelaru, Marcel V. 'From Divine Speech to National/Ethnic Self-Definition in the Hebrew Bible: Representation(s) of Identity and the Motif of Divine–Human Distancing in Israel's Story'. D.Phil. diss., Oxford University, 2008.
Măcelaru, Marcel V. *Identitatea între povară și privilegiu: Reprezentări ale poporului sfânt în literatura deuteronomistă.* Cluj-Napoca: Editura Risoprint, 2012.
Mays, James Luther. *Psalms.* IBC. Louisville: Westminster John Knox, 1994.
McKenzie, John L. *Myths and Realities: Studies in Biblical Theology.* Milwaukee: Bruce Publishing, 1963.
Mein, Andrew. 'The King's Justice? Early Modern Perspectives on the Ethics of Psalm 72'. Pages 93–111 in *Psalmody and Poetry in Old Testament Ethics.* Edited by Dirk J. Human. LHBOTS 572. London: T&T Clark, 2012.
Mitchell, David C. *The Message of the Psalter: An Eschatological Programme in the Book of Psalms.* JSOTSup 252. Sheffield: Sheffield Academic, 1997.
Mowinkel, Sigmund. *He That Cometh: The Messiah Concept in the Old Testament and Later Judaism.* Translated by G. W. Anderson. Oxford: Abingdon, 1956.
Murphy, Roland E. *A Study of Psalm 72 (71).* Washington: Catholic University of America Press, 1948.
Németh, Áron. *'Királyok zsoltára, zsoltárok királya': a 72. zsoltár előállása és teológiája a Zsoltárok könyve redakciójának tükrében* [*'Psalm of Kings, King of Psalms': The Formation and Theology of Psalm 72 in Light of the Redaction of the Psalter*]. Cluj-Napoca: Exit, 2018.
Obiorah, Mary Jerome. 'Prayer for Good Governance: A Study of Psalm 72 in the Nigeria Context'. *Open Journal of Philosophy* 3.1A (2013): 192–9.
Otto, Eckart. 'Political Theology in Judah and Assyria: The Beginning of the Hebrew Bible as Literature'. *SEÅ* 65 (2000): 59–76.
Paul, Shalom M. 'Psalm 72:5: A Traditional Blessing for the Long Life of the King'. *JNES* 31 (1972): 351–5.
Poorthuis, Marcel. 'King Solomon and Psalms 72 and 24 in the Debate between Jews and Christians'. Pages 257–78 in *Jewish and Christian Liturgy and Worship: New Insights into its History and Interaction.* Edited by A. Gerhards and C. Leonhard. Jewish and Christian Perspectives 15. Leiden: Brill, 2007.
Renaud, B. 'De la bénédiction du roi à la bénédiction de Dieu (Ps 72)'. *Bib* 70 (1989): 305–26.
Ricoeur, Paul. 'The Text as Dynamic Identity'. Pages 175–86 in *Identity of the Literary Text.* Edited by M. J. Valdés and O. Miller. Toronto: University of Toronto Press, 1985.

Salo, Reettakaisa Sofia. *Die judäische Königsideologie im Kontext der Nachbarkulturen: Untersuchungen zu den Königspsalmen 2, 18, 20, 21, 45 und 72*. ORA 25. Tübingen: Mohr Siebeck, 2017.

Saur, Markus. *Die Königspsalmen: Studien zur Entstehung und Theologie*. BZAW 340. Berlin: de Gruyter, 2004.

Sheppard, Gerald T. 'The Relation of Solomon's Wisdom to Biblical Prayer'. *TJT* 8 (1992): 7–27.

Smith, James K. A. *Desiring the Kingdom: Worship, Worldview and Cultural Formation*. Cultural Liturgies 1. Grand Rapids: Baker Academic, 2009.

Starbuck, Scott R. A. *Court Oracles in the Psalms: The So-Called Royal Psalms in their Ancient Near Eastern Context*. SBLDS 172. Atlanta: SBL, 1999.

Tamez, Elsa. *Bible of the Oppressed*. Translated by M. J. O'Connell. Maryknoll: Orbis, 1983.

Tate, Marvin E. *Psalms 51–100*. WBC 20. Dallas: Word, 1990.

Taylor, Charles. *Modern Social Imaginaries*. Durham: Duke University Press, 2004.

Taylor, Charles. *A Secular Age*. Cambridge: Belknap Press of Harvard University Press, 2007.

Wette, W. L. M. de, and J. C. W. Augusti. *Commentar über Die Psalmen*. Heidelberg: Mohr & Zimmer, 1811.

Willgren, David. 'Psalm 72:20: A Frozen Colophon?' *JBL* 135 (2016): 49–60.

Wesselschmidt, Quentin F., ed. *Psalms 51–150*. ACCS 8. Downers Grove: InterVarsity, 2014.

Zenger, Erich. *Dein Angesicht suche ich: Neue Psalmenauslegungen*. Freiburg: Herder, 1998.

Zenger, Erich. '"Es sollen sich niederwerfen vor ihm alle Könige" (Ps 72,11): Redaktionsgeschichtliche Beobachtungen zu Psalm 72 und zum Programm des messianischen Psalters Ps 2–89'. Pages 66–93 in *'Mein Sohn bist du' (Ps 2,7): Studien zu den Königspsalmen*. Edited by E. Otto and E. Zenger. SBS 192. Stuttgart: Verlag Katholisches Bibelwerk, 2002.

Zenger, Erich. '"So betete David für seinen Sohn Salomo und für den König Messias": Überlegungen zur holistischen und kanonischen Lektüre des 72. Psalms'. *JBTh* 8 (1993): 57–72.

LITERAL AND ALLEGORICAL READINGS
OF THE PSALMS:
IMAGINING THE PSALMIST*

John Barton

There is a long tradition in Christian interpretation of the Psalms that sees them as containing the whole of Christian truth, as a kind of Bible in miniature. St Ambrose, for example, wrote:

> In the Book of Psalms there is profit for all, with healing power for our salvation. There is instruction from history, teaching from the law, prediction from prophecy, chastisement from denunciation, persuasion for moral preaching... All with eyes to see can discover in it a complete gymnasium for the soul, a stadium for all the virtues, equipped for every kind of exercise; it is for each to choose the kind each judges best to help gain the prize.
> What am I to say of the grace of prophecy? We see that what others hinted at in riddles was promised openly and clearly to the psalmist alone: the Lord Jesus was to be born of David's seed, according to the word of the Lord: 'I will place upon your throne one who is the fruit of your flesh'.
> In the Psalms, then, not only is Jesus born for us, he also undergoes his saving passion in his body, he lies in death, he rises again, he ascends into heaven, he sits at the right hand of the Father. What no one would have dared to say was foretold by the psalmist alone, and afterward proclaimed by the Lord himself in the gospel.[1]

Much later, from the Anglican tradition, we may cite Richard Hooker:

---

* It is a great pleasure and privilege to dedicate this piece to Sue Gillingham, a friend and colleague for forty years, and the United Kingdom's leading Psalms expert.

1. Ambrose, *Commentary on Psalm 1*, CSEL 64, Chapters 4–8; quoted from *Celebrating the Seasons: Daily Spiritual Readings for the Christian Year*, compiled and introduced by Robert Atwell (Norwich: Canterbury, 1999), 357–8.

> The choice and flower of all things profitable in other books the psalms do both more briefly contain, and more movingly also express, by reason of that poetic form wherewith they are written. The ancient when they speak of the book of psalms use to fall into large discourses, showing how this part above the rest doth of purpose set forth and celebrate all the considerations and operations which belong to God... What is there necessary for man to know which the psalms are not able to teach? They are to beginners an easy and familiar introduction, a mighty augmentation of all virtue and knowledge in such as are entered before, a strong confirmation to the most perfect among others. Heroic magnanimity, exquisite justice, grave moderation, exact wisdom, repentance unfeigned, unwearied patience, the mysteries of God, the sufferings of Christ, the terrors of wrath, the comforts of grace, the works of providence over the world and the promised joys of that world which is to come, all good necessarily to be either known or done or had, this one celestial fountain yieldeth.[2]

For most modern readers this tradition – and especially in its assertion that details of the nature and life of Christ are narrated in the Psalms – is problematic. We may grant that many virtues and precepts can be found there, but we jib at the idea that the Psalms are messianic oracles foretelling the sufferings and glorification of Christ. What is more, there is much in the Psalms that most Christians find morally repugnant, especially the vituperation and cursing of enemies and the assertions of the psalmist's own virtue.

How then did ancient Christian readers and commentators manage to extract such edifying and Christocentric messages from this book? Most scholars would probably argue that it was through allegorization, either according to what became the formal fourfold scheme or, more informally, by looking for possible 'spiritual' applications of apparently 'carnal' passages. A classic case would be Origen's solution to the problem of Psalm 137, with its invitation to dash Babylonian babies against a rock. Origen proposes that the rock is taken to be Christ, and the babies to be inchoate evil thoughts and desires: then the scandal of the verse disappears:

> Blessed is the one who seizes the little ones of Babylon, which are understood to be nothing else but these 'evil thoughts' that confound and disturb our heart. For this is what Babylon means. While these thoughts are still small and just beginning, they must be seized and dashed against the 'rock' who is Christ [cf. 1 Cor. 10.4], and, by his order, they must be slain, so that nothing in us 'may remain to draw breath' [Josh. 11.14]. (Origen, *Homily on Joshua* 15.1)

---

2. Richard Hooker, *Of the Laws of Ecclesiastical Polity*, vol. 2, ed. A. S. McGrade (Oxford: Oxford University Press, 2013), 100–101 (§37).

This approach resurfaces in C. S. Lewis's *Reflections on the Psalms*:

> I can even use the horrible passage in 137 about dashing the Babylonian babies against the stones. I know things in the inner world which are like babies; the infantile beginnings of small indulgences, small resentments, which may one day become dipsomania or settled hatred, but which woo us and wheedle us with special pleadings and seem so tiny, so helpless that in resisting them we feel we are being cruel to animals… Against all such pretty infants…the advice of the Psalms is the best. Knock the little bastards' brains out.[3]

Lewis here misses Origen's Christological reference ('rock' is singular, not the plural 'stones' as Lewis renders it), though no doubt he would have accepted this reference too.

But Christology is central to much patristic allegorization of the Psalms, as it had already been in the New Testament. Psalm 110 had not been widely treated as messianic before the New Testament authors began to see it as referring to Christ, building on Jesus' reported saying 'How can the scribes say that the Messiah is the son of David? David himself, by the Holy Spirit, declared, "The Lord said to my Lord, 'Sit at my right hand, until I put your enemies under your feet'." David himself calls him Lord, so how can he be his son?' (Mk 12.35-37).[4] But there is evidence that the Psalm had already been seen as messianic at Qumran. In the Epistle to the Hebrews the psalm becomes central to the argument that Jesus is greater than the angels (Heb. 1.13).[5] Thus what was probably in origin an oracle to the earthly king is turned into a prophecy of the coming Messiah, who is Jesus Christ.

Such allegorization in Origen and in the Alexandrian school that followed his lead is often contrasted with the supposedly more 'literal' style of the school of Antioch (exemplified by John Chrysostom, Theodore of Mopsuestia, Diadore of Tarsus, and the later Theodoret of Cyrrhus). It is

---

3. C. S. Lewis, *Reflections on the Psalms* (London: Geoffrey Bles, 1958), 113–14.

4. See the discussion in Benjamin Sargent, *David Being a Prophet: The Contingency of Scripture upon History in the New Testament* (Berlin: de Gruyter, 2014).

5. See David Willgren Davage, '"As It Is Written Concerning Him in the Songs of David" [11Q13 2 9–10]: On the Role of Paratextual Activity in Shaping Eschatological Reimaginations of Psalm 82', in *David, Messianism, and Eschatology: Ambiguity in the Reception History of the Book of Psalms in Judaism and Christianity*, ed. David Willgren Davage and Erkki Koskenniemi, SRB 10 (Åbo: Åbo Akademi University, 2020), 3–44, and Adela Yarbro Collins and John J. Collins, *King and Messiah as Son of God: Divine, Human, and Angelic Messianic Figures in Biblical and Related Literature* (Grand Rapids: Eerdmans, 2008).

true that the Antiochenes often follow a more historical and less 'mystical' approach to the Psalms. They tend to interpret the Psalms as referring to events of Jewish history, rather than as messianic – to such an extent that in their day they were accused of 'judaizing'. They did not see the text as a tissue of symbols and figures, but attended to textual flow and argument, and this tended to replace Origen's interest in allegorical interpretation. Yet at times they can allegorize with the best. Thus Theodoret interprets the title of Psalm 30 (29 in Greek), 'A Psalm. A Song at the Dedication of the Temple', as referring to 'the restoration of human nature that Christ the Lord accomplished by accepting death on behalf of us and giving hope of resurrection'.[6] This is not what we would naturally call a literal interpretation. Diodore allows only four Psalms to be messianic (Pss. 2, 8, 45, and 110); yet in those psalms he treats 'historical' references as applying to Christ. With Psalm 2 he follows the interpretation of Heb. 1.5 and Acts 4.24-28, where it is taken to describe how the incarnate Christ suffered at the hands of Herod and Pilate.[7] The Antiochenes seem sometimes to allegorize and sometimes to give a 'plain' interpretation of the text; and that is also true of Origen, who was content to follow the text's argument when there was one – he did not allegorize St Paul, for example. In the Psalms allegorization was sometimes necessary and appropriate, as in the case of Psalm 137, which would otherwise be offensive, but at other times the natural sense of the text could be accepted. Sometimes interpretation might be 'historical', sometimes 'spiritual'. The schools of Alexandria and Antioch differed in emphasis, but they spoke the same language.

This makes me wonder whether the distinction between allegorization and accepting the text at face value – 'literally' – may be the wrong way of describing patristic psalm-exegesis. For Origen, and indeed for the Antiochenes, just as for the New Testament writers, a psalm like Psalm 110 referred *literally* to Christ – that was its natural meaning, not one that was being imposed on it by the interpreter as a reaction to a difficulty. Many passages in biblical books are allegorical in intent – consider the four beasts in Daniel 7, for example. Reading them as metaphors for world-empires is not allegorization in the sense of taking a literal text and reading it non-literally, but is an observation about the original intent of

---

6. Theodoret of Cyrus, *Commentary on the Psalms: Psalms 1–72*, trans. Robert C. Hill, Fathers of the Church 101 (Washington, DC: Catholic University of America Press, 2000), 187–91; see also Robert C. Hill, *Reading the Bible in Antioch*, The Bible in Ancient Christianity 5 (Atlanta: SBL, 2005).

7. For details see Susan Gillingham, *A Journey of Two Psalms: The Reception of Psalms 1 & 2 in Jewish and Christian Tradition* (Oxford: Oxford University Press, 2013), 50–1.

the text. So with the Psalms: for Theodoret Psalm 30 (29) really is about the restoration of human nature through Christ: this is not a meaning added on to some putative naturalistic sense. The term 'allegorization' implies that what we may think is the natural sense was also so perceived by the Fathers, who then reinterpreted it allegorically. But for them, on the contrary, the allegorical meaning simply was the meaning: the building of the temple in Psalm 30 (29) was just as much a symbol of the resurrection as the fourth beast of Daniel was a symbol of the empire of Antiochus IV Epiphanes. It looks to us like allegorizing a text whose intention was literal, but that is a misleading way of thinking about it, from a patristic perspective.

This can be seen, for example, in an Antiochene reading of Psalm 45, which all the Fathers of both schools agreed was Christological in meaning. As Sue Gillingham summarizes, Diodore of Tarsus takes the psalm as clearly referring to Jesus, not to Solomon, since the line 'Your throne, O God, is for ever and ever', cannot possibly refer to an earthly ruler like Solomon.[8] The psalmist (David) had Christ in mind when he wrote the psalm.

Is there a better way of describing the difference between us and the Fathers when it comes to the interpretation of the Psalms, and indeed of the Old Testament in general? Rather than driving a wedge between Alexandria and Antioch (and aligning ourselves more with the latter), we need to distinguish between how patristic interpretation looks from the outside, to us as modern readers, and how it seemed to them from inside the Church's interpretative community. The term 'allegorization' fudges this distinction, because it is our way of describing a process of thought that for them did not have two stages – first the perception of a natural sense, then a decision to interpret it allegorically – but was a seamless procedure, which came from reading the text in the light of the Church's rule of faith.

Perhaps we could deploy the social anthropologists' distinction between *emic* and *etic* approaches. An emic description of a society is the self-understanding or depiction the society gives of itself; an etic one is the society as observed by an outsider. Allegorization is a term applied in an etic way, which implies that if *we* were to read the Psalms as even the Antiochenes often did, we would be reading them allegorically rather than literally. But it does not capture the emic perspective, that of the

---

8. Susan Gillingham, *Psalms Through the Centuries: A Reception History Commentary on Psalms 1–72*, vol. 2 (Chichester: Wiley-Blackwell, 2018), 271.

Fathers themselves, who would have said simply that they were reading the Psalms as part of the Holy Scriptures of the Church and therefore naturally finding Christian references in them. Neither the etic nor the emic perspective is necessarily mistaken, but they are incommensurable, and cannot be described using the same terms.

From an emic point of view, the Fathers imagined David, the psalmist, as a prophet, who foretold the coming of Christ and even details of his life. That did not prevent him from foreseeing other things too, such as events in the history of Israel, and the Antiochenes were more interested in that than were the Alexandrians. But for both schools the straightforward or literal sense of the text of the Psalms was a prophetic sense, and often therefore included Christological references.

This can already be seen clearly in Acts 2.24-36, where Peter on the day of Pentecost interprets Psalms 16 and 110 as prophecies of the resurrection and ascension of Jesus:

> You that are Israelites, listen to what I have to say: Jesus of Nazareth, a man attested to you by God with deeds of power, wonders, and signs that God did through him among you, as you yourselves know – this man, handed over to you according to the definite plan and foreknowledge of God, you crucified and killed by the hands of those outside the law. But God raised him up, having freed him from death, because it was impossible for him to be held in its power. For David says concerning him,
> 'I saw the Lord always before me,
> for he is at my right hand so that I will not be shaken;
> therefore my heart was glad, and my tongue rejoiced;
> moreover, my flesh will live in hope.
> For you will not abandon my soul to Hades,
> or let your Holy One experience corruption.
> You have made known to me the ways of life;
> you will make me full of gladness with your presence.'
> Fellow Israelites, I may say to you confidently of our ancestor David that he both died and was buried, and his tomb is with us to this day. Since he was a prophet, he knew that God had sworn with an oath to him that he would put one of his descendants on his throne. Foreseeing this, David spoke of the resurrection of the Messiah, saying,
> 'He was not abandoned to Hades,
> nor did his flesh experience corruption'.
> This Jesus God raised up, and of that all of us are witnesses. Being therefore exalted at the right hand of God, and having received from the Father the promise of the Holy Spirit, he has poured out this that you both see and hear. For David did not ascend into the heavens, but he himself says,
> 'The Lord said to my Lord,

"Sit at my right hand,
  until I make your enemies your footstool"'.
Therefore let the entire house of Israel know with certainty that God has made him both Lord and Messiah, this Jesus whom you crucified.

From our own, etic, perspective, we might want to say that Psalm texts are being reinterpreted in the light of the resurrection and ascension as described by Luke. There are two givens: the events of Jesus' exaltation, and the text of the Psalms. The two have to be made to fit together. Thus the reference to 'not seeing corruption' is taken to imply, not – as probably originally intended – escaping death, but being restored to life after death. The argument is that the verses cannot refer to David himself, as one might think, because he did die and his flesh did 'see corruption'. Hence the text must refer to someone else, and this can only be the Messiah, which fits perfectly with the events being celebrated by the Church and recalled by Peter in this speech. The text is taken in a non-literal sense, which we could describe as allegorical, in order to make it conform to the events in question.

But seen emically, Peter in this passage is like any Christian preacher who naturally sees the Psalms as speaking of Christ. There is no sense that the meaning is being forced, or is somehow secondary to a 'natural' meaning in which the psalmist is talking about escaping premature death. On the contrary, it is self-evident that the Psalm speaks of Jesus, who died but did not corrupt in the grave, instead rising to new and eternal life. That is the obvious meaning of the Psalms quoted for Peter, and hence for any Christian reader. David was a prophet, who foretold Christ's sufferings, resurrection and ascension. The interpreter (Peter, Luke, the reader) sees straight to the spiritual sense of the Psalms, without having to go through a prior non-spiritual meaning and then cancelling it out.

This is the perspective of the Fathers, whether Alexandrian or Antiochene. At least in some cases the sense of the Psalms is spiritual or (as we should say) allegorical, referring to Jesus Christ or other features of the Christian dispensation. The allegorical sense is not added on, but is seen as itself the natural sense of the text. Where, as common in Antioch, the sense is primarily a moral (one might almost say halakhic) one rather than Christological or doctrinal, it still has its existence within a Christian framework: there is no sense that the Old Testament texts belong to a pre-Christian religion. Indeed, the Psalms are interpreted in Greek rather than in Hebrew, that being the Church's language, and their meaning derives from the semantic possibilities of Greek. The Psalms do not stand at a distance from the Christian reader, but are immediate in the same way as the New Testament is. They do not need to be allegor*ized* because they are already allegorical or spiritual in their natural sense. We see patristic writers as allegorizing, but they see themselves as tracing the mind of the psalmist, and hence the mind of the Holy Spirit.

Bibliography

Ambrose. *Commentary on Psalm 1*. Pages 357–8 in *Celebrating the Seasons: Daily Spiritual Readings for the Christian Year*. Compiled and introduced by Robert Atwell. Norwich: Canterbury, 1999.

Collins, Adela Yarbro, and John J. Collins. *King and Messiah as Son of God: Divine, Human, and Angelic Messianic Figures in Biblical and Related Literature*. Grand Rapids: Eerdmans, 2008.

Davage, David Willgren. '"As It Is Written Concerning Him in the Songs of David" [11Q13 2 9–10]: On the Role of Paratextual Activity in Shaping Eschatological Reimaginations of Psalm 82' Pages 3–44 in *David, Messianism, and Eschatology: Ambiguity in the Reception History of the Book of Psalms in Judaism and Christianity*. Edited by David Willgren Davage and Erkki Koskenniemi. SRB 10. Åbo: Åbo Akademi University, 2020.

Gillingham, Susan E. *A Journey of Two Psalms: The Reception of Psalms 1 & 2 in Jewish and Christian Tradition*. Oxford: Oxford University Press, 2013.

Gillingham, Susan. *Psalms Through the Centuries: A Reception History Commentary on Psalms 1–72, Vol. 2*. Chichester: Wiley-Blackwell, 2018.

Hill, Robert C. *Reading the Bible in Antioch*. The Bible in Ancient Christianity 5. Atlanta: SBL, 2005.

Hooker, Richard. *Of the Laws of Ecclesiastical Polity, Volume 2*. Edited by A. S. McGrade. Oxford: Oxford University Press, 2013.

Lewis, C. S. *Reflections on the Psalms*. London: Geoffrey Bles, 1958.

Sargent, Benjamin. *David Being a Prophet: The Contingency of Scripture upon History in the New Testament*. Berlin: de Gruyter, 2014.

Theodoret of Cyrus. *Commentary on the Psalms: Psalms 1–72*. Translated by Robert C. Hill. Fathers of the Church 101. Washington, DC: Catholic University of America Press, 2000.

Natural Theology?
Gerard Manley Hopkins and Psalm 19*

Peter Groves

The resonant influence of the Psalter upon the poetry and prose of Gerard Manley Hopkins is widely acknowledged. Allusions to the psalmists' words and images, variously received by Hopkins in English and Latin in particular, echo throughout the Jesuit poet's work. As well as the linguistic inheritance which the psalms and poems of the Hebrew Bible provide, Hopkins draws on the theological insight and attitudes of biblical authors in formulating his own poetic worldview. The doxological approach to the created world for which he is famous is too rich and complex a literary phenomenon to be limited to any single inspiration, but there can be little doubt that the Psalter is one of the more significant building blocks in the construction of Hopkins's theologically imaginative world.

The expressive joy and communicative power of Hopkins's poetic reflection on the natural world has led many to explore and discuss his interest in, and connections to, the task of natural theology. In so doing critics bring the reception of Hopkins into conversation with one of the major debates of twentieth-century theology. The present study participates in that conversation, with the help of Susan Gillingham's work on the reception history of the Psalms,[1] and the contribution of another major scholar of the Hebrew Bible, James Barr, whose Gifford Lectures offer a sustained critique of the rejection of natural theology in the work of Karl Barth. The contrasting approaches to Psalm 19 taken by Barth and later by

---

* It is a joy to contribute to this volume in honour of the most collegiate of colleagues and the dearest of friends.

1. Susan Gillingham, *Psalms Through the Centuries: A Reception History Commentary on Psalms 1–72, Vol. 2*, Blackwell Bible Commentaries (Oxford: Wiley-Blackwell, 2018).

Barr echo something of the attitude to the created world found in the great series of sonnets which Hopkins composed in the year 1877. Attention to those sonnets, and to two of them in particular, suggests the influence of Psalm 19 on Hopkins's choice of words and images, and also upon the poems' theological structure, where the contrast between octave and sestet allows an altered perspective, from which vantage point faith corrects and adds to the experience of a divinely created order. This dialogue between two ways of looking at the world resembles in part the final form of Psalm 19, a text in which two different hymns of praise, one concerning cosmology and the other the law, come together.

Barr, Barth and Natural Theology

Essential to the thought of Karl Barth is the contention that human concepts and knowledge, apart from revelation, are incapable of providing any information about the divine. Authentic theological discourse is only possible in so far as God, as subject, freely chooses to make himself the object of our knowledge, in revelation. This he does by speaking to us his Word, in Jesus Christ, in scripture and in proclamation.[2] In speaking this Word, however, in revealing himself, God must become other than he is, must assume a form we can comprehend: the human being Jesus of Nazareth, the printed words of the Bible and the articulations of the church constitute the threefold form of the Word of God. This 'veiled' Word of God is apprehended in faith, and the fact that it is concealed communicates to the believer both his or her inability to understand God himself in this finite world, and the mysteriousness of God which goes beyond what can be known or understood by faith. God's revelation of himself in Jesus Christ, and the witness to this revelation provided in scripture and in the proclamation of the church, are the only possible sources of proper theological knowledge.

However, much of Christian theological tradition and practice has disagreed, and engaged in the task of natural theology.[3] This Barth deplores.

---

2. Karl Barth, *Church Dogmatics*, ed. G. W. Bromiley and T. F. Torrance (Edinburgh: T. & T. Clark, 1936–77), I.1, 5£ (henceforth *CD*). Here Barth observes that the Word of God could come to us in any form – 'a burning bush, a flute concerto, Russian communism or a dead dog' – but that the three sources he outlines are the only safe bases for the theologian.

3. The phrase 'natural theology' refers to the claim that '"by nature", that is, just by being human beings, men and women have a certain degree of knowledge of God and awareness of him, or at least a capacity for such an awareness; and this knowledge or awareness exists anterior to the special revelation of God made

'Instead of finding God where he has sought us – namely in his objectivity – we seek him where he is not to be found'.[4] Natural theology is not something rightly engaged in by the Christian theologian. It cannot be a legitimate intellectual task, since it suggests that there is a second, or rival, source of knowledge about God, alongside the grace of God's revelation, and if there were any other access to knowing God apart from God's revelation, then that revelation must either be inadequate or unnecessary. Our knowledge of God is always mediated to us through his Word. Barth sees God both as subject and object within the act by which he is known: God the subject acts to present himself, through revelation, as the object of our knowledge. Natural theology, he thinks, claims immediate knowledge of God, and presents general worldly truths[5] about the divine, as opposed to the particular revelation of Jesus Christ.[6]

In 1991 James Barr delivered the Gifford Lectures, a series endowed to 'promote and diffuse the study of natural theology'. Published as *Biblical Faith and Natural Theology*, these lectures devote much space, attention and polemic to the rejection of the Barthian position through a scriptural hermeneutic. Given that Barth upholds revelation and its witness in scripture as the primary, indeed the only, possible source for Christian theology, his dismissal of natural theology must find a basis in this source, Barr argues (not unreasonably). If (as Barth freely admits)[7] scripture can be shown to contain or to sanction natural theology as a valid way of thinking about God (*however* partial), then Barth's position is called into serious question, and with close readings of the appeal to general revelation in Romans 1, and the Areopagus speech in Acts 17, Barr finds Karl Barth significantly wanting.[8]

In his chapter on natural theology within the Old Testament, Barr discusses several psalms, among them Psalm 19. The familiar opening

through Jesus Christ, through the Church, through the Bible' (James Barr, *Biblical Faith and Natural Theology: The Gifford Lectures for 1991, delivered at the University of Edinburgh* [Oxford: Clarendon, 1993], 1).

4. *CD* II.1, 11.

5. Note, for example, that Barth, in discussing the creation stories of the Old Testament, rejects the word 'myth' in favour of the word 'saga'. The former, he feels, smacks too much of the general. See *CD* I.1 §8.3, especially 326–9.

6. 'If God's revelation is alongside a knowledge of God proper to us as humans beings as such, even though it may never be advanced except as a prolegomenon, it is obviously no longer the revelation of God, but new expression (borrowed or even stolen) for the revelation which encounters us in our own reflection' (*CD* II.1, 139).

7. *CD* II.1, 99.

8. Barr, *Biblical Faith and Natural Theology*, 21–57.

words of this poem, 'the heavens are telling the glory of God, and the firmament proclaims his handiwork', might be thought to be among the clearest statements of natural theology within the Judaeo-Christian tradition. As Gillingham puts it, 'Psalm 19 is really two psalms in one', but the two are united by the theme of 'order, both in the natural world and in relation to the community'.[9] The first six verses of the psalm praise the creator, with specific reference to the sun and the heavens, and the remainder worship Yahweh as the giver of the law. The act of speaking binds the psalm together, as creation speaks in the first section, and Yahweh seems to speak concerning the law, before the psalmist speaks a petition for purity and innocence in conclusion.

Barth does not ignore Psalm 19, and his emphasis upon the unity of the poem as received enables him to stress the centrality of revealed divine teaching in the poem overall. Barr is dismissive of such an approach, accusing Barth of a refusal to accept the obvious import of a plain reading. Instead, Barr contends that the poem testifies to a universal knowledge of some sort: 'as everyone on earth receives the heat of the sun, we are entitled to conclude, so everyone on earth receives the language of the heavens or some impression of it'.[10] He then draws a link between the knowledge which the heavens declare, and the 'instruction' (*torah*) which is discussed later in the Psalm. He thus rejects Barth's plea that the apparent 'natural theology' of the Psalm be placed in the context of the Law of Moses and the history of Israel.[11]

However, Barth's position in relation to this text is not as vulnerable as might first appear. According to his view, there are not even any grounds for saying that God *exists* except through revelation. However, once somebody has encountered God in his revelation, once God has spoken his Word, her eyes may be opened to all sorts of things she did not see before. So the Psalmist, believing wholeheartedly in the God of Moses and Israel who created the heavens and the earth, can quite legitimately point to the effects of the creator God without being a 'natural theologian' – because he only knows that God is creator, in fact only knows of God's existence, through revelation. Thus Barth can defend himself, simply by saying that the effects of the heavens are not the starting point for the Psalmist's knowledge of the God of Israel. His 'theology of creation' is rather consequent upon that knowledge.

---

9. Gillingham, *Psalms Through the Centuries*, 2:122.
10. Barr, *Biblical Faith and Natural Theology*, 87–8.
11. Barth's discussion comes in *CD* II.1, 107–8.

Barth's argument can rest on the fact that, even if the Psalmist was appealing to a natural knowledge of God that all may possess, this is not conclusive in the text. All that the text of the Psalm shows us is an Israelite poet praising the wonderful works of his God, the creator. Barth can, and does, appeal to this question – where do we start? – over and again in discussing natural theology. In this instance, he can also draw upon the final form of the psalm, in other words to scripture as received, to bolster his point. The images or themes which he feels support natural theology in scripture he describes as 'sidelines' (*nebenlinie*) the interpretation of which is controlled by the 'mainline' of biblical revelation. Thus our reading of the creation theology in Psalm 19 is prevented from error (as Barth sees it) by the revelational emphasis of the second part of the poem.[12]

Hopkins and Psalm 19

The Psalter was basic to Gerard Manley Hopkins's literary world. Brought up in the mainstream of the Victorian Church of England, he enthusiastically imbibed Tractarianism as an undergraduate in Oxford, before being received into the Roman Catholic Church at the beginning of his final year at Balliol, and joining the Society of Jesus two years later. The Anglican liturgies with which he grew up at home, in school and at Balliol College, were dominated by the Coverdale Psalter in the *Book of Common Prayer* (*BCP*), and his life of private prayer and study as Jesuit was fashioned around the liturgy of the hours in the Roman Breviary. Hopkins did learn some Hebrew, and took a particular interest in Hebrew poetry and its structures. 'Hebrew poetry, you know, is structurally only distinguished fr. prose by its being paired off in parallelisms',[13] says Hopkins's 'Professor' in *On the Origin of Beauty: A Platonic Dialogue*, composed while he was an undergraduate. His repeated references to parallelism and its importance in poetry, display the clear influence of Robert Lowth's 1741 *Lectures on the Sacred Poetry of the Hebrews*.[14] But his encounter with the text of the Hebrew Bible was much more commonly in English and in Latin. Several scholars have observed the breadth of biblical

---

12. *CD* II.1, 107.
13. Lesley Higgins and Michael Suarez, S.J., eds., *The Collected Works of Gerard Manley Hopkins* (Oxford: Oxford University Press, 2006), IV, 158. Henceforth *CW*.
14. For discussion of Hopkins and parallelism, see Maria Lichtmann, *The Contemplative Poetry of Gerard Manley Hopkins*, Princeton Legacy Library (Princeton: Princeton University Press, 1989), and 108–9 for Lowth.

translation which remains throughout Hopkins's maturity,[15] and whilst the Latin Vulgate and the Douay-Rheims Bible are important for him,[16] the King James Bible and the Coverdale Psalter never disappear from their prominent position in his aural and poetic world.

So, for example, the early poem 'Barnfloor and Winepress' employs the joyful harvest imagery of Psalm 65 in its darker celebration of the passion of Christ.[17] The frequent biblical recourse to agrarian language is itself plentifully harvested by Hopkins in some of his favourite themes – sowing, gathering, threshing, gleaning – whilst the river of life which this Psalm describes haunts by its absence the picture of aridity presented in the late Dublin sonnets. In one such poem, 'My own heart let me more have pity on',[18] Psalm 121 and the act of lifting up one's eyes to the hills seem to underlie the encouragement to look up and beyond oneself towards the presence of God in beauty of the mountains. Allusion to the same text is more explicit in 'Hurrahing in harvest', where the lifting up of eyes is rewarded by the knowledge of Christ's presence in the 'azurous hung hills'.[19]

Susan Gillingham's *Psalms Through the Centuries* notes a number of similar echoes in 'The Wreck of the Deutschland', Hopkins's first great poem as a Jesuit, and his longest.[20] The God who for the Psalmist 'cast forth lightnings' (compare Hopkins's 'I did say yes /O at lightning and lashed rod')[21] is the one who delivers from the waters of chaos in Psalm 18 and becomes for Hopkins the 'master of the tides', even as the apparent tragedy of five nuns drowning in a shipwreck becomes the triumphant storm of passion through which they are raised to union with Christ. The

---

15. See, for example, Martin Dubois, *Gerard Manley Hopkins and the Poetry of Religious Experience* (Cambridge: Cambridge University Press, 2017), 27–49; and James Finn Cotter, 'Hopkins and the Bible', *Religion & Literature* 45, no. 2 (2013): 161–6.

16. See, for example, his discussion of Latin Bible versions in an 1887 to Alexander Baillie, *CW* II, 867–8.

17. W. H. Gardner and N. H. Mackenzie, eds., *The Poems of Gerard Manley Hopkins* (Oxford: Oxford University Press, 1967), 16. Henceforth *Poems*. See Paul Fiddes, 'Gerard Manley Hopkins', in *The Blackwell Companion to The Bible in English Literature* ed. Rebecca Lemon, Emma Mason, Jonathan Roberts and Christopher Rowland (Oxford: Wiley-Blackwell, 2012), 565.

18. *Poems*, 62–3.

19. 'Hurrahing in Harvest', l. 9, *Poems*, 70.

20. Gillingham, *Psalms Through the Centuries*, 2:120, see also Fiddes, 'Gerard Manley Hopkins', 571.

21. Psalm 18.14 (*BCP*). Cf 'The Wreck of the Deutschland' st.2 l.1-2, Gardner and Mackenzie, eds., *The Poems of Gerard Manley Hopkins*, 52.

precarious situation of those on board is brought out in the poet's address to the God who stills storms – 'O Father, not under thy feathers'. Here the image of safety depends specifically on Coverdale's Psalm 91 ('He shall defend thee under his wings, and thou shalt be safe under his feathers'). The Latin *Psalterium Gallicanum*, which he knew, has *scapulis* – shoulders – rather than the feathers which are a favoured metaphor for Hopkins[22] (recurring several times in the sonnet 'Henry Purcell', for example).[23] The relevant verse is doubly resonant for Christians by virtue of its appearance in the temptation narratives of Matthew and Luke.

Psalm 19 itself makes a number of allusive appearances in the poems, and notably so in 'The Wreck' where the extent of Christ's redemptive reach is presented through the image of the harrowing of hell, Christ's descent to the realm of the 'spirits in prison' (1 Pet. 3.19) which breaks open the kingdom of death and offers salvation to those who seemed beyond the help of prayer. The image of resurrection is baptismal – Christ is the 'passion plunged giant risen'[24] whose rescue of the patriarchs in limbo anticipates the salvation received by the nuns who have perished in the waters. The use of 'giant', closely following 'uttermost' in the previous line, suggests Coverdale's 'rejoiceth as a giant to run his course. It goeth forth from the uttermost part of the heaven…'[25] The giant of the psalm is the sun, whose rising is a long-established image of the resurrection of Christ.[26]

This psalm informs Hopkins's oeuvre with more than just literary allusion, however. It features, for example, in the notes he wrote as 'Instructions', based on the *Spiritual Exercises* of St Ignatius, probably for use in a Jesuit mission in Maryport, in which Hopkins participated in 1882. These appear as a parallel in miniature of the earlier 'Commentary on the Spiritual Exercises' which he wrote on retreat in 1880. There he responds to the phrase *homo creatus est* (Man was created) by noting 'We may learn that all things are created by consideration of the world without or of ourselves the world within'.[27] In the simpler catechetical instructions he does not describe the task of natural theology but concentrates instead

---

22. Dubois, *Gerard Manley Hopkins and the Poetry of Religious Experience*, 31–2.

23. *Poems*, 80.

24. 'The Wreck of the Deutschland' st.33 l.7, *Poems*, 62.

25. Psalm 19.5-6 (*BCP*).

26. See James Finn Cotter, *Inscape: The Christology and Poetry of Gerard Manley Hopkins* (Pittsburgh: University of Pittsburgh Press, 1972), 164.

27. *CW* V, 348.

on the divine glory. God 'meant the world to give him praise, reverence and service; to give him glory'.[28] He repeats the word glory several times before moving from allusion to quotation: 'The sun and stars shining glorify God. They stand where he placed them, they move where he bid them. "The heavens declare the glory of God". They glorify God but they do not know it.'[29]

The introduction of creaturely ignorance in relation to the purposeful praise of that which God has made is a reflection on the continuation of the psalm. Although knowledge is poured out day after day, the telling which the heavens are doing is silent: 'There is no speech, nor are there words; their voice is not heard; yet their voice goes out through all the earth, and their words to the end of the world'.[30] Thus, the opening of Psalm 19 is used in a familiar fashion as an item of foundational natural theology, suggesting the very beginnings of faith – the created world exists to praise God, but dumb creatures must do so without knowing it. Human beings, on the other hand, are called to greater praise, a praise which Hopkins goes on to set out.

This almost casual invocation of the psalm is evidence not just of Hopkins's familiarity with the text, but also of its status for him as a proof text of Christian reflection on creation. The first verse in particular is as much a theological disposition for Hopkins as an item of scripture (to be read, studied, prayed and performed). The comment above concerning 'consideration of the world without or of ourselves the world within' is developed in the 'Commentary on the *Spiritual Exercises*' into an intense reflection on selfhood and the uniqueness of human nature which is 'more highly pitched, selved and distinctive than anything in the world'. He goes on 'Nothing else in nature comes near this unspeakable stress of pitch, distinctiveness and selving, this selfbeing of my own'.[31] The consciousness of self in relation to the world throws up a uniquely powerful self-knowledge which nevertheless depends on differentiation from the other. The connection with Hopkins's account of selving, which we encounter in the 1877 sonnets, is anticipated in his undergraduate essay, 'On the Probable Future of Metaphysics',[32] and the slightly later notes on Parmenides.[33] In these early texts we find Hopkins's first account

28. *CW* V, 524.
29. *CW* V, 525.
30. Psalm 19.3-4 (NRSV).
31. *CW* V, 349.
32. *CW* IV, 287–91.
33. *CW* IV, 311–17.

of 'instress', which along with its companion term 'inscape', has caused such fascination among his interpreters. 'Inscape' we may take broadly to mean the unique essence of a thing (seen by some as a version of the Scotist's 'thisness'[34]), while 'instress' communicates both the manner in which that essence is held together in the qualities of the thing itself, and the act of observing or recognizing the inscape of a particular thing, an act which in turn affects the agent who is observing. Among the hints at natural theology provided by this conceptual framework is his remarking, in the Parmenides essay, on the 'stem and stress between us and things'.[35]

The relationship between observer and created thing is not always expressed with such complexity, however. Indeed, the place of Psalm 19 in Hopkins's worldview might be summarized by a journal entry for 1874: 'As we drove home the stars came out thick: I leant back to look at them and my heart opening more than usual praised our Lord to and in whom all that beauty comes home'.[36] This simplest of theological acts – observing the beauty of the world and offering praise to its creator – underlies each of the great sonnets of 1877, a particularly fecund poetic year for Hopkins (which unfortunately for him coincided with his failure in theology and subsequent departure from the Jesuit college of St Beuno a year earlier than intended). One of those sonnets, 'The Starlight Night', begins

> Look at the stars! Look, look up at the skies!
> O look at all the fire-folk sitting in the air!
> The bright boroughs, the circle-citadels there!
> Down in the dim woods the diamond delves! the elves'-eyes![37]

Hopkins's affirmation of the Psalmist's claim that 'the heavens are telling the glory of God' is never more enthusiastically expressed than in this rapturous opening.

---

34. See, for example, Norman White, *Hopkins: A Literary Biography* (Oxford: Clarendon, 1992), 275–6. However, Hopkins sets out his terminology in the Parmenides notes, before his first encounter with the writings of Scotus. See the detailed discussion in Daniel Brown, *Hopkins Idealism: Philosophy, Physics, Poetry* (Oxford: Clarendon, 1997), especially 197–8. See also Bernadette Waterman Ward, *World as Word: Philosophical Theology in Gerard Manley Hopkins* (Washington, DC: The Catholic University of America Press, 2002), Chapter 7; and Trent Pomplun 'The Theology of Gerard Manley Hopkins from John Duns Scotus to the Baroque', *JR* 95 (2015): 1–34.

35. *CW* IV, 313.
36. *CW* III, 592.
37. 'The Starlight Night', l. 1–4, *Poems*, 66.

'But the beholder wanting': Two Ways of Seeing

Hurrahing in Harvest

Summer ends now; now, barbarous in beauty, the stooks rise
Around; up above, what wind-walks! what lovely behaviour
Of silk-sack clouds! has wilder, wilful-wavier
Meal-drift moulded ever and melted across skies?

I walk, I lift up, I lift up heart, eyes,
Down all that glory in the heavens to glean our Saviour;
And, éyes, heárt, what locks, what lips yet gave you a
Rapturous love's greeting of realer, of rounder replies?

And the azurous hung hills are his world-wielding shoulder
Majestic – as a stallion stalwart, very-violet-sweet! –
These things, these things were here and but the beholder
Wanting; which two when they once meet,
The heart rears wings bold and bolder
And hurls for him, O half hurls earth for him off under his feet.[38]

In a letter of 16 July 1878 to Robert Bridges, Hopkins described this poem as 'the outcome of a half an hour of extreme enthusiasm as I walked home alone one day from fishing in the Elwy'.[39] The intensity of poetic vision bears this out: the sheaves of wheat, with their bearded appearance, reach up towards the clouds which drift into and out of formless beauty. The glory in the heavens to which the poet lifts his eyes is more than the glory told by the opening of Psalm 19, for its gleaning presents salvation as well as creation. The poet responds to the truth of God's creation in the ecstatic beauty of the scene, and receives in turn the excessive response of grace, which reveals the presence of Christ in the entirety of the world observed. The transformation which takes place occurs within the onlooker – 'these things were here and but the beholder / Wanting' – the enjambed lines running the reader on towards the goal of the vision revealed, the reception of Christ in the mind and the heart of the beholder. The coming together of viewer and viewed produces an incarnational ambiguity: the heart is, perhaps, both the sacred heart of Christ, the seat of the compassion which envelops the world in his passionate love, and also and more clearly the heart of the onlooker stirred itself to passionate response as if all earth were cleared before him and the glory of the heavens entirely manifest.

---

38. *Poems*, 70.
39. *CW* II, 308.

This poem, dated 1 September 1877, is the latest of the great nature sonnets which emerged from that year. It presents themes common to them all – the ultimate inscape of created things is revealed to be Christ, whose incarnate presence in the material world is depicted through the bringing together of sound, word and image that is the poem's own construction, itself a living utterance which testifies to the eternal Word. Scholarly reflection on Hopkins as natural theologian has tended, understandably, to concentrate on his reception of and response to Darwinism, a subject in which he took a close interest.[40] In an important article,[41] Daniel Williams has argued for a reassessment of that response, seeing two of the 1877 sonnets, 'The Sea and the Skylark' and 'The Caged Skylark', as evidence for a tightly designed theological poetics which steers a middle way between the rational sterility of a Paley-type natural theology, and an orderless universe promulgated by an extreme Darwinism.

Any sense of design or order communicated through these poems depends on an approach to seeing the world, an approach which is not a sole possibility of seeing,[42] just as James Barr and Karl Barth find different approaches to natural theology in Psalm 19 from their different starting points. The sonnets of this period – including some of Hopkins's most famous poems: 'God's grandeur', 'Spring', 'The Windhover', 'As Kingfishers Catch Fire' – share an attitude which presents the glory of nature as expressive of something beyond itself, and then moves on to draw more specifically Christian conclusions.[43] The discovery of Christ

---

40. See, for example, the letter to his mother of 20–21 August 1872, *CW* I, 237, and to Bridges on 18–19 August 1888, *CW* II, 948. See also Jude V. Nixon, *Gerard Manley Hopkins and his Contemporaries: Liddon, Newman, Darwin and Pater* (New York: Garland, 1994), and Jill Muller, *Gerard Manley Hopkins and Victorian Catholicism: A Heart in Hiding* (London: Routledge, 2003), 69–100.

41. Daniel Williams, 'Stem and Skein: Order and Evolution in Hopkins', *Victorian Poetry* 53, no. 4 (2015): 423–54.

42. For Hopkins and vision, Catherine Phillips, *Gerard Manley Hopkins and the Victorian Visual World* (Oxford: Oxford University Press, 2007), in particular Chapter 7. See also Katherine Bubel, 'Nature and Wise Vision in the Poetry of Gerard Manley Hopkins', *Renascence* 62, no. 2 (2010): 117–40, and Laurie Camp Hatch, 'Gerard Manley Hopkins and Victorian Approaches to the Problems of Perception: Affirming the Metaphysical in the Physical', *Christianity & Literature* 65, no. 2 (2016): 170–94.

43. See Lichtmann, *The Contemplative Poetry of Gerard Manley Hopkins*, 177–86; and also Hilary Fraser, 'Aesthetics, Visuality and Feelings in the Natural Theology of Gerard Manley Hopkins and Alice Meynell', in *Form and Feeling in*

in nature is a corrective to the act of seeing itself – the moment of recognition serves as a re-evaluation of what has already been processed, and so the act of theological poetics, where the poem read and heard becomes ever more communicative of the infinite divine Word, is never exhausted. Instead, the coming together of the beholder and the saviour whose presence transforms the beholding creates new moments of possibility at every iteration. The wonder of the incarnation brings heaven and earth together in a manner reflected by the falcon in flight but also by the plough as its blade strikes the earth.

Commenting on Psalm 19 and its loving devotion to the law itself, Gillingham cites one of Hopkins's own favourite poets, George Herbert.[44] His 'The Holy Scriptures (I)' makes use of 'the form of secular love poetry to praise the Bible (not just the Torah) as an object of desire'. In this poem, Herbert describes scripture as 'the thankful glasse / That mends the lookers eyes'.[45] The line is strongly reminiscent of another and more famous Herbert poem, 'The Elixir'.

> A man that looks on glass
> On it may stay his eye
> Or if he pleaseth, through it pass
> And then the Heav'n espy.[45]

Here are two ways of looking and seeing, one of which reaps eternal reward. The Holy Scriptures serve, for Herbert, as a prompt to the better way of looking, a lure away from the dull materialism which sees the object before it and nothing within or beyond that object. The first six verses of Psalm 19 can serve as a quasi-rationalist natural theology which observes the heavens and draws the conclusion that they are created. But, as Karl Barth would urge, the psalm as received presents us with much more – a theological reading of the heavens which is encouraged and formed by the devotion to the law (whether the law of the universe or specifically the Torah) of Yahweh, the God of Israel.

Modern Literature: Essays in Honour of Barbara Hardy, ed. W. Baker and Isobel Armstron (London: Maney, 2013), 88–99.

44. Gillingham, *Psalms Through the Centuries*, 2:127. For Hopkins's praise of Herbert see, for example, the letter to Richard Watson Dixon of 27 February–13 March 1879, *CW* I, 343–9.

45. Helen Wilcox, ed., *The English Poems of George Herbert* (Cambridge: Cambridge University Press, 2007), 208.

46. Ibid., 638.

In Hopkins's 1877 sonnets, the move from wonder at creation to more thoroughly theological truths could be seen as this sort of prompting, or corrective.[47] In particular, the move from octave to sestet in the sonnets functions theologically in this manner. 'God's Grandeur' moves from the physical contrast of divine superabundance and human drudgery, to the realization of 'the dearest freshness deep down things',[48] the pneumatological creativity of the Holy Spirit's inbreathing; 'Spring' records the ecstatic energy of new life in the natural world, and progresses in the sestet to a mariological image of Edenic innocence offered in the incarnation; the curtal sonnet 'Pied Beauty' moves from particular to universal as it draws from individual observation the twofold incarnate presence of the divine; 'The Starlight Night' cries out with wonder at the starry heavens above, and goes on to celebrate a Christian life in response to this manifestation of divine creativity, a life which will bring one to the feast of the Kingdom to which Christ and his Mother offer invitation.

The pattern is clear. There is truth to be found in nature, by virtue of God's creation, but there is more truth to be found once we discern the presence of Christ and recognize, or instress, the incarnational inscape of created objects. The idea is expressed most fully in another famous sonnet, also from 1877.[49]

> As kingfishers catch fire, dragonflies draw flame;
> As tumbled over rim in roundy wells
> Stones ring; like each tucked string tells, each hung bell's
> Bow swung finds tongue to fling out broad its name;
> Each mortal thing does one thing and the same:
> Deals out that being indoors each one dwells;
> Selves – goes itself; myself it speaks and spells,
> Crying Whát I dó is me: for that I came.
>
> I say móre: the just man justices;
> Keeps grace: thát keeps all his goings graces;
> Acts in God's eye what in God's eye he is –
> Chríst – for Christ plays in ten thousand places,
> Lovely in limbs, and lovely in eyes not his
> To the Father through the features of men's faces.[50]

---

47. Hopkins uses the word 'corrective' to describe grace in the 'Commentary on the Spiritual Exercises', *CW* V, 392.

48. 'God's Grandeur', l. 10; *Poems*, 66.

49. For the dating of this undated sonnet, see Norman H. MacKenzie, *A Reader's Guide to Gerard Manley Hopkins*, 2nd ed. (Philadelphia: St Joseph's University Press, 2008), 145.

50. *Poems*, 90.

In this, perhaps the most aurally sophisticated of Hopkins's sonnets, two ways of seeing are related to the differing vocations within the order of creation. Inanimate and non-human creatures express their true selves in the motive energy of the world which they constitute. We may see this selving as expressive of an ordered universe without drawing any more than the barest theological conclusions (that there is a creator, for example). But attention to humanity, as the recipient of God's grace, allows the poet to 'say more'. The grace-filled activity of the just points us beyond the world of self and refocuses our attention on the source of selving itself, the creative energy of the divine, whose character is revealed in the sacrificial love of Christ for the world.[51]

Here, as before, the sestet interprets and corrects the reported observations of the octet. The selving which the poet describes is not untheological, except insofar as we are not yet ready to speak of it theologically. As with theological debates concerning revelation, either/or will not quite do. A stark division between 'natural' and 'revealed' theology does not do justice to the joyful and gracious unfolding which Hopkins, inspired by the psalmist, seeks poetically to celebrate. In Psalm 19, the silence of the heavens, which are nevertheless 'telling the glory of God', is filled with the language of instruction which is God's gracious gift to his people in the law. For Gerard Manley Hopkins, the incompleteness of natural theology in the things of the world and their self-expression is brought to fulfilment by the instress of the presence of Christ.

Bibliography

Barr, James. *Biblical Faith and Natural Theology: The Gifford Lectures for 1991, delivered at the University of Edinburgh.* Oxford: Clarendon, 1993.

Barth, Karl. *Church Dogmatics.* Edited by G. W. Bromiley and T. F. Torrance. Edinburgh: T&T Clark, 1936–77.

Brown, Daniel. *Hopkins Idealism: Philosophy, Physics, Poetry.* Oxford: Clarendon, 1997.

Bubel, Katherine. 'Nature and Wise Vision in the Poetry of Gerard Manley Hopkins'. *Renascence* 62.2 (2010): 117–40.

Cotter, James Finn. 'Hopkins and the Bible', *Religion & Literature* 45, no. 2 (2013): 161–6.

Cotter, James Finn. *Inscape: The Christology and Poetry of Gerard Manley Hopkins.* Pittsburgh: University of Pittsburgh Press, 1972.

Dubois, Martin. *Gerard Manley Hopkins and the Poetry of Religious Experience.* Cambridge: Cambridge University Press, 2017.

---

51. Compare the discussion of free will in the 'Commentary on the Spiritual Exercises', *CW* V, 385–6. See also Catherine Pickstock's discussion of the 'natural theology' of Rowan Williams, in C. J. C. Pickstock, 'Matter and Mattering: The Metaphysics of Rowan Williams', *Modern Theology* 31, no. 4 (2015): 599–616 (616).

Fiddes, Paul. 'Gerard Manley Hopkins'. Pages 563–76 in *The Blackwell Companion to the Bible in English Literature*. Edited by Rebecca Lemon, Emma Mason, Jonathan Roberts and Christopher Rowland. Oxford: Wiley-Blackwell, 2012.

Fraser, Hilary. 'Aesthetics, Visuality and Feelings in the Natural theology of Gerard Manley Hopkins and Alice Meynell'. Pages 88–99 in *Form and Feeling in Modern Literature: Essays in Honour of Barbara Hardy*. Edited by W. Baker and Isobel Armstrong. London: Maney, 2013.

Gardner, W. H., and N. H. Mackenzie, eds. *The Poems of Gerard Manley Hopkins*. Oxford: Oxford University Press, 1967.

Gillingham, Susan. *Psalms Through the Centuries: A Reception History Commentary on Psalms 1–72, Vol. 2*. Blackwell Bible Commentaries. Oxford: Wiley-Blackwell, 2018.

Hatch, Laurie Camp. 'Gerard Manley Hopkins and Victorian Approaches to the Problems of Perception: Affirming the Metaphysical in the Physical'. *Christianity & Literature* 65, no. 2 (2016): 170–94.

Higgins, Lesley, and Michael Suarez S.J., eds. *The Collected Works of Gerard Manley Hopkins*. Oxford: Oxford University Press, 2006.

Lichtmann, Maria. *The Contemplative Poetry of Gerard Manley Hopkins*. Princeton Legacy Library. Princeton: Princeton University Press, 1989.

MacKenzie, Norman H. *A Reader's Guide to Gerard Manley Hopkins*. 2nd ed. Philadelphia: St Joseph's University Press, 2008.

Muller, Jill. *Gerard Manley Hopkins and Victorian Catholicism: A Heart in Hiding*. London: Routledge, 2003.

Nixon, Jude V. *Gerard Manley Hopkins and his Contemporaries: Liddon, Newman, Darwin and Pater*. New York: Garland, 1994.

Phillips, Catherine. *Gerard Manley Hopkins and the Victorian Visual World*. Oxford: Oxford University Press, 2007.

Pickstock, C. J. C. 'Matter and Mattering: The Metaphysics of Rowan Williams'. *Modern Theology* 31, no. 4 (2015): 599–616.

Pomplun, Trent. 'The Theology of Gerard Manley Hopkins from John Duns Scotus to the Baroque'. *JR* 96 (2015): 1–34.

Ward, Bernadette Waterman. *World as Word: Philosophical Theology in Gerard Manley Hopkins*. Washington, DC: The Catholic University of America Press, 2002.

White, Norman. *Hopkins: A Literary Biography*. Oxford: Clarendon, 1992.

Wilcox, Helen., ed. *The English Poems of George Herbert*. Cambridge: Cambridge University Press, 2007.

Williams, Daniel. 'Stem and Skein: Order and Evolution in Hopkins'. *Victorian Poetry* 53, no. 4 (2015): 423–54.

Part III

REIMAGING THE PSALMS IN LITERATURE,
MUSIC AND VISUAL ARTS

Three Renditions of the Three Breaths in Psalm 39*

John Jarick

Psalm 39 is unique in the Psalter in containing three resonant instances of the evocative Hebrew word הבל, 'breath' or 'vapour'. It comes first in v. 5 of the psalm,[1] in the expression אך כל־הבל כל־אדם נצב ('Surely all of a breath, all of humanity stands');[2] then a second time in the very next verse, v. 6, in the expression אך־הבל יהמיון ('Surely a breath, they struggle');[3] and a third time in v. 11, essentially repeating the initial expression, אך הבל כל־אדם ('Surely a breath, all of humanity').[4]

---

* This is a modified version of a paper delivered to the 23rd Congress of the International Organization for the Study of the Old Testament at the University of Aberdeen in August 2019. It is a pleasure to present it in this volume as a tribute to Sue Gillingham, whose scholarship I have much admired and whose collegiality I have much appreciated over the years.

1. I cite the verses of this psalm in terms of the standard English enumerations, in which the superscription ('To the leader; to Jeduthun; a psalm of David') is not included in the verse-count. In the Hebrew Bible, since the superscription counts as v. 1, all subsequent verses are accordingly one number higher than in English Bibles, and thus, e.g., v. 5 cited here is v. 6 in the Hebrew.

2. John Goldingay, *Psalms, Vol. 1*, Baker Commentary on the Old Testament Wisdom and Psalms (Grand Rapids: Baker Academic, 2006), 558, translates this as 'Yes, every human being standing firm [is] every breath', and comments that 'presumably the idea is that even human beings who stand firm, people in good health who look destined to live a long life (unlike the suppliant?), are quite evanescent and might die at any moment'.

3. Goldingay, *Psalms, Vol. 1*, gives this expression as an example of the 'elliptical' style of Ps. 39, and explicates as follows: '"a breath they hustle" (v. 6) presumably means, "They hustle, but it is only for a breath [something transitory]"' (555).

4. Rolf A. Jacobson, 'Psalm 39: From Silence to Speech to Silence', in *The Book of Psalms*, by Nancy DeClaissé-Walford, Rolf A. Jacobson, and Beth Laneel Tanner,

The context for these three evocations of what might be called the *hebel*-ness or breathiness of human life is the psalmist's meditation upon the transient nature of human existence, the puniness of mortal, powerless, swiftly vanishing creatures over against an immortal, almighty, all-consuming God.[5] The psalmist cries (as translated by the New Revised Standard Version, vv. 4-6, with italics added here to indicate the rendering of the expressions containing the word הבל):

> LORD, let me know my end,
>   and what is the measure of my days;
>   let me know how fleeting my life is.
> You have made my days a few handbreadths,
>   and my lifetime is as nothing in your sight.
> Surely everyone stands *as a mere breath*.
>   Surely everyone goes about like a shadow.
> Surely *for nothing* they are in turmoil;
>   they heap up, and do not know who will gather.

And then, lamenting a somewhat unspecified situation of distress, the psalmist pleads with the deity (vv. 10-11):

NICOT (Grand Rapids: Eerdmans, 2014), translates both of these occurrences as 'Surely every person is futile', and astutely notes that it functions as a refrain which both times (i.e. in vv. 5 and 11) is 'followed by the enigmatic liturgical marker *selah*', thus marking the end of a section or stanza (360). Our honoree is also alert to this aspect, commenting on 'the liturgical style' of Ps. 39, 'evident in the repeated refrain "everyone is a mere breath" in vv. 5 and 11, each ending with *selah*' (Susan Gillingham, *Psalms Through the Centuries: A Reception History Commentary on Psalms 1–72, Vol. 2*, Wiley Blackwell Bible Commentaries [Chichester: Wiley-Blackwell, 2018], 237). It is also seen as a structural device by Samuel Terrien, *The Psalms: Strophic Structure and Theological Commentary* (Grand Rapids: Eerdmans, 2003), 330.

5. This is of course a common theme in ancient Near Eastern wisdom traditions. Witness for example Shiduri's words to Gilgamesh: 'When the gods created mankind, they also created death, and they held back eternal life for themselves alone. Humans are born, they live, then they die, this is the order that the gods have decreed' (Stephen Mitchell, *Gilgamesh: A New English Version* [New York: Free Press, 2004], 168). Note also the lines in 'The Ballad of Early Rulers': 'The fates are determined by Ea, the lots are drawn according to the will of the gods, since always so it was… Life is but a swivel of an eye, life of mankind cannot [last] forever' (Yoram Cohen, *Wisdom from the Late Bronze Age* [Atlanta: SBL, 2013], 141). I am indebted to Mark Sneed for the latter reference.

Remove your stroke from me;
  I am worn down by the blows of your hand.
You chastise mortals
  in punishment for sin,
consuming like a moth what is dear to them;
  surely everyone *is a mere breath.*

And the psalm ends (v. 13) with a heartfelt plea:

Turn your gaze away from me, that I may smile again,
  before I depart and am no more.

In deploying and redeploying this word *hebel* in a depiction of the sorry state of humanity – at least as it appears to someone suffering the slings and arrows of outrageous fortune – the poet who crafted Psalm 39 is drawing upon a term that appears to have been something of a favourite image among the sages of ancient Israel. Among the aphorisms collected in the book of Proverbs are such sayings as 'The getting of treasures by a lying tongue is *a fleeting vapour and a snare of death* (הבל נדף מבקשי־מות)' (Prov. 21.6), and '*Charm is deceitful, and beauty is vain* (שקר החן והבל היפי), but a woman who fears the LORD is to be praised' (Prov. 31.30). And within the grand poetic speeches of Job are such lines as 'I loathe my life, I would not live forever; let me alone, *for my days are a breath* (כי־הבל ימי)' (Job 7.16), and 'I shall be condemned: *why then do I labour in vain?* (למה־זה הבל איגע)' (Job 9.29).

But the most sustained application of the image is in the book of Ecclesiastes,[6] where the writer (or the editor of the book) encapsulates the thesis of the work in a motto, stated at the beginning (Eccl. 1.2) and again at the end (12.8) of the treatise, הבל הבלים הכל הבל ('Breath of breaths,

---

6. Steven J. L. Croft, *The Identity of the Individual in the Psalms*, JSOTSup 44 (Sheffield: Sheffield Academic, 1987), in his comments on Ps. 39, notes that the psalm 'uses, with emphasis, the term הבל, in vain, beloved by Ecclesiastes' (168); and James L. Crenshaw, within a chapter on Ecclesiastes' use of *hebel* (Chapter 3, 'Elusive Essence', in his work *Qoheleth: The Ironic Wink*, Studies on Personalities of the Old Testament [Columbia: The University of South Carolina Press, 2013], 33–48), traces a number of affinities between the two compositions in a section on 'Qoheleth and Psalm 39' (pp. 40–8). I have written on certain aspects of Ecclesiastes' resonant use of the term in my essay, 'The Hebrew Book of Changes: Reflections on *hakkōl hebel* and *lakkōl zᵉmār* in Ecclesiastes', *JSOT* 90 (2000): 79–99. For a recent survey of views on this key-word in Ecclesiastes, see Russell L. Meek, 'Twentieth- and Twenty-first-century Readings of *Hebel* (הבל) in Ecclesiastes', *CurBR* 14 (2016):

all is a breath' – traditionally rendered 'Vanity of vanities, all is vanity', or 'Futility of futilities, all is futility'). It is a theme constantly worked over in the book, with the frequent conclusion to various observations of human toil and trouble that 'this too is a breath', or 'this too is vanity' (גם־זה הבל, e.g. 2.15, 19, 21), and from time to time a particular collocation of 'all is vanity and a chasing after wind' (הכל הבל ורעות רוח, 1.14; 2.11, 17) – clearly denoting an aimless and futile striving after something transitory and unattainable, the empty pursuit of the insubstantial.

הבל, then, the notion of 'breath' or 'vapour', functions in many cases in the biblical corpus with a decidedly figurative meaning of transience and insubstantiality, or more particularly of emptiness and futility; hence the tradition since Jerome of rendering it as *vanitas* or 'vanity' in many instances.[7] But it seems indeed to be something of a catch-all term for whatever is deemed to be unsatisfactory about human life and experience. Nevertheless, the specific idea of transience is often particularly relevant to the usage of the word, presumably connected to the disturbing thought that the breath of life will inevitably be snuffed out of each individual sooner or later. Perhaps there is an allusion to the first human to die, according to Israelite mythology, namely a character who bears the very name הבל, known in English Bibles as Abel, the second son of Adam (Gen. 4.2).[8] We are all, in Hebrew thinking, children of Adam, each of us a בן־אדם (or a בת־אדם), but in this connection it might rather be said that every human being is an Abel, a mortal who draws breath only for a short span of time. Indeed, Psalm 39 seems to say just that in its phrasing אך הבל כל־אדם, which might be rendered as 'Surely every Adam is Abel'. (I mean here of course the name spelt A-B-E-L, not the adjective spelt A-B-L-E – though a pun might be made in English by saying that 'Surely no Adam is able to avoid the day of death'.)

Now, in fact, this is not the only place in the Psalter where this poetic play-on-words occurs. Witness Ps. 144.4, where readers are told as it were that Adam should be likened to Abel: אדם להבל דמה – which the NRSV

279–97; and note in particular the monographs of Daniel C. Fredericks, *Coping with Transience: Ecclesiastes on Brevity in Life*, BibSem 18 (Sheffield: JSOT, 1993), and Douglas B. Miller, *Symbol and Rhetoric in Ecclesiastes: The Place of Hebel in Qohelet's Work*, SBLAcBib 2 (Atlanta: SBL, 2002).

7. Meek, 'Twentieth- and Twenty-first-century Readings of *Hebel*', 283.

8. See the discussion on 'Cain and Abel: Unexpected Outcomes', 252–5, of Russell L. Meek, 'The Meaning of הבל in Qohelet: An Intertextual Suggestion', in *The Words of the Wise Are like Goads: Engaging Qohelet in the 21st Century*, ed. Mark. J. Boda, Tremper Longman III, and Cristian G. Rata (Winona Lake: Eisenbrauns, 2013), 241–56.

renders as '[Mortals] are like a breath', with the parallel line 'their days are like a passing shadow'.⁹ And note, too, the analogous formulation in Ps. 62.9, where the poet brings all humanity, that is all descendants of Adam, under the Abel umbrella: אך הבל בני־אדם – which the NRSV renders as 'Those of low estate are but a breath', a somewhat puzzling restriction of the reference to only some of the בני־אדם. But for my present purposes, I want simply to note the affinity of that psalm's expression אך הבל בני־אדם with the formulation in Psalm 39, אך הבל כל־אדם – 'surely everyone is a mere breath'.

Having dipped into this intriguing aspect of Psalm 39, with its threefold deployment of the term הבל, and the light shed upon that term by the wider biblical depiction of the *hebel*-ness of the human condition, let me now make a foray into the reception history of the psalm in question. I want to consider how three modern poetic treatments of this psalm have dealt with this notion of the breath, breath, breath to be encountered in Psalm 39.

The reworkings under consideration here are those of Leslie Brandt (in his collection *Psalms/Now* of 1973),¹⁰ Juanita Colón (in her collection *The Manhattan Psalter* in 2002),¹¹ and Edward Clarke (in his collection *A Book of Psalms* for 2020).¹² Their poems each in their own way present a reimagining of 'how the psalmist might speak if he faced our anxious, depersonalised, and lonely world' (as Leslie Brandt's enterprise has been described),¹³ or an appropriation of the Psalter for a personal enclosed life (as in the case of Juanita Colón), or a set of 'conversations with, and hesitations about, these ancient texts' (as Edward Clarke depicts his

---

9. Robert Alter, *The Book of Psalms: A Translation with Commentary* (New York: Norton, 2007), 496, translates 144.4 as 'The human is like unto breath', and comments that 'the Israeli scholar Gershon Brin has made the ingenious proposal that the previous verse and this one allude punningly to the first three generations of humankind: *'adam* ("the human", or "Adam"), *hevel* ("breath", or "Abel"), and *ben 'enosh* ("the son of man", or "Enosh")'.

10. Leslie F. Brandt, *Psalms/Now* (St Louis: Concordia, 1973), 62–3.

11. M. Juanita Colón, ocso, *The Manhattan Psalter: The Lectio Divina of Sister Juanita Colón* (Collegeville: Liturgical Press, 2002), 61.

12. Edward Clarke, *A Book of Psalms* (Brewster: Paraclete, 2020), 50–1. I am grateful to Edward Clarke for having provided me with a pre-publication copy of his rendition of Ps. 39, which enabled me to make use of it in the preparation of this paper.

13. Quoting the publisher's blurb for Brandt, *Psalms/Now*.

reworkings of the Psalms).[14] The remainder of the present paper, then, offers, as it were, a further conversation between the ancient text of Psalm 39 and these three modern renditions of the resonant motif of the nature of humanity as an all-too-briefly-breathing species.

Taking the three modern works in chronological order, I begin with the rendition of Leslie Brandt, a Lutheran pastor in the suburbs of Los Angeles in the latter years of the twentieth century. He described his enterprise in the following terms:

> In the twentieth year of my ministry I began to 'rewrite' a few of [the psalms] for my church bulletin [and] these were eventually published… I have tried to express what these Psalms say to me and about me. It is just possible that they may reveal to other readers something about themselves and give them a means of expressing their actual feelings in their conversations with God. These offerings are by no means an attempt to be scholarly or textual. On the other hand, they ought to indicate something of the honesty and humanity of the psalm-writers in their daily conflicts, and to encourage us to be honest in our pursuit of truth and our walk with God.[15]

With that description in mind, an inspection of the third stanza of Brandt's rendition of Psalm 39 will be pertinent. This is where he wrestles with the imagery of vv. 4-6 of the psalm, with its talk of the fleeting nature of life and the first two of its three deployments of the *hebel* motif. Brandt's lines run:

> O God, demonstrate some concern for me.
> Give me some reason for this incessant conflict,
>   some objective for this fast-ebbing life of mine.
> You made me what I am – a bubble or a bag of gas,
>   and the span of my existence
>   is but a speck of dust to You.
> It is true about every man.
> He is no more than a smidgen of moist air
>   or a shadow without lasting substance.
> Man enters and endures this temporal turmoil
>   for no reason whatsoever.
> He agonizes and toils
>   only to leave the fruits for someone else to enjoy.[16]

---

14. Edward Clarke, 'New Songs of Praise', *Oxford Mail*, 13 September 2018 (www.oxfordmail.co.uk/news/16858968.new-songs-of-praise-oxford-writer-edward-clarke-pens-new-book-of-psalms/).

15. Brandt, *Psalms/Now*: 'Preface', 5.

16. Ibid., 62.

The direct equivalent of the first *hebel* here is the expression 'a smidgen of moist air', which captures an image that may well in antiquity have contributed to the notion of the breath as emblematic of transience, insofar as one can see one's exhaled breath for a moment on a cold winter's day before it dissipates into thin air. It may even be that Brandt is continuing that image in his following expression 'without lasting substance', though he poetically applies the latter phrase to the phenomenon of the shadow. Both of those images – 'a smidgen of moist air' and 'without lasting substance' – are likewise supporting and reiterating his earlier description of the human being as 'a bubble or a bag of gas', two equally evocative pictures that fall well within the semantic field of *hebel*.[17]

Meanwhile the second instance of *hebel* in the original psalm receives a far less striking accord in this rendition: in keeping with standard English translations of this second instance as 'Surely *for nothing* they are in turmoil', Brandt tells his readers that 'Man enters and endures this temporal turmoil *for no reason* whatsoever'. Yet this forms a telling counterpoint to the plea with which Brandt had begun this stanza, with the earnest request to the deity to 'give me *some reason* for this incessant conflict, some objective for this fast-ebbing life of mine'.

Moving to the fourth stanza, and taking its latter half – where Brandt gives his version of vv. 10-11 of the psalm, with its talk of the blows inflicted by God and culminating in the third deployment of the *hebel* motif – further creative reworkings are to be found:

> Lift Your heavy hand from me;
>   I am utterly weary of its oppressing weight.
> When You punish a man
>   with judgment of his failures,
>   You suck up like a tornado
>   everything that is precious to him.
> Surely man is no more than a passing cloud
>   on the eternal horizon.[18]

---

17. Meek, 'Twentieth- and Twenty-first-century Readings of *Hebel*', 291, cites two scholars who argue that 'bubble' accurately captures the meaning of הבל, namely F. C. Burkitt ('Is Ecclesiastes a Translation?', *JTS* 23 [1921]: 22–8, specifically 28) and Charles F. Whitley (*Koheleth: His Language and Thought*, BZAW 148 [Berlin: de Gruyter, 1979] – Meek cites the latter as p. 68, but this appears to be in error for p. 7, where Whitley approvingly presents Burkitt's opinion).

18. Brandt, *Psalms/Now*, 63.

'A passing cloud on the eternal horizon' seems a splendid way to re-express the earlier idea of 'a smidgen of moist air' as variations on the theme of human *hebel*-ness, the mortal over against the Immortal, with God's breath by contrast being compared to a roaring tornado sucking up everything in which puny humans might take delight.

The Manhattan Psalter of the Cistercian Sister Juanita Colón emerged from her life as a contemplative nun singing the psalms in cloistered worship at St Mary's Abbey in Wrentham, Massachusetts, each day throughout the last decades of the twentieth century – though the title of the work reflects her background as a New Yorker. The Abbey's abbess, Mother Agnes Day, described the enterprise as follows:

> Sister Juanita began writing the psalms in her own words in the late spring of 1982. She was working on typing the fifth and final draft in the Infirmary a week before she died [of multiple myeloma in the summer of 1999]. The psalms reflect the reality of Israel's relationship with God. They were Jesus' prayers as a good Jew, and they are the heritage of both Jews and Christians. Sister Juanita entered into them in the same honest way, not withholding from God any of her humanity. As a contemplative nun she prayed them for all the people on earth in all their various situations. She also prayed them for her own interior battles with the forces within herself. That is why her version of the Psalter is so very alive.[19]

For a taste of that vitality, a consideration of the second paragraph of Colón's rendition of Psalm 39, her equivalent of vv. 4-6, will be worthwhile:

> 'God', I roared, 'how much longer? Is this what you call living? Tell me, when is it all going to end? Tell me it won't be long now. What good are these few miserable days on earth? Compared with yours, my lifespan doesn't amount to a thing. Even at its best, humanity is a nothing, a nothing, emptiness and hollow show. We rush around, poor fools, like headless chickens, darting here and there in a senseless lather, piling up possessions we don't know what to do with once we have them. I ask you, is this living?'[20]

Notice that twofold designation of humanity as 'a nothing, a nothing', as well as 'emptiness and hollow show'. Might that twice-told 'nothing' be Colón's recognition of the twofold use of *hebel* in the pair of verses at hand, or is it simply an evocative repetition for its own purposes,

---

19. M. Agnes Day, OCSO, 'Introduction', in Colón, *The Manhattan Psalter*, 9.
20. Colón, *The Manhattan Psalter*, 61.

quite coincidental to the cadences of the Hebrew text? Perhaps indeed 'senseless' is her reflection of the second *hebel* in this passage, since her phrasing about people 'darting here and there in a senseless lather' seems to reflect the standard English phrasing of 'for nothing they are in turmoil' for הבל יהמיון.

Now the third paragraph, in its latter half, Colón's equivalent of vv. 10-11:

> Mercy, Lord, make it stop, Lord; you've hammered me practically into the ground! When you decide to make people pay for their sins, you can really wither them with your reproof and strip them of their blown-up ideas about themselves. Oh yes, vanity gets us all in the end.[21]

'Vanity gets us all in the end'. Here Colón has fallen back on the traditional English rendering of *hebel*, leaving the notion of a breath out of the picture – at least temporarily, since she picks the idea up into her last sentence, her dying breath as it were as far as this psalm is concerned, at the end of the final paragraph, where she pleads with the Almighty, 'Turn those accusing eyes from me for the space of a breath or I'm finished!'.[22]

Finally I come to a consideration of the rendering of this psalm made by Edward Clarke, an Oxford-based poet and teacher of English literature and creative writing, who, when he turned 40, decided to read his way through the King James Bible at the rate of an hour a day. Particularly impressed by the Psalms, he began to write a series of poems, some of them being direct responses to the biblical text while others were more oblique commentaries or outright departures.[23] At first he published a small collection called *Eighteen Psalms*,[24] which did not include Psalm 39,

---

21. Ibid.
22. Ibid. Colón's return to the motif of 'breath' at the end of her rendition of the psalm nicely matches an observation made by Peter C. Craigie, *Psalms 1–50*, WBC 19 (Waco: Word, 1983), that 'though the psalm ends in fairly conventional prayer (vv. 13-14), it ends with a twist – it is the kind of prayer that Qoheleth might have prayed, if he could have summoned sufficient faith' (308). Robert Alter also deploys 'breath' in his translation of the final verse of the psalm: 'Look away from me, that I may catch my breath before I depart and am not' (Alter, *The Book of Psalms*, 140) – rendering the disputed verb ואבליגה as 'catch my breath'.
23. This description of Clarke's enterprise is based on that of D. J. Taylor, 'Chapter and Verse: Spinning Poetry from the Psalms' (a review of the BBC Radio 4 programme 'Clarke's Psalter' broadcast on 9 September 2018), *The Tablet*, 13 September 2018, 17.
24. Edward Clarke, *Eighteen Psalms* (Plymouth: Periplum Poetry, 2018).

but he has now published a full collection called *A Book of Psalms*, which engages with all 150 psalms.

Concerning his wider enterprise for *A Book of Psalms*, Edward Clarke has written that 'I love engaging with the Psalms because they are so old and strange and mysterious. But they are also so familiar to us today as if already internalised.' His own renditions, he notes, 'are not translations and versifications. They are conversations with, and hesitations about, these ancient texts.'[25] And concerning his rendition of Psalm 39, he told me in a personal communication that this particular poem was written

> before I fully understood that I had a book on my hands, when I was selecting individual psalms for treatment. Very soon after writing this poem, my work on the Psalms intensified greatly and didn't stop until the book was finished [in March 2019]. When I was revising the book recently I decided to let the poem stand in its original state because it seemed so embryonic to me: so full of what was to come. In fact, it was written just before, and is partially about, the delayed birth of my second son who grows up through the book into a significant emblem within it.[26]

When one looks at Clarke's rendition of this psalm, it is immediately apparent that it is a poem of two halves, a first section of four stanzas of four lines each, and then 'another go' (as it is called in the third line of Part 2), a set of five stanzas of six lines each with a more creative system of indentations. First, for the present purposes, a consideration of the second and third stanzas of Part 1, where the reflection of those key vv. 4-6 is to be seen, is in order.

> But do not tell me too exactly
> The measure of my days, the end
> You have ordained for me so flatly,
> My days are frail, their breadth an hand.
>
> My lines are like a warehouse where
> I worked, in hands of the receiver,
> Man's life is but the building's air
> We helped to raze the summer after.[27]

Here the 'breath' has become the 'air' of a transient building in which the poet had worked and in the dismantling of which he had participated.

---

25. Ibid.
26. Edward Clarke, personal communication, 4 April 2019.
27. Clarke, *A Book of Psalms*, 50.

As buildings rise and fall, so do individual human lives come into being and fall out of being. As it happens, Ecclesiastes appears to make a connection between these analogous happenings in his famous Poem of the Alternating Times (Eccl. 3.1-8, specifically in vv. 2a over against 3b)[28] and arguably also in his equally famous Poem of the End Times (12.1-7, in which the fall of an estate has often been interpreted as an allegory of the aging of a human body).[29] So Clarke's analogy that 'man's life is but the building's air' is well fitted to the biblical wisdom tradition's depiction of the *hebel*-istic aspect of such enterprises. It is indeed the case for every human being, as Clarke had intoned just before this image, that 'my days are frail, their breadth an hand' (drawing upon the psalmist's lament that 'you have made my days a few handbreadths, and my lifetime is as nothing in your sight', Ps. 39.5).[30]

As for the psalm's other use of *hebel*, in the sense of human toil being in vain, this finds an echo in Clarke's Part 2.

> I lost my way through nights and hills
>   In boots and shoes and black tie.
> I tore my back while heaping up
>   The treasure of the magpie.
> But I was careless about my storing of it
> And everything was scattered to no one's profit.[31]

'Careless' could be taken as an interesting spin on the notion of 'purposeless', 'meaningless', 'pointless' or the like that various scholars have seen in the application of the term *hebel* in the Hebrew Bible.[32]

---

28. See my comments about this 'parallelism' in Jarick, 'The Hebrew Book of Changes', 94, within the wider analysis of the poem (86–99).

29. For a useful recent discussion of this poem, see the section 'The Final Poem (12:1-7)' in Mette Bundvad, *Time in the Book of Ecclesiastes*, Oxford Theology and Religion Monographs (Oxford: Oxford University Press, 2015), 61–72.

30. Our honoree has noted that this verse of the psalm provides a clear example of how Shakespeare freely used psalmody in his plays, given that Ps. 39.5's description of life as 'a few handbreadths' evidently resonates with the phrase in *Othello* (ii.3.72) which compares life to a 'span of a hand' (Susan Gillingham, *Psalms Through the Centuries, Vol. 1*, Blackwell Bible Commentaries [Oxford: Blackwell, 2008], 173). I add the note here that both Shakespeare and Clarke speak of the span/breadth as being that of a single hand rather than the plural expression deployed by the psalmist (טפחות), thus diminishing the human lifespan even further.

31. Clarke, *A Book of Psalms*, 51.

32. Meek notes such disparate interpreters as Gregory of Nyssa, Diethelm Michel, J. A. Loader, and R. B. Y. Scott (Meek, 'Twentieth- and Twenty-first-century Readings

Especially since the 'careless[ness]' here is connected to the poet's 'storing' of 'the treasure of the magpie', a reader with the idea of *hebel*-ness in mind might well think of Ecclesiastes' picture of the quintessential hoarder acquiring a considerable amount of treasure (Eccl. 2.4-7) only to find that it can all be lost (e.g. 5.14; 9.11) and thus that it is all *hebel* (2.11 etc.). Ecclesiastes had followed up his headline statement that 'All is *hebel*' (1.2) with the rhetorical question, 'What do people gain from all the toil at which they toil under the sun?' (1.3); Clarke follows up his lament on the loss of his 'treasure' with the observation that 'everything was scattered to no one's profit'.

I suggest that readers' appreciation of the *hebel* motif in Psalm 39 can be enhanced by this consideration of the reworkings of the psalm at the hands of Leslie Brandt, Juanita Colón, and Edward Clarke. Whether it be 'a smidgen of moist air', 'without lasting substance', 'for nothing', or 'a passing cloud on the eternal horizon' in the phrasing of Brandt; 'a nothing, a nothing, emptiness and hollow show', 'a senseless lather', 'vanity get[ting] us all in the end', or 'the space of a breath' in the phrasing of Colón; or nothing but 'air' and 'careless[ness]', 'to no one's profit', in the phrasing of Clarke – the imagery of the 'breath' or 'vapour' deployed by the psalmist has resonated effectively in these three modern renditions of the psalm. Each of these poets' conversations with the ancient psalmist has highly effectively echoed that psalmist's resounding phrase: אך הבל כל-אדם, 'surely everyone is a mere breath'.

Bibliography

Alter, Robert. *The Book of Psalms: A Translation with Commentary.* New York: Norton, 2007.
Brandt, Leslie F. *Psalms/Now.* St Louis: Concordia, 1973.
Bundvad, Mette. *Time in the Book of Ecclesiastes.* Oxford Theology and Religion Monographs. Oxford: Oxford University Press, 2015.
Burkitt, F. C. 'Is Ecclesiastes a Translation?', *JTS* 23 (1921): 22–8.
Clarke, Edward. *A Book of Psalms.* Brewster: Paraclete, 2020.

---

of *Hebel*', 282, 286, 287, and 288 respectively). See also more recently Mark Sneed, 'הבל as "Worthless" in Qoheleth: A Critique of Michael V. Fox's "Absurd" Thesis', *JBL* 136 (2017): 879–94 (responded to by Michael V. Fox, 'On הבל in Qoheleth: A Reply to Mark Sneed', *JBL* 138 [2019]: 559–63). Sneed credits Klaus Seybold, 'הבל *hebhel*', *TDOT* 3:318–20 (specifically 319), for the idea of *hebel* as 'that which yields no results'; Seybold in turn credits Kurt Galling, 'Der Prediger', in *Die Fünf Megilloth*, ed. Ernst Würthwein, Kurt Galling, and Otto Plöger, 2nd ed., HAT 1/18 (Tübingen: Mohr Siebeck, 1969), 73–125 (specifically p. 79), for the idea.

Clarke, Edward. *Eighteen Psalms* Plymouth: Periplum Poetry, 2018.
Clarke, Edward. 'New Songs of Praise'. *Oxford Mail*, 13 September 2018, www. oxfordmail.co.uk/news/16858968.new-songs-of-praise-oxford-writer-edward-clarke-pens-new-book-of-psalms/.
Cohen, Yoram. *Wisdom from the Late Bronze Age*. Atlanta: SBL, 2013.
Colón, M. Juanita, ocso, *The Manhattan Psalter: The Lectio Divina of Sister Juanita Colón*. Collegeville: Liturgical Press, 2002.
Craigie, Peter C. *Psalms 1–50*. WBC 19. Waco: Word, 1983.
Crenshaw, James L. *Qoheleth: The Ironic Wink*. Studies on Personalities of the Old Testament. Columbia: The University of South Carolina Press, 2013.
Croft, Steven J. L. *The Identity of the Individual in the Psalms* JSOTSup 44. Sheffield: Sheffield Academic, 1987.
Fox, Michael V. 'On הֶבֶל in Qoheleth: A Reply to Mark Sneed'. *JBL* 138 (2019): 559–63.
Fredericks, Daniel C. *Coping with Transience: Ecclesiastes on Brevity in Life*. BibSem 18. Sheffield: JSOT, 1993.
Galling, Kurt. 'Der Prediger'. Pages 73–125 in *Die Fünf Megilloth*. Edited by Ernst Würthwein, Kurt Galling, and Otto Plöger. 2nd ed. HAT 1/18. Tübingen: Mohr Siebeck, 1969.
Gillingham, Susan. *Psalms Through the Centuries, vol. 1*. Blackwell Bible Commentaries. Oxford: Blackwell, 2008.
Gillingham, Susan. *Psalms Through the Centuries. VOLUMA Reception History Commentary on Psalms 1–72, vol. 2*. Wiley Blackwell Bible Commentaries. Chichester: Wiley-Blackwell, 2018.
Goldingay, John. *Psalms, vol. 1*. Baker Commentary on the Old Testament Wisdom and Psalms. Grand Rapids: Baker Academic, 2006.
Jacobson, Rolf A. 'Psalm 39: From Silence to Speech to Silence'. Pages 360–70 in *The Book of Psalms*, by Nancy DeClaissé-Walford, Rolf A. Jacobson, and Beth Laneel Tanner. NICOT. Grand Rapids: Eerdmans, 2014.
Jarick, John. 'The Hebrew Book of Changes: Reflections on *hakkōl hebel* and *lakkōl zᵉmān* in Ecclesiastes'. *JSOT* 90 (2000): 79–99.
Meek, Russell L. 'The Meaning of הֶבֶל in Qohelet: An Intertextual Suggestion'. Pages 241–56 in *The Words of the Wise Are like Goads: Engaging Qohelet in the 21st Century*. Edited by Mark J. Boda, Tremper Longman III and Cristian G. Rata. Winona Lake: Eisenbrauns, 2013.
Meek, Russell L. 'Twentieth- and Twenty-first-century Readings of *Hebel* (הֶבֶל) in Ecclesiastes'. *CurBR* 14 (2016): 279–97.
Miller, Douglas B. *Symbol and Rhetoric in Ecclesiastes: The Place of Hebel in Qohelet's Work*. SBLAcBib 2. Atlanta: SBL, 2002.
Mitchell, Stephen. *Gilgamesh: A New English Version*. New York: Free Press, 2004.
Seybold, Klaus. 'הֶבֶל *hebhel*'. *TDOT* 3:318–20.
Sneed, Mark. 'הֶבֶל as "Worthless" in Qohelet: A Critique of Michael V. Fox's "Absurd" Thesis'. *JBL* 136 (2017): 879–94.
Taylor, D. J. 'Chapter and Verse: Spinning Poetry from the Psalms'. *The Tablet*, 13 September 2018, 17.
Terrien, Samuel. *The Psalms: Strophic Structure and Theological Commentary*. Grand Rapids: Eerdmans, 2003.
Whitley, Charles F. *Koheleth: His Language and Thought*. BZAW 148. Berlin: de Gruyter, 1979.

Handel-ing the Psalms:
Reception-Historical Reflections on
Handel's Chandos Anthems

Deborah W. Rooke

Handel's Chandos Anthems are a collection of eleven choral psalm-settings.[1] They were written between 1717 and 1718 for James Brydges, Earl of Caernarvon and later Duke of Chandos,[2] to be used in the Duke's private chapel at his estate in Cannons Park, located near the village of Edgware to the north-west of London. My motivation for discussing the Chandos Anthems in the present context is two-fold. The first reason is of course to honour Professor Sue Gillingham, who was my doctoral supervisor in Oxford, by undertaking a study that encompasses her passion for the Psalms, my passion for Handel, and our shared passion for Old Testament reception history. The second reason relates to James Brydges' estate at Cannons Park,[3] where in the 17-teens Brydges built an enormous Palladian mansion. Sadly, Brydges' changing financial fortunes and spendthrift son meant that the mansion barely outlasted its builder, being sold and dismantled for architectural salvage in 1747–48.[4] But the site

---

1. Handel's Chandos or Cannons corpus of church music also includes a choral setting of the liturgical statement known as the 'Te Deum', giving a total of twelve individual pieces. Given that it is not based on a psalm text, the 'Te Deum' is not included in the present discussion.

2. For brief details of Brydges, see Joan Johnson, 'Brydges, James, first duke of Chandos (1674–1744)', in *Oxford Dictionary of National Biography* (Oxford: Oxford University Press, 23 September 2010).

3. The spelling 'Cannons' reflects the eighteenth-century convention. Today, the name of the estate and adjoining Underground station is spelt with a single 'n' ('Canons Park').

4. For details of the mansion see Ian Dunlop, 'Cannons, Middlesex: A Conjectural Reconstruction', *Country Life*, 30 December 1949, 1950–4; Kerry Downes, 'Cannons',

was purchased by William Hallett, a successful cabinet maker, who in the 1750s erected a much more modest house on the mansion's foundations.[5] That house still remains, and today forms the core premises of the North London Collegiate School for Girls, where as a sixth-former I studied classics and prepared for the Cambridge entrance exam. So, in gratitude for benefits received, from both the North London Collegiate School at Canons and from Sue's supervision at Oxford, it is my privilege to offer this short study of the Chandos Anthems.

As already noted, the collection of psalm settings referred to as the Chandos Anthems – or the Cannons Anthems, from the place of their composition – was prepared for James Brydges in the late 17-teens.[6] Born in 1674, Brydges was the product of landed gentry – the eighth Baron Chandos – on his father's side and merchant bankers on his mother's side, and put his natural talents and connections to good use to better his situation. His financial breakthrough came when in 1705 he was appointed Paymaster General of Queen Anne's forces, a post he held until he resigned it in 1713, £600,000 better off than when he had started. The estate at Cannons Park belonged to the family of Brydges' first wife, Mary, and Brydges bought it from her uncle, though he did not actually move into the house until after both Mary and her uncle had died (she in 1712, he in 1713).[7] Brydges' rise through the ranks of the nobility began when in 1714 his father, Baron Chandos, died the day after royal approval was granted for the Baron to receive an earldom. Brydges himself thus received the title Earl of Caernarvon instead of his father.[8] Five years later he was made Duke of Chandos in recognition of his services to the state.

in *The Cambridge Handel Encyclopedia*, ed. Annette Landgraf and David Vickers (Cambridge: Cambridge University Press, 2009), 116.

5. See 'Hallett, William Snr & Jnr (1730–d.1767)', *British and Irish Furniture Makers Online*, https://bifmo.history.ac.uk/entry/hallett-william-snr-1707-81.

6. The biographical details in this paragraph are summarized from Johnson, 'Brydges, James, first duke of Chandos (1674–1744)'.

7. Details of the complicated process by which Brydges acquired Cannons can be found in C. H. Collins Baker and Muriel I. Baker, *The Life and Circumstances of James Brydges, First Duke of Chandos, Patron of the Liberal Arts* (Oxford: Clarendon, 1949), 13–16.

8. Baker and Baker explain that this was in fact a strategy to allow Brydges himself to receive the earldom without attracting unwanted attention, because 'the paymaster's accounts [from Brydges' tenure of that position], so pregnant with charges of corruption, had not yet passed the auditors. To receive marked favours from the new King would court publicity, which of all things had better be avoided at present' (*Life and Circumstances*, 96).

Having attained wealth and title, Brydges cultivated a lifestyle to match, and this is where the Handelian connection comes in. As well as building a magnificent house at his newly acquired Cannons Park estate, Brydges was a patron of art and music, and the records for the household at Cannons show that he employed a bevy of vocalists, instrumentalists and composers who provided entertainment for the Duke and his guests as well as music for services held in the estate's private chapel.[9] For a short period of time Handel was part of this musical establishment as a composer-in-residence, and his Chandos Anthems were liturgical compositions for use in the Duke's chapel. Incidentally, too, Handel's very first Israelite oratorio *Esther* was one of two small-scale musical dramas written for performance at Cannons to entertain the Duke's guests (the other was the Greek mythological story *Acis and Galatea*).[10]

This, then, is the context in which the Chandos Anthems were written; so, what of the anthems themselves? An anthem is a choral composition which forms a musical interlude in the liturgy, and which consists of scriptural or liturgical texts set to music. The Chandos compositions are anthems on a grand scale: they are verse anthems, which means that they each have several alternating movements for solo voice and chorus,[11] and all but one of them have an introductory instrumental sonata, which means that they take between 20 and 30 minutes each in performance.[12] All eleven anthems use material from the Psalms, but they differ in the immediate source from which that material is taken. Eight of the eleven (nos. 1, 3, 4, 5, 7, 8, 10 and 11) use the Psalms translation published by Miles Coverdale in 1535, which was subsequently incorporated into the

---

9. A detailed description of the Cannons musical establishment and its fortunes is given from the Cannons household records of the time by Graydon Beeks, 'The Chandos Anthems and Te Deum of George Frideric Handel (1685–1759)' (Ph.D. diss., University of California Berkeley, 1981), 15–36.

10. A summary of Handel's time at Cannons is provided by Donald Burrows, *Handel*, 2nd ed., The Master Musicians (Oxford: Oxford University Press, 2012), 103–5.

11. The alternative form to a verse anthem is a 'full anthem' or 'motet', in which the entire text is sung through by the choir rather than being broken into separate solo and choral movements.

12. They may have been modelled on the Latin anthems that Handel wrote in 1707 while in Rome (*Dixit Dominus*; *Laudate pueri*; *Nisi Dominus*), which have a similarly elaborate structure. See Howard Cox, 'Handel's Text Selection Procedures in the Chandos Anthems', *Bach* 24, no. 1 (1993): 21–34 (21). Such compositions would have been entirely appropriate for performance in the newly rebuilt church of St Lawrence, which was to serve as Brydges' private chapel and was renovated and decorated in the Italian style (see Beeks, 'Chandos Anthems', 14–15).

Great Bible of 1539 and then into the 1662 *Book of Common Prayer*. It was thus the most well-known, readily available and liturgically appropriate version of the Psalms for Handel to use. A further two of the eleven anthems (nos. 2 and 9) use the metrical version of the Psalms produced in 1696 by the Irish Protestants Nahum Tate, poet laureate for William III, and Nicholas Brady, a royal chaplain.[13] Although not quite as entrenched in the Anglican psyche as the Prayer-Book version of the Psalms, Tate and Brady's paraphrase was widely known and used. Finally, one anthem (no. 6) is based on a combination of material from the Prayer-Book Psalms translation and a psalm paraphrase by Dr John Arbuthnot, physician to Queen Anne.[14] Arbuthnot's text had been set to music as an anthem for use in the Chapel Royal, and this is the context in which Handel most probably encountered it, since he himself had worked for the Chapel Royal between 1712 and 1714, producing there as his first-ever English verse anthem a setting of the same text as he later used for Chandos Anthem 6.[15]

This leads us quite naturally to the question of which psalm texts were used in the anthems, and what prompted their choice. Only one of the anthems sets a complete psalm, and that is Anthem 1, which is a setting

---

13. Nahum Tate and Nicholas Brady, *A New Version of the Psalms of David, in English Metre, fitted for Public Use* (London, 1696). The book is prefaced with a royal commendation letter declaring that 'His Majesty…is pleased to Order in Council, that the said *New Version of the Psalms in English Metre* be, and the same is hereby Allowed and Permitted to be used in all Churches, Chappels, and Congregations, as shall think fit to receive the same'.

14. So Beeks, 'The Chandos Anthems', 434. The words of the Arbuthnot version are printed in *Divine Harmony; or a New Collection of Select Anthems, Us'd at Her Majesty's Chappels Royal, Westminster Abby, St. Pauls, Windsor, Both Universities, Eaton, and Most Cathedrals in Her Majesty's Dominions. Publish'd with the Approbation of the Subdean of Her Majesty's Chappel Royal, and of Several of the Greatest Masters* (London: printed and sold by S. Keble at the Turks-Head in Fleetstreet, C. King in Westminster-Hall, and J. Hazard, at the Golden Bible in Stationers Court near Ludgate, 1712), 102. For a brief biography of Arbuthnot, see Angus Ross, 'Arbuthnot [Arbuthnott], John', in *Oxford Dictionary of National Biography*, rev. ed. (Oxford: Oxford University Press, 23 Sept. 2004). A different view of Anthem 6 is taken by Howard Cox, who argues that Handel used phrases from Tate and Brady in conjunction with the Prayer-Book version of Ps. 42 ('Handel's Text Selection Procedures', 23).

15. For details of this period in Handel's life and career, see Donald Burrows, *Handel and the English Chapel Royal*, Oxford Studies in British Church Music (Oxford: Oxford University Press, 2005), 54–137. Arbuthnot was also a member of the artistic circle associated with Cannons, and may have had a hand in providing the libretto for the oratorium *Esther*.

of Psalm 100, together with the liturgical text 'Glory be to the Father and to the Son...' Three anthems use a selection of verses from a single psalm: Anthems 3 (Ps. 51), 6 (Ps. 42), and 7 (Ps. 89). Three further anthems use selections from one psalm for most of their text but add a single verse from another psalm; these are Anthems 4 (Ps. 96 plus a single verse from Ps. 93), 5 (Ps. 145 plus a single verse from Ps. 144), and 11 (Ps. 68 plus a single verse from Ps. 76). The remaining four anthem texts are more complicated. Anthem 2 alternates verses from Psalm 11 with those from Psalms 9, 12 and 13, all in the versions found in Tate & Brady's paraphrase except for the opening verse (11.1) which is from the Prayer Book version. Anthem 8 uses verses from Psalms 95, 96, 97, 99 and 103. Anthem 9 uses verses from Psalms 135, 117 and 148 in Tate & Brady's paraphrase version; and Anthem 10, the most complex, uses verses from Psalms 27, 18, 20, 34, 29, 30 and 45. Based on a range of criteria these final three anthems are probably the latest to have been written, suggesting that Handel was becoming more adventurous and experimental in his text selection processes.[16]

Identifying the 'what' of the texts brings us to the 'why'. What motivated Handel's precise choice of psalm texts for setting to music? Some of the psalms used have established liturgical connections, making them an obvious choice. A good example of this is Anthem 1, which sets Psalm 100 in its entirety. The psalm is known as the Jubilate, from its first line in the Vulgate, and is set in the Prayer Book liturgy as an alternative canticle to be read at Morning Prayer. Other psalms with established liturgical connections that appear in the Chandos Anthems are Psalm 95, used daily at Morning Prayer; Psalm 89, used on Christmas Day Evening Prayer; Psalm 68, used at Whit Sunday Morning Prayer; Psalm 145, used at Whit Sunday Evening Prayer; and Psalm 51, used at the beginning of Lent. Between them these psalms account for the entirety of Anthems 1, 3 and 7, all but one movement of Anthems 5 and 11, and about half of Anthem 8. There is no immediately obvious liturgical connection for the remaining psalms used; that said, the more elaborate combinations of verses comprising some of the anthems are taken from psalms located quite close to each other, and therefore appointed to be read on the same or successive days. For example, the psalms used in Anthem 2 (Pss. 9, 11, 12, 13) are all set for reading on the second day of the monthly psalm reading cycle. Likewise, the psalms used in Anthems 4 and 8 (Pss. 93, 95, 96, 97, 99, 103) are all set to be read between the 18th and 20th

---

16. For a discussion of those processes, see Cox, 'Handel's Text-Selection Procedures'.

days of the monthly cycle. This proximity was probably a factor in their being combined. A third consideration is that the texts used in several of the anthems had been set by composers prior to Handel, thereby establishing precedents and giving models on which Handel could build. Aside from the Jubilate (Ps. 100; Anthem 1) which has been set multiple times because of its liturgical use, seven of the other ten anthems use texts of psalms that had already been set either in whole or in part by two or more previous composers: Anthems 3 (Ps. 51), 4 (Ps. 96), 5 (Ps. 145), 6 (Ps. 42), 7 (Ps. 89), 9 (Pss. 135, 117) and 11 (Ps. 68).[17] So there is both liturgical and compositional precedent for much of the general content of the Chandos Anthems.

From the components of the anthems, then, we can move on to consider the resulting compositions. Eight of them are anthems of praise, while three have a more meditative or introspective mood, but in both the more upbeat and the more meditative compositions the idiom and modes of expression have what might be termed a conventional feel. In other words, and not necessarily surprisingly, despite the psalms' origins as expressions of devotion to a pre-Christian Semitic deity in an ancient Near Eastern context, the language and sentiments in the psalm verses chosen for the Anthems reflect those of what would have been conventional eighteenth-century Christian devotions, and indeed, what have continued to be standard tropes in Western Christian worship. Consider, for example, the opening words of Anthem 7, taken from Psalm 89:

> My song shall be alway of the loving kindness of the Lord; with my mouth will I ever be shewing thy truth from one generation to another. The Heavens shall praise thy wondrous works, and thy truth in the congregation of the saints. (Ps. 89.1, 5)

Or this from Anthem 8, taken from Psalm 97:

> The Lord preserveth the souls of the saints, he shall deliver them from the hand of the ungodly. (Ps. 97.10)

Praising God for showing faithfulness and saving those whom he loves is a fundamental element of Christian worship, and these texts, devoid as

---

17. The texts and compilers for these settings can be found in *Divine Harmony*, as follows: Ps. 51: p. 21 (Humphrys, Weldon); Ps. 96: pp. 69 (Clarke, Croft), 80 (Weldon, Isham, Brind); Ps. 145: pp. 54 (Turner), 83 (Croft); Ps. 42: pp. 24 (Humphrys), 102 (Arbuthnot); Ps. 89: pp. 12 (Goldwin), 55 (Purcell), 82 (Croft, Tudway); Ps. 135: pp. 6 (Child), 25 (Humphrys, Weldon); Ps. 117: pp. 4–5 (Batten); Ps. 68: pp. 33 (Blow), 101 (Brind, Davis), 103 (King, Purcell).

they are of elements that might undermine their relevance for specifically Christian devotions, lend themselves readily to being used for this purpose.

Another fundamental element of Christian worship that appears in the anthems is what might be termed creation-related praise, in other words, declaring God to be creator and curator of the world. Turning once more to Anthem 7, we find the following lines:

> The heavens are thine, the earth also is thine; thou hast laid the foundation of the round world. (Ps. 89.12)

And Anthem 8 proclaims,

> Tell it out among the heathen, that the Lord is King, and that he made the world so fast it cannot be moved. (Ps. 96.10)

Alongside these declarations of praise, there is the inevitable sprinkling of fire and brimstone to punish the wicked; thus, for example, in Anthem 5, using Psalm 145, we hear,

> The Lord preserveth all them that love him, but scatt'reth abroad all the ungodly. (Ps. 145.20)

Rather more sulphurous is Anthem 2, which uses the Tate & Brady paraphrases and includes this verse from Psalm 11 speaking of divine vengeance on the wicked:

> Snares, fire and brimstone on their heads
> Shall in one tempest show'r:
> This dreadful mixture his revenge
> Into their cup shall pour. (Ps. 11.6 in Tate & Brady version)

And, along similar lines, in Anthem 10 comes this combination of verses from Psalm 18:

> The earth trembled, and quak'd, the very foundation also of the hills shook, and were removed; (Ps. 18.7) / he cast forth lightnings, and gave his thunder, and destroy'd them. (Ps. 18.13-14)

Alongside these concepts that, regardless of their pre-Christian origin, fit quite readily within a Christian framework, one potentially more exotic image used in the anthems is that relating to the sea. Thus, we find in Anthem 4 a verse from Psalm 93:

> The waves of the sea rage horribly, but yet the Lord who dwells on high is mightier. (Ps. 93.5)

Another more obscure example is in Anthem 10, from Psalm 29:

> It is the Lord that ruleth the sea, the Lord sitteth above the water flood, and the Lord remaineth a king forever. (Ps. 29.4a, 9)

Since the rediscovery of materials from a range of ancient Near Eastern civilizations, modern scholarship often associates the psalmic stress on calming the sea with the calming of chaos forces which are conceptualized throughout the ancient Near East in monstrous and supernatural terms. Additionally, in a specific example of such conceptualization, it is common to attribute the imagery in Psalm 29 (cited above) to the psalmist's re-use of a hymn originally written to the Ugaritic storm-god Baal.[18] But in the eighteenth century where no such background information was available, the idea of God having power over the sea might well be deemed comforting to members of a maritime nation for which the sea was a significant factor in both politics and trade. As long as the Lord whom Britons worshipped was the Lord who ruled the sea, they could presumably rely on his favour when it came to their seafaring activities, including battles with their European neighbours.[19]

As is the case for the anthems of praise, examples of generic expressions can be given from the more meditative anthems. The language of Psalm 51 in Anthem 3 is a classic expression of the sinner pleading for forgiveness from a merciful deity:

> Have mercy upon me, O God after thy great goodness: according to the multitude of thy mercies do away mine offences. (Ps. 51.1)

---

18. A helpful summary of this scholarly position, together with some additional bibliography, can be found in Dennis Pardee and Nancy Pardee, 'Gods of Glory Ought to Thunder: The Canaanite Matrix of Psalm 29', in *Psalm 29 through Time and Tradition*, ed. Lowell K. Handy (Cambridge: James Clark & Co., 2009), 115–25.

19. An alternative way of reading this maritime imagery is to understand the raging sea as a metaphor for the floods of raging enemies that potentially threaten the Lord and his chosen ones, a threat to which the Lord is more than equal. See, for example, J. Clutterbuck, *A brief explanation of the obscure phrases in the book of Psalms, collected out of the writings of the Right Revd Bishop Patrick the Reverend Doctor Henry Hammond, and others. Together with the titles and arguments of each psalm* (London: William Keblewhite, at the Swan in St. Paul's Church-Yard, 1702), 87 (on Ps. 93).

And even a text like this one from Psalm 42 in Anthem 6 can readily be parsed in Christian terms:

> Now when I think thereupon, I pour out my heart by myself, for I went with the multitude and brought them out into the house of God;
> In the voice of praise and thanksgiving among such as keep holy-day. (Ps. 42.4-5)

The 'house of God', presumably an Israelite temple, can be understood in terms of a Christian church, and 'holy-days' are observed by Christians just as they were by the psalmist.

It should be said, of course, that the generic flavour of the texts is partly a function of using an English, Christian translation which renders the original psalm texts in a way that fits with how the translation's target audience conceptualizes its religious understanding. This is particularly evident in two terms that appear in the foregoing examples, namely, 'saints' and 'heathen'. 'Saints' appears four times in the anthems, in verses taken directly from the Coverdale translation of the Psalms, that is, in Pss. 30.4; 89.5, 7; and 97.10. Given Coverdale's known reliance on versions other than the Hebrew,[20] the term 'saints' is probably based on the Vulgate rendering *sanctus* which appears in all four of these verses. In a Christian context the term 'saint' means either the faithful departed who are alive in heaven with God, or the faithful believers here on earth. This is not necessarily, however, what the underlying Hebrew texts of these verses mean. In two of the four verses (Pss. 30.4; 97.10), the Hebrew term underlying the English word 'saints' is חסידיו, which could reasonably be rendered 'his (i.e. God's) saints' in the sense of 'his faithful ones'. But in the other two verses (Pss. 89.5, 7) the Hebrew term underlying 'saints' is קדשים, 'holy ones', and in the context this is much more likely to refer to heavenly beings who are not – and who never have been – human. The term 'saints' here thus disguises the true nature of the Hebrew text in a way that makes it seem much more obviously Christian than it actually is.

A similar comment could be made about the term 'heathen', which appears twice in the anthems (once in Anthem 4 and once in Anthem 8), both times in verses taken from Psalm 96 (vv. 3, 10). 'Heathen' is another loaded term that has distinctly Christian overtones, and in Psalm 96 it is a rendition of the Latin *gens*, which in turn renders the Greek ἔθνος (from the Septuagint). The underlying Hebrew is גוי, with its overtones of

---

20. For a brief description of the main characteristics of Coverdale's translation, especially of the Psalms, see Gordon Campbell, *Bible: The Story of the King James Version, 1611–2011* (Oxford: Oxford University Press, 2010), 15–18.

non-Israelite nations, so to that extent 'heathen' is a comparable concept in that it makes a binary division between insiders and outsiders, those who are like us and those who are not. Nevertheless, its Christian overtones make it anachronistic in a translation of the Psalms. This is powerfully highlighted in the explanatory comment reported by Clutterbuck on the phrase 'Say among the heathen' in Ps. 96.10:

> Let the People of the *Jews* instruct the *Heathen* World in these great Articles of their Creed, concerning God the Father, and God the Son, &c.[21]

The comment paints the psalmist and his contemporaries as proto-Christians who would be in a position to convey to the rest of the world some at least of the truths of the Christian faith. It thus equates non-Christian cultures with heathen, a stance that would have been meaningful to the Christian readership for which the translation was prepared, but which makes no sense in the original context of the Psalms.

The real fascination, though, is with what does *not* find its way into the anthem texts. Very few of the psalms used are set in their entirety because they are simply too long. This means that a selection of verses has to be made, and when we look at the psalms in their complete forms as opposed to the edited highlights that appear in the Chandos Anthems, it is noticeable that certain elements are absent from the anthems as compared with the full biblical text – or, indeed, with earlier anthems based on the same and other psalms.

The first of these missing elements is what might be termed 'ritualism'. Despite the psalms from which the anthems are composed containing references to ritualistic activity, those references are not included in the anthems. A good example is Ps. 51.7, 'Purge me with hyssop and I shall be clean; wash me, and I shall be whiter than snow'. The commentator John Clutterbuck in his comments on this verse remarks, '*Hyssop* and *Water* were appointed by God in all solemn Purifications (*Levit.* 14. 6. *Numb.* 19. 17, 18.) as a Sign and Seal of Inward Cleansing'.[22] The biblical references given here in parentheses are to the ceremonies of cleansing for lepers and for people affected by corpse contamination, both of which involve using hyssop to sprinkle the ritual detergent on the person to be cleansed. The Chandos version of this psalm, however, omits the reference to 'purification with hyssop', even though it is included in the version of the psalm that is said during the liturgy of Commination at the beginning of Lent and in the version which is said once a month as the psalms are

21. Clutterbuck, *A Brief Explanation*, 90.
22. Ibid., 43.

read through from beginning to end on a thirty-day cycle. Interestingly, a setting of Psalm 51 by Pelham Humphrey, a Chapel Royal composer of the 1660s and 70s, includes v. 7 and the reference to cleansing with hyssop; but John Weldon, a Chapel Royal man from about 1700, omits it, using a selection of verses to which Handel's text corresponds almost exactly.[23] This points to the omission of the verse as something deliberate on Handel's part.

Nor are there any references to sacrifice in the Chandos Anthems, even though such references appear in other composers' anthems. The only possible exception to this observation is a reference in Anthem 10 to an 'oblation', taken from Ps. 27.7:

> I will offer in his dwelling an oblation with great gladness, I will sing and speak praises unto the Lord.

It is true that the underlying Hebrew does speak of 'sacrificing joyful sacrifices' and so clearly has a ritual action in mind; but by using the terminology of 'offering an oblation' Coverdale's translation obscures the literal force of the language,[24] so that what is offered can then be interpreted as the praises mentioned in the second half of the verse. In addition, references to the divine 'tabernacle' or 'temple' or 'dwelling', as here, can readily be equated with the Christian place of worship without necessarily implying any particularly ritualistic activity. In this respect, then, for all the extravagance of their musical settings the Chandos Anthems display a decidedly low-church theology.

It is also noteworthy that nowhere in the Chandos Anthem texts is there any terminology relating to biblical characters and places; thus, there is no mention of Israel or Judah or Zion or Jerusalem or David or Moses or of any other biblical person or place who appears in the Psalms from which the anthem texts are taken. This is in contrast with some other composers' anthems; it is also in contrast with Handel's later Israelite oratorio libretti, where the whole premise of the works is that eighteenth-century Britain is the modern equivalent of biblical Israel – in other words, the Protestant Britons are God's chosen people, surrounded by heathen idolatrous (i.e. Catholic) peoples, but enjoying God's protection against those heathen idolatrous peoples so long as they maintain the

---

23. The words for both these anthems are in *Divine Harmony*, 21–2.

24. Compare the Latin, *Circuivi, et immolavi in tabernaculo eius hostiam vociferationis*; and the LXX, ἐκύκλωσα καὶ ἔθυσα ἐν τῇ σκηνῇ αὐτοῦ θυσίαν ἀλαλαγμοῦ. Both of these versions use explicitly sacrificial vocabulary, *immolavi* and *hostiam* in the Vulgate and ἔθυσα and θυσίαν in the LXX.

true faith and rely on God.[25] In the oratorios, the whole point is to speak of biblical people and places because they are seen as in some sense representing the people of Britain. No such paradigm is evident in the Chandos Anthems, though. To be fair, in the majority of cases, there is no such mention in the source texts for a given anthem, which may in itself be one of the features that dictated Handel's choice of those particular psalms as a source. Nevertheless, there are some cases where it seems fairly obvious that a potential such reference has been passed over when selecting verses for inclusion. One example is Anthem 7, which is based on Psalm 89. In the full text of the psalm, laced in between the verses that have been chosen for the anthem are other verses that include references to David, Rahab (translated as 'Egypt' in the Coverdale version), Tabor and Hermon, none of which have been included in the anthem.[26]

But the most fascinating and, dare I say, most significant omissions of specific Old Testament names are in Anthems 9 and 11. Anthem 9 is based on Psalms 135, 117 and 148 in Tate and Brady's metrical translation. The first four movements of the anthem are Psalm 135, vv. 1-3 and 5, omitting v. 4. In Tate and Brady the omitted verse reads:

> For God his own peculiar choice
> The sons of Jacob makes;
> And Isr'el's offspring for his own
> Most valu'd treasure takes.

The equivalent in the Coverdale (Prayer-Book) version reads:

> For why? The Lord hath chosen Jacob unto himself: and Israel for his own possession.

Omitting this verse from the anthem therefore means that explicit references to the historical, Israelite context for which the psalm was originally written are removed, allowing the fiction that it is a specifically Christian composition to be preserved. But there is another suggestive consideration. When the Chandos Anthems were being written in 1717–18, the

---

25. See Ruth Smith, *Handel's Oratorios and Eighteenth-Century Thought* (Cambridge: Cambridge University Press, 1995); Deborah W. Rooke, *Handel's Israelite Oratorio Libretti: Sacred Drama and Biblical Exegesis* (Oxford: Oxford University Press, 2012), esp. xxi.

26. Another composer, Mr Goldwin, similarly omitted the references to David and to Tabor and Hermon, but included the reference to Egypt in his setting (*Divine Harmony*, 12).

Jacobite riots of 1715 were not that far away, and there was continuing tension over the fact that the German Protestant Hanoverian King George I, who succeeded Queen Anne in 1714, had displaced the legitimate Stuart (though Catholic) line from the British throne while the Stuart heir James was alive in exile. Given the fact that 'Jacobus' is the Latin equivalent of the name 'James', giving rise to the terminology of 'Jacobites' for supporters of James Stuart's cause, it seems a real possibility that the reference to 'Jacob' in this verse of the psalm was what caused it to be omitted from Handel's anthem. Indeed, the Tate and Brady paraphrase makes the reference even more pointed than it is in the Prayer Book; the paraphrase speaks of God making the '*sons* of Jacob' his own peculiar choice, which in the context is as good as saying that not just the individual James but his entire line were chosen for the throne. Little wonder, then, that the verse does not appear in Handel's anthem.

This is, of course, an argument from silence, and without further supporting evidence it is notoriously difficult to prove the intentionality of absences. But there is another place in the Anthems where the intentionality of the omission is difficult to refute. This is in Anthem 11, which uses Psalm 68 and then a single verse from Psalm 76, and has the following text:

> Let God arise, and let his enemies be scatter'd; let them also that hate him, flee before him.
> Like as the smoke vanisheth, so shalt thou drive them away; like as wax melteth at the fire, so let the ungodly perish at the presence of God.
> Let the righteous be glad, and rejoice before God; let them also be merry and joyful.
> O sing unto God, and sing praises unto his name.
> Praised be the Lord! At thy rebuke, O God, both the chariot and the horse are fall'n.
> Blessed be God. Alleluja.

As it stands, this is a perfectly generic expression of God's support for the righteous and punishment of the 'ungodly', as the language of the Prayer Book has it, giving no intimation of precisely who the righteous and the ungodly are. But two considerations hint at a more political significance for the anthem. The first is that Ps. 68.1a in Latin – *exurgat Deus, dissipentur inimici* – was used several times as a motto on coins, initially by Mary Queen of Scots in 1565, then by James I in 1603–4 on his accession to the English throne, and later by Charles I during the Civil War when he had his capital in Oxford (and a mint in the city's New Inn Hall St) (1642–46). All were periods when the monarch's position was insecure, and so all three monarchs used the monetary motto to declare their God-given legitimacy.[27] The second consideration is that when we compare the text of Handel's anthem with the Prayer-Book version of the psalm from which it is taken, there is one small but important omission. The first four movements are taken almost exactly from Ps. 68.1-4a, except that the setting of v. 3 drops the word 'But' with which the Prayer-Book text begins. The final movement, though, 'Praised be the Lord!', consists of Ps. 76.6 bookended by laudatory phrases, and this is where our interest is piqued. Between the movement's opening and closing expressions of praise, the text that is taken from Ps. 76.6 reads like this:

At thy rebuke, O God, both the chariot and the horse are fall'n.

But the full text of Ps. 76.6 found in the *Book of Common Prayer* is,

At thy rebuke, O God of Jacob: both the chariot and horse are fallen.

It seems fairly evident that the reference to Jacob here has been deliberately dropped from Handel's text. That could be because it links the text too closely to its ancient (i.e. pre-Christian) context. But it could also be because it risked linking the text too closely to the recent context, in which talk of the God *of Jacob* rebuking human cavalry, together with the prayer for God's (that is, the king's) enemies to be scattered, might be seen as expressing approval of those who had attempted to disrupt the establishment of a Protestant monarchy by putting the exiled James Stuart on the throne.[28] The Hanoverian rule was still in its infancy, unpopular and politically vulnerable, and James Brydges was dependent on its favour for his elevated social status. Given the influential circles in which Brydges moved, his physical and political proximity to the royal court, and the flow of eminent guests through his establishment at Cannons, the last thing he needed was for the equilibrium of his position to be disturbed by a carelessly worded anthem. So, by means of a politically significant psalm combined with some discreet textual editing, Handel's anthem not only avoids any possible offence to the Hanoverian king but also embodies a dramatic declaration of God's power to overcome that king's

---

27. For comments on the phrase's use on coins of James I and Charles I, see F. Stroud, 'Brief Musings on the Exurgat Money', *BNJ* 1 (1903): 163–7.

28. Compare Howard Cox's listing of this omission as a 'minor contraction' under the heading of 'Omissions for Brevity', presumably for metrical or artistic reasons (Cox, 'Handel's Text Selection', 30).

enemies,[29] thereby safeguarding the positions of both Handel and Brydges with regard to their future relationships with the monarchy.

It is also worth briefly considering Handel's musical setting of these words from Psalm 76, a setting which by its wonderful tone-painting contributes enormously to the drama of that declaration. The text may originate from an Israelite monarchic-era psalm, but the musical idiom is pure eighteenth-century opera, and in an era when cavalry (though, admittedly, not chariotry) was still very much a part of warfare the anthem's original audience would have little difficulty in seeing a contemporary scenario pictured in the anthem. Particularly striking are repeated descending melismatic motifs illustrating the word 'fall'n' that run through both the vocal and the instrumental parts, with the polyphonic fugal style of the composition evoking a chaotic scene of massed horses and chariots collapsing into disarray. Equally effective, though in the opposite manner, is the four-times repeated homophonic statement 'fall'n' followed each time by two beats' rest (fall'n – fall'n – fall'n – fall'n), and the section's dramatic ending with a decisive block-harmony declaration that 'both the chariot and horse are fall'n'. The effect is of the Lord's rebuke throwing the enemy cavalry into utter turmoil, which gradually subsides until the last of the foe falls still and silent and the victors declare the battle won. Whether or not the defeat of Jacobite forces was at the back of Handel's mind for this composition, it is not hard to imagine it being evoked in the minds of his audience.

Much more could be said about the Chandos Anthems and their use of texts from the Psalms, as also about their musical exegesis of those texts, but enough has been said to give a sense of how in the Anthems material that could well have originated in eighth- or seventh-century BCE Israel has been presented in the verbal and musical idioms current in seventeenth- and eighteenth-century CE England and thereby given new meaning; in other words, how texts from an ancient religious and cultural milieu have been re-imagined in a manner that speaks to their subsequent readers and hearers, thereby bridging the gap of two millennia between such texts' origins and their Handelian re-use. This type of analysis, it seems to me, is at the heart of the reception historical enterprise: first, working to gain a critical understanding of the biblical text in its historical context, and then looking to establish not only *how* the text has been

---

29. It is interesting to observe that Ps. 76 refers to God's miraculous protection of Zion from enemy attack; so using Ps. 76.6, in which God disempowers the enemy troops besieging Zion, has a particular resonance for an anthem asserting the current king's divinely approved right to rule in the context of a recent unsuccessful military challenge to his reign.

re-imagined in subsequent eras but *why* it has been so re-imagined. As a central element in Christian devotion, the Psalms have a particularly rich and fascinating history of re-use, to which Professor Gillingham has sought to draw our attention in a critical and yet imaginative way; and I hope that this short study in her honour on a small corner of that history of re-use is sufficiently critical and imaginative to be able to fill out a little more of the picture she has been drawing.

Bibliography

Baker, C. H. Collins, and Muriel I. Baker. *The Life and Circumstances of James Brydges, First Duke of Chandos, Patron of the Liberal Arts*. Oxford: Clarendon, 1949.
Beeks, Graydon. 'The Chandos Anthems and Te Deum of George Frideric Handel (1685–1759)'. Ph.D. diss., University of California Berkeley, 1981.
Burrows, Donald. *Handel*. 2nd ed. The Master Musicians. Oxford: Oxford University Press, 2012.
Burrows, Donald. *Handel and the English Chapel Royal*. Oxford Studies in British Church Music. Oxford: Oxford University Press, 2005.
Campbell, Gordon. *Bible: The Story of the King James Version, 1611–2011*. Oxford: Oxford University Press, 2010.
Clutterbuck, J. *A brief explanation of the obscure phrases in the book of Psalms, collected out of the writings of the Right Revd Bishop Patrick, the Reverend Doctor Henry Hammond, and others. Together with the titles and arguments of each psalm*. London: William Keblewhite, at the Swan in St. Paul's Church-Yard, 1702.
Cox, Howard. 'Handel's Text Selection Procedures in the Chandos Anthems'. *Bach* 24, no. 1 (1993): 21–34.
Divine Harmony; or a New Collection of Select Anthems, Us'd at Her Majesty's Chappels Royal, Westminster Abby, St. Pauls, Windsor, Both Universities, Eaton, and Most Cathedrals in Her Majesty's Dominions. Publish'd with the Approbation of the Subdean of Her Majesty's Chappel Royal, and of Several of the Greatest Masters. London: printed and sold by S. Keble at the Turks-Head in Fleetstreet, C. King in Westminster-Hall, and J. Hazard, at the Golden Bible in Stationers Court near Ludgate, 1712.
Downes, Kerry. 'Cannons'. In *The Cambridge Handel Encyclopedia*. Edited by Annette Landgraf and David Vickers. Cambridge: Cambridge University Press, 2009.
Dunlop, Ian. 'Cannons, Middlesex: A Conjectural Reconstruction'. *Country Life*, 30 December 1949, 1950–4.
'Hallett, William Snr & Jnr (1730-d.1767)'. *British and Irish Furniture Makers Online*, https://bifmo.history.ac.uk/entry/hallett-william-snr-1707-81.
Johnson, Joan. 'Brydges, James, first duke of Chandos (1674–1744)'. In *Oxford Dictionary of National Biography*. Rev. ed. Oxford: Oxford University Press. 23 September 2010.
Pardee, Dennis, and Nancy Pardee. 'Gods of Glory Ought to Thunder: The Canaanite Matrix of Psalm 29'. Pages 115–25 in *Psalm 29 through Time and Tradition*. Edited by Lowell K. Handy. Cambridge: James Clark & Co., 2009.
Rooke, Deborah W. *Handel's Israelite Oratorio Libretti: Sacred Drama and Biblical Exegesis*. Oxford: Oxford University Press, 2012.
Ross, Angus. 'Arbuthnot [Arbuthnott], John'. In *Oxford Dictionary of National Biography*. Rev. ed. Oxford: Oxford University Press. 23 September 2004.

Smith, Ruth. *Handel's Oratorios and Eighteenth-Century Thought.* Cambridge: Cambridge University Press, 1995.

Stroud, F. 'Brief Musings on the Exurgat Money'. *BNJ* 1 (1903): 163–7.

Tate, Nahum, and Nicholas Brady. *A New Version of the Psalms of David, in English Metre, fitted for Public Use*. London: T. Hodgkin for the Company of Stationers, 1696.

Visualizing Psalm 23:
Pastoral Idylls, Protectors and Shadows of Death

Natasha O'Hear

Introduction

It is an honour to be a participant in this volume celebrating Professor Sue Gillingham. I was lucky enough to be an undergraduate student of Sue's at Worcester College, Oxford in the 2000s and later her research assistant and colleague as I was undertaking doctoral and post-doctoral work. I consider her as one of my foremost academic mentors and also as a dear friend. Her encouragement and support of young female academics in particular has been second to none in the field of Theology, a fact that is attested to by the number of her ex-students who are active in academic Theology today (as well as in associated fields).

However, this volume celebrates Gillingham not as a tutor and mentor but as a leading scholar of the Psalms, as well as something of a pioneer in the field of biblical reception history. Her multi-volume Wiley-Blackwell Commentary on the Psalms, an undertaking of Herculean proportions, will soon be complete.[1] It is an invaluable guide to the multifaceted Jewish, Christian and cultural history of the Psalms. As well as her more in-depth study of Psalms 1 and 2, Gillingham has also written several illuminating articles on her approach to reception history.[2]

---

1. Susan E. Gillingham, *Psalms Through the Centuries, Vol. 1*, Blackwell Bible Commentaries (Malden: Blackwell, 2008), and *Psalms Through the Centuries. Volume 2*, Wiley-Blackwell Bible Commentaries (Chichester: Wiley-Blackwell, 2018). Volume 3 is forthcoming in 2022.

2. Susan E. Gillingham, *Jewish and Christian Approaches to the Psalms: Conflict and Convergence* (Oxford: Oxford University Press, 2013); Gillingham, 'Biblical

Exploration of the visual history of the Psalms has been a key part of Gillingham's approach to their reception and there is a section on the visual reception of each Psalm in Volume 2 of the Blackwell Commentary. She argues that the visual reception of the Psalms offers us an important (alternative) perspective on these texts and how they have been 'viewed' and used throughout their complex history.[3] As a visual reception historian (more usually accustomed to working with Revelation and other apocalyptic texts) it made sense for me to engage with the visual history of a Psalm for this contribution. Having selected Psalm 23 on the basis of its rich and varied visual history, as well as its status as a 'cultural icon', I was able to use Gillingham's own meticulous research into its visual history as a springboard into some further explorations of two particular visual strands.[4] The first strand relates to the different traditions that arose within medieval manuscript illustrations of the Psalter, as well as later Psalms cycles. After the *Utrecht Psalter* of c. 820–30, which visualized the Psalm in its entirety, we see different elements of the Psalm (what we might crudely refer to as the 'positive' or pastoral versus the darker dimensions) being given visual emphasis according to the interpretative emphases of the different Psalms cycles. Secondly, I will explore some highlights from the visual history of the motif of the 'valley of the shadow of death' (Ps. 23.4), a motif that eventually becomes decontextualized from the Psalm itself. The historical context of each visualization is considered in order to facilitate exploration both of the way in which it functioned as an interpretation of Psalm 23 within its own context, as well as the ways that it may continue to illuminate the Psalm for us today (something that I

Studies on Holiday? A Personal View of Reception History', in *Reception History and Biblical Studies: Theory and Practice*, ed. Emma England and William John Lyons, LHBOTS 615/Scriptural Traces 6 (London: T&T Clark, 2015), 3–13; Gillingham, 'Reception History, Biblical Studies and the Issue of Multivalency: Annual Aquinas Lecture, Faculty of Theology, University of Malta', *Melita Theoligica* 68 (2018): 1–15. Gillingham reflects helpfully on the young discipline of reception criticism in Gillingham, 'Biblical Studies on Holiday?', 22–7. She gives an overview of four of the main criticisms leveled at the field, as well as ways of 'doing' reception history in a way that avoids common pitfalls.

3. See Gillingham, 'Reception History, Biblical Studies and the Issue of Multifvalency', 6, 8.

4. Mark Roncace, 'Psalm 23 as Cultural Icon', 2019, https://www.bibleodyssey.org/en/passages/related-articles/psalm-23-as-cultural-icon; see also Karl Jacobson, 'Through the Pistol Smoke Dimly: Psalm 23 in Contemporary Film and Song', in *SBL Forum*, 2009, http://sbl-site.org/Article.aspx?ArticleID=796.

refer to in my own work as *visual exegesis*).⁵ Most of the visual examples are drawn from the Western Christian tradition with two examples woven in from the Jewish tradition.

Psalm 23: The Text and Its History

Gillingham rightly stresses the importance of keeping the biblical text firmly in view when 'doing reception history', lest it turn into 'the reception of the interpreters' rather than the reception of the text.⁶ This is what she is referring to when she talks of the 'critical imagination'. Exploration of the history of imaginative engagement with the Psalms must always be brought back to the text itself in order to maintain the 'critical' dimension.

Gillingham's section on Psalm 23 in her Wiley-Blackwell Commentary provides an excellent overview of the text of Psalm 23 and its non-visual reception.⁷ In short, by virtue of its use in funeral services since the early twentieth century, Psalm 23 is now usually associated with death and 'the next life'.⁸ However, prior to the twentieth century, this short and lyrical psalm of only six verses, which oscillates between states of calm joy and darkness, had more varied connotations. What we now take to be the well-known 'valley of the shadow of death' of Ps. 23.4 comes from the Hebrew, צלמות, meaning deep or death-like shadow.⁹ It was the Greek and Latin translations that changed the meaning to an encounter with death, rather than just darkness, although the emphasis was very much on having the encounter in this life, rather than the next. Similarly, the reference to 'returning' (Hebrew) or 'dwelling' (Greek/Latin) with God in 23.6 was understood in the sense of having had a close encounter with death but now being safe for the rest of one's days. Thus, for most of its history, it was understood as a pastoral Psalm about confidence and trust in God

---

5. See Natasha O'Hear and Anthony O'Hear, *Picturing the Apocalypse: The Book of Revelation in the Arts over Two Millennia* (Oxford: Oxford University Press, 2015), 284–7. See also J. Cheryl Exum, *Art as Biblical Commentary: Visual Criticism from Hagar the Wife of Abraham to Mary the Mother of Jesus*, LHBOTS 694 (London: Bloomsbury T&T Clark, 2019).

6. Gillingham, 'Biblical Studies on Holiday?', 21.

7. Gillingham, *Psalms Through the Centuries*, 2:144–53.

8. Brent A. Strawn, 'The Lord Is My Shepherd (Ps 23)', 2019, https://www.bibleodyssey.org/passages/main-articles/lord-is-my-shepherd.

9. Gillingham, *Psalms Through the Centuries*, 2:145.

(akin to Pss. 16 and 22).[10] It was when the Psalm was included in the order for the burial of the dead in the *Book of Common Prayer* (alongside Pss. 39 and 90) from 1928 onwards that it became widely read in a metaphorical sense as referring entirely to the life beyond.[11]

Jewish interpreters framed the Psalm as representing the experience of hope in exile as well as later the hope for restoration.[12] In several New Testament texts, Jesus is cast as the Shepherd-protector of Ps. 23.1-2 (see Jn 10.11; 1 Pet. 2.25; 5.4; Rev. 7.17), although early Christian writers were more interested in the sacramental qualities of the Psalm, and, from Origen onwards, in its potential practical and pastoral applications (building on the sheep/church and Shepherd/Christ typology).[13] Although the Psalm was not used in the burial liturgy until 1928, certain verses were used as antiphons and the whole Psalm often used in prayers before the Eucharist. In the Jewish tradition Psalm 23 was also integrated into the funeral service at the end of the nineteenth century, and before that had been prominent in customs connected with meals.[14]

As Gillingham elucidates, Psalm 23 has had a lively musical history, as well as a significant literary one. Bunyan's use of the journeying theme of vv. 4ff. and the specific motif of the 'valley of the shadow of death', in his *Pilgrim's Progress* of 1678, had a far-reaching literary and wider cultural impact.[15] Two images from the many illustrated editions of the *Pilgrim's Progress* will be considered below. Tennyson's use of the motif of the 'valley of the shadow of death' in Stanza 1 of his *Charge of the Light Brigade* of 1854 will also be considered below in relation to a photographic image from the Crimean War. Gillingham summarizes some of the many (and occasionally surprising) uses of Psalm 23 in popular culture, such as in the films *Titanic* (1997) and *Dangerous Minds* (1995), and Roncace and Jacobson present some additional strands of popular reception (such as in hip-hop music) in their respective articles.[16]

10. Strawn, 'The Lord Is My Shepherd (Ps 23)'.
11. There is some is some scattered evidence that Ps. 23 was used as a Psalm of consolation for those facing martyrdom or death prior to the twentieth century (Hannibal Hamlin, *Psalm Culture and Early Modern English Literature* [Cambridge: Cambridge University Press, 2004], 167–8).
12. Gillingham, *Psalms Through the Centuries*, 2:146.
13. Ibid., 147.
14. Ibid., 148.
15. See Hamlin, *Psalm Culture and Early Modern English Literature*, 165–8. See also David Jasper, 'The Twenty-Third Psalm in English Literature', *Religion & Literature* 30 (1998): 1–11.
16. Gillingham, *Psalms Through the Centuries*, 2:152–3; Roncace, 'Psalm 23 as Cultural Icon'; and Jacobson, 'Through the Pistol Smoke Dimly'.

Visualizing Psalm 23

A Google image search of Psalm 23 or its opening line, 'The Lord is My Shepherd' reveals a plethora of kitsch images featuring some or all of the text of Psalm 23 overlaid over bucolic images of lakes, sheep and shepherds (who themselves resemble the archetypical Western Jesus). While these images bear little resemblance to the strands of the historical visual reception of Psalm 23 that we will explore below, they do have a link with the earliest known images connected with the Psalm. Images of a Hellenized 'Christ-as-Shepherd' were found at the third-century Priscilla Catacombs in Rome. They were inspired by the Early Christian identification of Christ as the Shepherd-protector who is described and addressed throughout the Psalm.[17] The 'Christ-as-Shepherd' visual motif was rarely taken up by the Medieval Psalters in their visualizations of Psalm 23 (see the *Stuttgart Psalter* below as a notable exception), but was of interest to many later artists such as William Blake (*The Shepherd*, 1789), Eastman Johnson (in his politically charged post-emancipation painting, *The Lord is My Shepherd* of 1863), and many pastoral works, such as *The Sunday at Home*, an illustrated version of Psalm 23 from 1880. *The Sunday at Home: A Family Magazine for Sabbath Reading* was a weekly magazine published by the Religious Tract Society in London (from 1854–1940). As one might expect, the images accompanying Psalm 23 in this publication are two rather clichéd depictions of a Christ-like shepherd leading his sheep across imagined 'biblical' landscapes. This tradition perhaps reaches its zenith in Walter Sallman's *The Lord is My Shepherd* of 1943, prints of which still hang in Sunday school classrooms and even children's bedrooms across America.[18] Such images, part of devotional visual culture, are the iconographical precursors to the aforementioned montages of Psalm 23 available via a Google Image search today.[19]

While tracing the visual history of the 'Christ-as-shepherd' motif is interesting, its path is somewhat fragmented and it is not always clear whether the artists in question are drawing on Psalm 23, John 10 or Revelation 7. More interesting in interpretative terms is the rich visual

---

17. See Ethel Ross Barker, 'The Symbolism of Certain Catacomb Frescoes-I', article, *The Burlington Magazine for Connoisseurs* 24, no. 127 (1913): 43–5, 47–50, 48. See also Steve Werlin, 'Shepherds in the Bible and in Art', 2019. https://www.bibleodyssey.org/passages/related-articles/shepherds-in-the-bible-and-in-art.

18. David Morgan, *Visual Piety: A History and Theory of Popular Religious Images* (Berkeley: University of California Press, 1998), 21.

19. See also Oxford artist Roger Wagner's image of Ps. 23 which features a woodcut of Christ-as-Shepherd herding sheep (Roger Wagner, *The Book of Praises: A Translation of the Psalms* [Oxford: Besalel Press, 1994]).

reception of the Psalm found in illustrated Psalters from the ninth century onwards. I have grouped my chosen medieval images of Psalm 23 (from the *Utrecht, Stuttgart, Parma* and *Luttrell Psalters* respectively) together with some images from two twentieth-century Psalms cycles into one strand. Images taken from a Psalms cycle (in which at least thirty Psalms are visualized) are necessarily very different from 'stand alone' images, or images from different cycles, such as the illustrated *Pilgrim's Progress*. Illustrated Psalters and Psalms cycles are not intended to be viewed in isolation and have to be understood as part of a series of images tackling the daunting task of visualizing this set of non-narrative poems. What also unites these visual interpretations of Psalm 23 is their (with the exception of the *Stuttgart Psalter*) emphasis on the 'this worldly' and 'positive' aspects of the Psalm. The 'valley of the shadow of death' (of Ps. 23.4) is alluded to in some of the images but not allowed to dominate the visual field. This stands in contrast to our second main strand of visualizations, those images which focus only on the 'valley of the shadow of death'.

Illustrated Psalters: An Overview

There are many extant Psalters from around the ninth to the fifteenth centuries, testament to their popularity and the sense of prestige attached to them during this period. Illustrated Psalms cycles could of course appear within illustrated Bibles but stand-alone Psalters were more common.[20] There were liturgical Psalters for use in the Liturgy of the Hours and Canonical Psalters for private devotion. These 'Canonical Psalters' were divided into five sections, with Psalms 1, 41, 72, 89 and 106 all marking new sections (although later they would be divided into as many as ten sections). Psalters for lay use tended to be the most lavishly illustrated and also often served as a primer for learning letters.[21]

In the later medieval period, in the Latin Psalters, certain iconographic conventions began to become more prominent. For example, the opening initial of the Psalms became more ornate and marginalia of animals and other items, such as trumpets, began to be included. Prefatory miniatures, such as life cycles of Christ and Lives of the Virgin, were included in many

---

20. See Rosemary Muir Wright, 'Introducing the Medieval Psalter', in *Studies in the Illustration of the Psalter*, ed. Brendan Cassidy and Rosemary Muir Wright (Stamford, UK: Shaun Tyas, 2000), 1–11; and Sally Dormer, 'Illuminated Psalter Manuscripts', Transcript of Lecture given at the Museum of London on 29 May 2012, https://www.gresham.ac.uk/lectures-and-events/illuminated-psalter-manuscripts for introductory material on Medieval Psalters.

21. Wright, 'Introducing the Medieval Psalter', 5.

Psalters from the twelfth century onwards, evidence of the popularity of the 'typological way' of reading the Psalms. Typological readings of the Psalms were often echoed by illustrators in their visualizations. Other illustrators were more preoccupied with the figure of David while others made visual links between the Psalms and historical or contemporary events.

Perhaps the most common way in which the task of visualization was approached, however, was via 'literal' illustrations, which were designed to elucidate the meaning of the Psalms texts for the reader, and possibly serve as mnemonic aids. 'Literal' is something of a vexed term in studies of the Illustrated Psalter, both because it can be applied to many different ways of illustrating a Psalm (from expansive images that attempt to cover the whole Psalm to images that focus on only one 'literal' detail) and because it implies a mode of illustration akin to that of the literal narrative illustration.[22] In a literal medieval illustration of a biblical narrative, such as the opening of the first four seals of Rev. 6.2-8 in the thirteenth-century *Trinity Apocalypse*, for example, one finds a sequence of images (f. 5v-6v) that closely follow the detail of the text. The illustrations of the Four Horsemen unfold episodically and chronologically. Different versions and translations of Rev. 6.2-8 tend not to produce very different images because the overall narrative remains broadly identical. But the Psalms are different. They are (on the whole) non-narrative and tend to reflect and evoke human emotion rather than events. As Freeman Sandler argues, 'Direct illustration of the [Psalms] text produces not narrative but word images'.[23] And different translations of the Psalms produce quite different 'word images'. Thus scholars of illustrated Psalters tend to speak in terms of *imagines verborum*, or word pictures generated by specific words or phrases in a Psalm.

The Utrecht Psalter, *c. 1820–30, 33 × 25.8 cm*

The *Utrecht Psalter* is widely acknowledged as one of the greatest illustrated manuscripts of the Carolingian Renaissance, not only in terms of the richness and complexity of the illustrations contained therein but

---

22. See Koert van der Horst, William Noel, and Wilhelmina C. M. Wüstefeld, *The Utrecht Psalter in Medieval Art: Picturing the Psalms of David* (London: Harvey Miller, 1996), 55–6; Wright, 'Introducing the Medieval Psalter', 7; William Noel, 'Medieval Charades and the Visual Syntax of the Utrecht Psalter', in Cassidy and Wright, eds., *Studies in the Illustration of the Psalter*, 34–41; Lucy Freeman Sandler, '"The Images of Words in Gothic English Psalters": The Saunders Lecture 1997', in Cassidy and Wright, eds., *Studies in the Illustration of the Psalter*, 67–86 (67–77).

23. Sandler, '"The Images of Words in Gothic English Psalters"', 69.

also on account of its legacy in terms of Psalter iconography.[24] It was produced at the monastery of Hautvilliers, near Reims, probably under the patronage of Archbishop Ebbo as a gift for Charlemagne's son or for his wife Judith.[25] For reasons unknown, the *Utrecht Psalter* was moved to Canterbury around 1000 and a direct line of influence can be traced to manuscripts as late as the Paris Psalter of around 1200 (MS Lat. 8846), via other key Psalters such as the eleventh-century Harley Psalter and the twelfth-century Eadwine Psalter. The illustrations found therein take specific 'word images' contained in each Psalm, and weave them into wider, well-balanced compositions, of which there are 166 in total (one for each of the 150 Psalms plus sixteen further canticles). The images appear to have moved through several stages of composition, from rough initial drawings to completion in a dilute and then a darker ink.[26] The overall effect on each page is of a wide monochrome composition placed either at the top, bottom or in the middle of three columns of Psalm text. The Psalms are all written using rustic capitals (possibly used to give the Psalter an antique appearance).[27] Noel and Van der Horst both speculate further that the images in the *Utrecht Psalter* (hereafter referred to as *Utrecht*) and its descendants would almost certainly have been used as *aides memoires* when people (both clergy and lay) meditated on the Psalms and sung them.[28] The detailed and legible nature of the compositions would have recommended themselves to this practice and no doubt contributed to the enduring appeal of the *Utrecht* iconography.

As with all of the Psalms in this manuscript, the text of Psalm 23 appears in its entirety *below* the image evoking it (Fig. 12.1, f.13r). Thus the image *precedes* the text, both literally and potentially metaphorically.[29] Starting at the upper register of the image (*Utrecht* is famed for its lively upper register, signifying the Divine realm), we see the giant hand of God stretching down from the sky in the direction of the Psalmist who is sitting just right of centre on a bank next to a stream (the 'still waters' of Ps. 23.2).

24. Van der Horst, Noel, and Wüstefeld, *The Utrecht Psalter in Medieval Art*, 55.
25. Bart Jaski, 'The Utrecht Psalter', 2013, https://bc.library.uu.nl/utrecht-psalter.html.
26. Van der Horst, Noel, and Wüstefeld, *The Utrecht Psalter in Medieval Art*, 46.
27. Ibid., 168.
28. Ibid., 81.
29. Lucy Freeman Sandler, 'The Word in the Text and the Image in the Margin: The Case of the Luttrell Psalter', *The Journal of the Walters Art Gallery* 54 (1996): 87–99 (87).

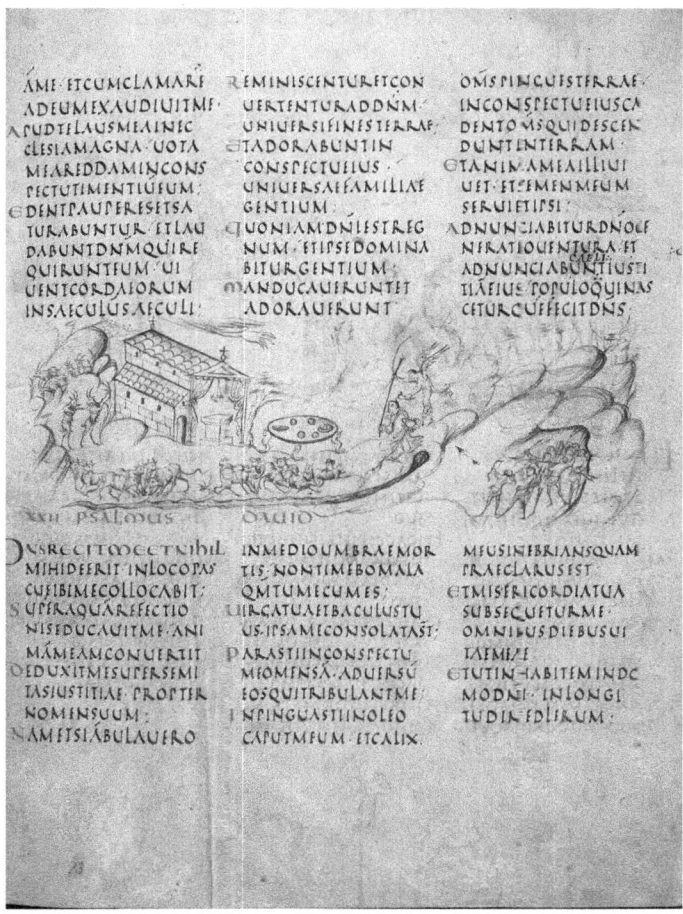

Figure 12.1. Utrecht Psalter, *Ms. 32, fol. 13r, 33 × 25.8 cm.*
Utrecht University Library.

The Psalmist holds a cup in his left hand and a staff in his right (see Ps. 23.4). The divine provenance of these items is underlined by the presence of the angel holding the staff behind the Psalmist. The angel is also anointing the Psalmist in accordance with Ps. 23.5. To the left of the composition goats, cattle and sheep graze the 'green pastures' of Ps. 23.2. These animals surround a tabernacle, an evocation of the 'house of the Lord' mentioned in Ps. 23.6. And to the right of the tabernacle, there is a table that has been prepared with food (Ps. 23.5). At the far right of the image are the 'stock enemies' of *Utrecht* firing arrows in the direction of the Psalmist (see Ps. 23.5, 'in the presence of my enemies'), who is protected from their onslaught by the cave-like structure of the bank.[30]

In interpretative terms, as with nearly all the *Utrecht* images, the inclusion of so many textual details as 'word pictures' in an elaborate landscape setting creates an interesting synchronicity. Rather than attempting to impose a linear narrative structure that doesn't exist in the text, this image presents the images described in the Psalm as all happening simultaneously, but in three distinct groupings.[31] The pastoral and feasting elements, which appear at the beginning and end of the Psalm have all been grouped together on the left of the image, the Psalmist (the uniting voice of the Psalm) appears in the middle and the 'enemies' and the 'valley of the shadow of death' are on the right. Noel argues that we would do best to view the *Utrecht* images not as literal illustrations but as 'charade illustrations', which, like charades, visualize words and phrases 'quite out of their textual context'.[32] He argues further that visual proximity in these images refers not to proximity in a spatial or temporal sense but to conceptual proximity.[33] Thus, by separating off the 'enemies' of Ps. 23.5 in the lower right-hand register of the image, their symbolic distance from God and the Psalmist is emphasized. The main visual emphasis is firmly on the idea of God and his angels as protectors and providers of peace and plenty. And the proximity of the Psalmist to the angel underlines his special status in this schema. This image of Psalm 23, therefore, whilst superficially a literal rendering of all the 'elements' of the Psalm, can be seen to convey the essence of the Psalm 23, described by Gillingham as 'confident trust in God' as both protector and provider, through its careful placement of the different 'word pictures' engendered by the text.[34]

The Stuttgart Psalter, *c. 820, 26.5 × 17.5 cm*

We turn now to a completely different yet almost contemporaneous image of Psalm 23. *The Stuttgart Psalter* was produced around 820 at another religious institution which enjoyed the patronage of Charlemagne, the scriptorium at St. Germain-des-Prés in Paris. There is, however, no clear iconographical link between these two Psalters. The Psalter contains 316 images, with many Psalms illustrated with more than one image. In

30. See 'Psalm 22', *The Annotated Utrecht Psalter*, 2013, http://psalter.library.uu.nl/page?p=32&res=1&x=0&y=0.
31. Although see Hamlin, *Psalm Culture and Early Modern English Literature*, 166, on the inherent narrative stages of Ps. 23, the 'resting place' and the 'journey'.
32. Noel, 'Medieval Charades and the Visual Syntax of the Utrecht Psalter', 37–8.
33. Ibid., 39.
34. Gillingham, *Psalms Through the Centuries*, 2:144.

contrast to the complex and highly detailed 'charade' images *Utrecht*, the images in the *Stuttgart Psalter* (hereafter referred to as *Stuttgart*) are far simpler, although not necessarily 'simple'. Only one incident or idea is visualized in each image and the style is heavier, bolder and clearer. The images have also been carefully coloured.

Figure 12.2. Stuttgart Psalter, *Cod. bibl. fol. 23, f. 28v, 26.5 × 17.5 cm. Wuerttembergische Landesbibliothek.*

The image accompanying Psalm 23 (f. 28v) takes up around one third of the page and has been inserted into the Latin text of the Psalm (Fig. 12.2). The simple composition is dominated by the central figure of the Shepherd/Christ, recognizable by his halo and crossed staff or *ferula*. The figure is rather naively conceived and has an almost classical appearance due to his draped, toga-like garments. The 'still waters' (Ps. 23.2) are represented by the stream to the right and the 'green pastures (also of Ps. 23.2) via the two green trees (drawn in very different styles). A small and pale but clearly visible snake is wrapped around the base of the right-hand tree and the Jesus/Shepherd figure appears to be subduing it with his left hand. Bradley argues that the tree represents the tree of knowledge of good and evil of Gen. 2.17 and that the serpent should be viewed through this prism as a bringer of death to humankind.[35] Thus this is a symbolic representation of Christ offering protection from the 'valley of the shadow of death' of Ps. 23.4. Bradley argues further that this image should be seen as a representation of Christ's defeat of 'eschatological death' and that the image can be seen as a gloss of the reference to the 'restoration of the soul' (*ainimam meam convertit*) in Ps. 23.3. The concept of Christ overcoming death in an eschatological sense via the defeat of a serpent is also found on f. 16v in the image accompanying Ps. 15.4, where the snake appears wound around the arm of a demon looking on in dismay as the Christ figure 'saves' three human figures.[36]

We have therefore moved some way from the more 'balanced' pastoral visualization of Psalm 23 found in *Utrecht*. And the fact that this is the only representation of Psalm 23 in this Psalter means that the image and its foregrounding of death/the serpent acquires a heightened importance. The Psalm has been distilled down to one element, that of the ability of the Shepherd/Christ to overcome death in all its aspects. The 'provider' aspect of the Shepherd/Christ that was so prominent in the *Utrecht* image, as well as the foregrounding of the pastoral imagery, has been sacrificed here.

The Parma Psalter, *c. 1280, 13.5 × 10 cm*

We move now to the Late Medieval Period and the thirteenth-century *Parma Psalter*, a very rare example of a Jewish illustrated Psalter made during a period of Jewish persecution.[37] Other Italian Hebrew Psalters were produced at this time but they were not illustrated.[38] Interestingly there is no trace here of the prohibition of human representation that characterized other Ashkenazi manuscripts of the thirteenth and fourteenth centuries.[39] The (comparatively small) *Parma Psalter* (hereafter referred to as *Parma*) boasts 102 irregularly distributed illustrations (they don't start at the beginning of the Psalter) which don't seem to follow a particular

---

35. Jill Bradley, *"You Shall Surely Not Die": The Concepts of Sin and Death as Expressed in the Manuscript Art of Northwestern Europe, c. 800–1200*, Library of the Written Word 4 (Leiden: Brill, 2008), 105.

36. Ibid., 103.

37. See Malachi Beit-Arié, Emanuel Silver, and Thérèse Metzger, *The Parma Psalter: A Thirteenth-Century Illuminated Hebrew Book of Psalms with a Commentary by Abraham Ibn Ezra* (London: Facsimile Editions, 1996). for an in-depth study of this Psalter as well as a complete facsimile of the entire work.

38. Ibid., 103.

39. Ibid.

programme.[40] Additionally there are no clear iconographic antecedents for these illustrations in the Christian Western European Psalters. The images seem rather to be responses to the individual Psalms by one artist who had a deep understanding of the Hebrew texts of the Psalms.[41] Half of the illustrations reflect a general theme found in the Psalm, while the other half visualize a single unit of text (or single, motif, figure or instrument). There are some common themes across the illustrations. Landscape plays a very important part in determining the overall mood of the image. More distinctive is the artist's frequent use of human figures, humanized animal figures and animal-faced human figures. It is not easy to determine the function of these figures. They often represent believers at prayer, leaders of the choir and singers. Beit-Arié et al. suggest that their presence conveys 'the idea – which pervades the Psalms – that every creature participates in some way in the universal praise of God's glory'.[42]

Whatever their function, the inclusion of these figures makes the *Parma* illustrations distinctive, and as Gillingham states, almost serves to 'jollify' the image accompanying Psalm 23.[43] Gone is the identification of the Shepherd figure with Christ that we witnessed in *Stuttgart*. Here we see a human figure with an animal head wearing a round brown hat with a distinctive rim (Fig. 12.3 f. 29a).

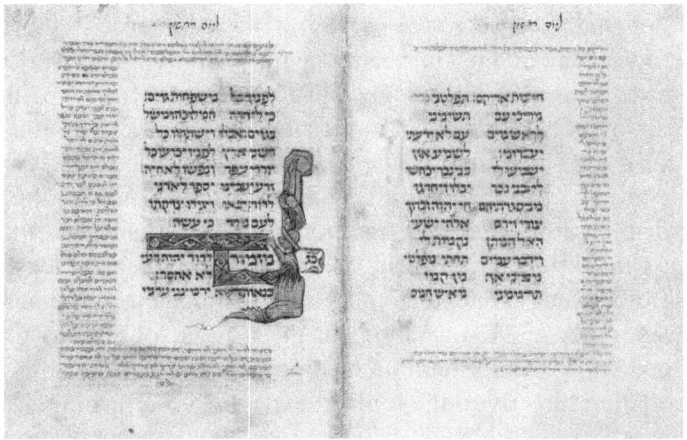

Figure 12.3. Parma Psalter, *fol.29a, c. 1280, 13.5 × 10 cm. From the facsimile of the* Parma *Psalter, www.facsimile-editions.com/en/pp/.*

40. Ibid., 106–7.
41. Ibid., 115.
42. Ibid., 103.
43. Gillingham, *Psalms Through the Centuries*, 2:149.

The figure's hands are raised in prayer or supplication as he stands on a grassy river bank which gives way to the 'still waters' of Ps. 23.2. The whole image, which also includes two decorative panels and a bird-like figure flying upwards from the Psalmist's hat, is itself almost intertwined with the Hebrew text of the Psalm. As is usual in *Parma*, the lower part of the Psalmist's body is concealed and the animal head resembles a dog's head (this is the most common animal head in *Parma*). The calm landscape of the grassy bank and the river signifies to the reader/viewer that this is a peaceful scene and helps to convey the idea of confidence in divine providence. There is no visual reference either to the 'valley of the shadow of death' or even the 'enemies' that were a key part of the *Stuttgart* image. This image could in some ways be categorized as a mirror-image of the *Stuttgart* image of Psalm 23. Where the *Stuttgart* image focused solely on the 'shadow of death' found in the Psalm, the *Parma* image is preoccupied only with the pastoral imagery of the opening of the Psalm and the confidence in God that this signifies. While this could be critiqued as only a partial representation of Psalm 23, it reminds us of the much wider range of responses that can be evoked by a Psalm, as opposed to a narrative biblical text.

The Luttrell Psalter, *c. 1335–40, 35 × 24.5 cm*

We will conclude our selective survey of the Medieval Psalters with a brief consideration of the fourteenth-century *Luttrell Psalter* (hereafter referred to as *Luttrell*). This richly illustrated manuscript was made for English landowner Geoffrey Luttrell around 1335–40.[44] The illustrations mostly consist of marginalia, which contain a variety of 'every-day' scenes, religious vignettes, parodies and also scenes containing a range of fantastical creatures.[45] It has traditionally been argued that the marginalia bear very little relation to the Psalms themselves, or at least that the relationship between the textual and visual component of the manuscript is somewhat opaque.[46] Explanations of the purpose of Gothic marginalia have ranged from seeing them as meaningless decoration to moralizing (but not relating directly to the biblical text) to 'life-affirming' to playing

---

44. See Michelle Brown, *The Luttrell Psalter: A Facsimile* (London: The British Library, 2006), Michael Camille, *Mirror in Parchment: The Luttrell Psalter and the Making of Medieval England*, Picturing History (London: Reaktion, 1998), and Sandler, 'The Word in the Text and the Image in the Margin', for more detail on *Luttrell*.

45. Sandler, 'The Word in the Text and the Image in the Margin', 88.

46. Ibid.

a protective function towards the text (hence the monstrous and fantastical creatures).[47] However, Freeman Sandler has countered persuasively that in the case of over forty of the illustrated Psalms in *Luttrell*, the marginalia function as a, sometimes incisive, gloss on the Psalms texts.[48] She distinguishes several different categories of interpretative visualization, including 'literal' visualization of words or phrases from the Psalms, what she calls 'visual syllabification (visualization of syllables from nouns found in the individual Psalms), images inspired by verbs of action found in the Psalms (sometimes presented in a decontextualized way that bears no relation to the Psalm) and more complex images based on the notion of 'visual counterparts' and 'the concentration of disparate words into a single marginal entity'.[49] Following Sandler, Noel has stated that *Luttrell* is the true descendent of *Utrecht* in terms of the complexity and depth of the gloss that it offers on the Psalms texts.[50] Freeman Sandler argues that the '*Luttrell imagines verborum*...provide a heightened and intensified experience of reading, through the discovery and appreciation of all the riches both apparent and concealed in the words'.[51] Thus, like the *Utrecht* images these images are not included just for mnemonic purposes but for enhancing the reader/viewer's understanding of the Psalms.

In terms of Psalm 23, *Luttrell* spreads the text of the Psalm over three pages (folios), thus allowing for three pages of accompanying marginalia (f. 45v-f. 46v). On the first page of Psalm 23 (f. 45v), aside from the historiated initial, at the bottom of the page, underneath the opening of the Psalm, is a small image of St Christopher carrying the Christ-child (Fig. 12.4). At the bottom of f. 46r is a king, who Brown identifies as St Edmund (Fig. 12.5). At the bottom of f. 46v we see St Michael defeating the dragon, although this is most likely a gloss on Ps. 24.3.[52] How then to interpret f. 45v and f. 46r in relation to Psalm 23? The figure of St Christopher on f. 45v, well-known as the patron saint of travellers, corresponds to both the journeying motif found in Psalm 23, as well as the notion of a protector figure found therein. Thus this image can be seen as a gloss on Ps. 23.3-4 in particular, helping to bring out the themes of guidance and protection. The image of St Edmund at the bottom of f. 46r is less straightforward to interpret.

47. Ibid., 88–9.
48. Ibid., 88.
49. Ibid., 88–97.
50. Noel, 'Medieval Charades and the Visual Syntax of the Utrecht Psalter', 41.
51. Sandler, 'The Word in the Text and the Image in the Margin', 97.
52. Brown, *The Luttrell Psalter*.

208 Psalms and the Use of the Critical Imagination

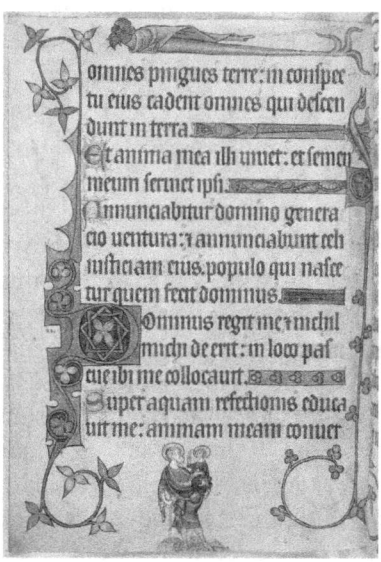

Figure 12.4. Luttrell Psalter, *fol. 45v*, 35 × 24.5 cm.
Credit: British Library, London, UK. © British Library Board.
All Rights Reserved/Bridgeman Images.

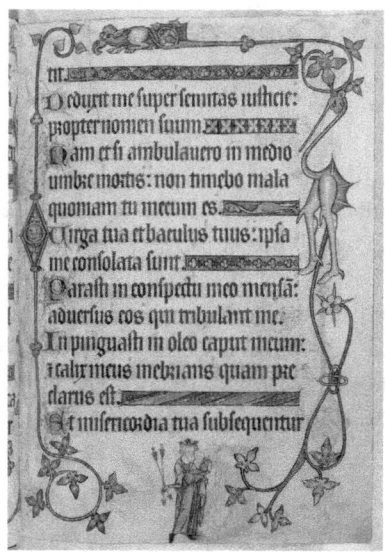

Figure 12.5. Luttrell Psalter, *fol. 46r*, 35 × 24.5 cm.
Credit: British Library, London, UK. © British Library Board.
All Rights Reserved/Bridgeman Images.

However, Brown, one of the foremost experts on the manuscript, argues that the image is likely intended to be juxtaposed with or viewed in conjunction with Ps. 23.5. As king and martyr (he was shot with arrows and beheaded by the Danes in c. 869), Edmund would have been anointed as ruler and then by virtue of his martyrdom would sit at the 'table of the Lord'.[53] Thus Edmund appears here to be acting as a stand-in for the Psalmist. In terms of Sandler Freeman's aforementioned categories, these two images are examples of 'visual counterparts' to the text. They serve to make the text relevant to a medieval audience and help to bring out its meaning in a non-literal way.

Twentieth-century Psalm Cycles

In all four of the visualizations explored thus far different aspects of the Psalm have received visual attention, ranging from the very detailed 'charade-style' illustration of *Utrecht* to the 'pared down' visualizations of *Stuttgart* and *Parma* and the opaque but potentially illuminating marginalia of *Luttrell*. While it would be misguided to attempt to draw any sort of direct line from these Psalters to twentieth-century works, any twentieth-century artist attempting a Psalms cycle will in some sense have a relationship with the great medieval Psalters. The two Psalms cycles explored below had very different creators. Arthur Wragg was a young Christian Socialist at the start of his career. He was preoccupied with what we would now refer to as 'social justice'. Whereas Chagall, who undertook the Psalms commission near the end of his long life when he was already a celebrated artist, who is far more reflective and spiritual in his approach. Both artists can certainly be seen as standing outside the 'mainstream' of their respective faiths. It is striking that they both undertook illustrated Psalms cycles during the twentieth century, an era in which most artists had comprehensively turned their back on what we might term 'biblical art'. This is in striking contrast to the medieval Psalters, which were produced during a time when all art was essentially religious in one form or other.

Arthur Wragg, The Psalms for Modern Life, *1933, 18.5 × 12 cm*. Arthur Wragg (1903–76), whose work features heavily in Volume 2 of Gillingham's Wiley-Blackwell commentary, was a twentieth-century British artist and illustrator. He is best known for *The Psalms for Modern Life*, a modern Psalter, complete with bold black and white cartoons accompanying a selection of the Psalms, which was reprinted ten times

---

53. Email discussion with Professor Emeritus Michelle Brown, November 2019.

between 1933 and 1936. The work was commissioned by Robert Lusty of Selwyn and Blount Publishers. Lusty was struck by Wragg's uncompromising approach to the social injustices of the 1930s.[54] Wragg's sample cartoon of Psalm 142 ('I cried unto thee, O Lord'), depicted a young homeless man sitting next to a dustbin. Lusty describes how the images, so shocking at the time, now seem strangely dated. Writing in the 1970s he claimed that, 'its diminished impact today derives from the fulfilment, at least to a heartening extent, of its purposes forty years ago'.[55] Against the background of the *The Sunday at Home*-style illustrations of the Psalms (discussed above) which typically accompanied the Psalms in the 1930s, one can see how this image would have appeared irreverent, shocking even. Wragg himself has written of how the Psalms began to take on a new significance in his eyes, as if they had been written for 'this particular moment in history'.[56] He places himself (albeit probably subconsciously) within the medieval tradition of 'charade illustration' (discussed above) when he writes that, 'words and sentences seemed to isolate themselves and stand out from the rest of the text, like telegrams'.[57] Some of the initial images were deemed 'too modern' and borderline offensive by Rusty, hardly surprising perhaps, given that Psalms 4 and 6 were visualized with scenes of a pregnant teenager and a male 'punter' looking for a prostitute in a lavatory, respectively. An introduction by the Reverend Dick Sheppard of St Martin-in-the-Fields was also appended to the book in order to give the work respectability in the eyes of a general religious audience, and among the clergy. Sheppard writes of how, on first viewing (having initially been reluctant to be part of the project), Wragg's illustrations 'pierced his soul like bullets'.[58] He refers to Wragg as a 'prophet', with something to 'reveal'. Wragg also seems to allude to this when he speaks of 'prophecy' creating his images.[59] The book was a commercial success and very well reviewed, with one reviewer, a J. A. Hutton, writing in *British Weekly*, claiming that reading the Psalms alongside Wragg's images had moved him as they never had done before in a church setting.[60]

54. Judy Brook, *Arthur Wragg: Twentieth-Century Artist, Prophet and Jester* (Bristol: Sansom & Co., 2001), 49.
55. Ibid., 50.
56. Ibid.
57. Ibid.
58. Arthur Wragg, *The Psalms for Modern Life* (London: Selwyn & Blount, 1933), 3.
59. Ibid., 4; Brook, *Arthur Wragg*, 50.
60. Brook, *Arthur Wragg*, 64.

Figure 12.6. *Arthur Wragg*, Psalm 23; *18. 5 × 12 cm in Arthur Wragg, The Psalms for Modern Life. London: Selwyn & Blount, 1933.*

Wragg's illustration for Psalm 23 is a good example of his unconventional approach to his source-text. He has not attempted to visualize the whole Psalm but has focused on just one verse. That verse is Ps. 23.4, which Wragg has inscribed below the image in the King James version of the text: 'Yea, though I walk through the valley of the shadow of death, I will fear no evil'. The pen and ink drawing, with its dramatic chiaroscuro almost resembles a woodcut image (Fig. 12.6). The composition shows a patient (whose head is on the far left of the image) lying on an operating table, surrounded by six doctors and nurses. A wide shaft of light cascades down on the centre of the image, illuminating both the patient and medical staff, and another light shaft enters the scene at a diagonal from the upper right corner. To the far right stands a trolley with operating equipment. The 'shadow of death' is thus here conceived of not as a threat from an enemy or a serpent but as an operation. Perhaps this is a life-saving operation (without which the patient would die) or a very dangerous operation (or both). The divine protection implicit in the rest of Ps. 23.4 ('you are with me') is signified by the shafts of light which form a sort of protective aura around the patient. While not an example of Wragg's more scathing social commentary, this image does encapsulate the intersection between the ancient Psalms and the modern age (here evoked by this scene from modern medicine) that Wragg felt so keenly as he was working on the illustrations for the book. As Gillingham points out, the overall effect is about (a perhaps unexpected) rescue in this life, rather than the eschatological rescue implied in an image such as the *Stuttgart* version of Psalm 23.[61]

Marc Chagall, Psaumes de David, *1978, 29.5 × 22 cm*. Chagall, the prolific Russian-Jewish artist (1887–1985) is known as the father of modernism and yet also as one who repeatedly engaged with biblical themes, at a time when it was not fashionable to do so. He worked on his celebrated Bible illustrations (*L'Ancien Testament, La Genèse, L'Exode, La Cantique des Cantiques* in 105 coloured plates) from 1931 to 1956 as well as a series of large-scale stained glass windows from 1956 onwards (located in Metz Cathedral and the United Nation Buildings, among many other locations).[62] He also donated seventeen monumental paintings illustrating Genesis and Exodus to the French state in 1966, around which the Musée National Message Biblique in Nice was designed.[63] He viewed art as a link with the Bible which he described as, 'the greatest source of poetry the world has ever known', and also as, 'the world's greatest work of art'.[64] He was also influenced by the Hassidism of his childhood which taught of the profound unity of the world and that God's presence was everywhere and in everything. This mingling of the supernatural and the natural and the idea that there is neither 'top nor bottom' to the world pervades Chagall's art and his biblical scenes in particular.[65]

The Psalms cycle, known as the *Psaumes de David*, consist of thirty illustrated Psalms produced using the 'aquatint technique' on sand-coloured paper. This technique visually captures the light and shade he perceived as existing in the Psalms themselves. Chagall saw his images as 'picture meditations' in which he brings forth the 'inner pictures' created by his engagement with the Psalms into external images.[66] In keeping with his earlier work inspired by the Bible, he saw his images as providing a visual commentary on the biblical text.

61. Gillingham, *Psalms Through the Centuries*, 2:149.
62. See Marc Chagall, *L'Ancien Testament: La Genèse, l'Exode, le Cantique des Cantiques* (Paris: Chêne, 2005).
63. See Jean-Michel Foray and Françoise Rossini-Paquet, *National Museum Message Biblique Marc Chagall* (Paris: Réunion des musées nationaux, 2000), 9–14.
64. Foray and Rossini-Paquet, *National Museum Message Biblique Marc Chagall*, 9.
65. Ibid., 17.
66. Klaus Mayer and Marc Chagall, *Psalmen in Bildern* (Würzberg: Echter, 1995), 7.

Figure 12.7. *Marc Chagall*, Psaumes de David, *29.5 × 22 cm.*
© *ADAGP, Paris. Localisation: Nice, musée national Marc Chagall, Photo*
© *RMN-Grand Palais, (musée Marc Chagall) / Adrien Didierjean*

The image he created for Psalm 23, apparently one of Chagall's favourite Psalms, is, in keeping with the layout and style of the entire work, a full-page aquatint drawing (Fig. 12.7). The overall effect is of a monochrome drawing not completely dissimilar in style and technique to *Utrecht*. The colour palette is similar to that of *Utrecht* and the image also has a hurried, sketch-like feel. The painter sitting on his stool, at his easel in the centre of the lower half of the image fulfils the role of the Psalmist. Instead of the 'green pastures' and 'still waters' of Ps. 23.1-2, the soul of this 'Psalmist' (surely Chagall himself) is restored via his painting equipment (the palette, brush, easel, canvas etc.) and his ability to paint. The flowers that have already been committed to the easel perhaps hint at the 'green pastures'. The painter sits with his hand not on the paintbrush but turned upwards, indicating that his talent is 'God-given' and in keeping with Chagall's notion that, in these images, he is bringing forth his 'inner pictures' of the Psalms.[67] Thus, this image evokes 'confident trust in God' in a metaphorical way. New visual elements not found in the text of the Psalm serve to extend the metaphor further. There are observers to the left of the painter and also behind the easel, indicating that he does not paint for himself alone. More significant is the large winged figure of a woman descending downwards towards the painter. This woman is almost certainly an evocation of Chagall's beloved second wife, Valentina (Vava) Brodsky. Her presence in his life is being presented as another example of God's shepherding care. Finally, the winged angel in the upper right-hand corner of the image with an outstretched right arm brings us back to the text and the claim that the Psalmist is led along the 'right paths' by the Shepherd/Lord (Ps. 23.3). Thus in this image Chagall is expressing his understanding of Psalm 23 as an acknowledgement of God's shepherding care in all areas of his life.[68] The mingling of the heavenly and the earthly in this image, both in the person of Vava and via the presence of the angel alongside the other figures, reflects the influence of Hassidism and Kabalistic thought described above. Glueck also picks up on the intermingling between the visual symbols of 'old Vitebsk', the Russian town where Chagall spent his youth, and the Psalms, in this and the other Psalms images.[69] As with the thirteenth-century Jewish *Parma Psalter* (discussed above) there is no hint here of the deathly shadow of Ps. 23.4 or the 'enemies' of 23.5 and the symbolic threat of death that were often an integral part of Christian visualizations of this Psalm. Glueck finds the images ultimately unconvincing as interpretations of the Psalms but that is perhaps to miss the point. Like the *Parma* artist this is a very personal response to Psalm 23, which can be viewed in part as a reaction, perhaps even a corrective, to the dominant Christian modes of visualizing the Psalm, which had gradually become less celebratory in tone.

A Selective Survey of the Visual Reception of Psalm 23.4, 'The Valley of the Shadow of Death'

Alongside images of Psalm 23 found within Psalters and Psalms cycles, another distinctive strand of visual reception of Psalm 23 developed, that of a range of literature, images, music and later, other audio-visual

67. Mayer and Chagall, *Psalmen in Bildern*, 28.
68. Ibid.
69. Grace Glueck, 'Chagall's Prints at Modern Museum', *New York Times Archives*, 1979.

media inspired (either directly or indirectly) solely by Ps. 23.4.[70] We have already explored two images from Psalms cycles inspired by this verse: the *Stuttgart* image (f. 28v, Fig. 12.2) and Wragg's illustration for Psalm 23 (Fig. 12.6). The *Stuttgart* image seemed to imply protection from both the evils of this life and also from 'eschatological death', whereas the Wragg image implied divine protection in this life. We will now look at four images which use Ps. 23.4 as inspiration and which are a key part of the reception history of the verse, pointing the way to its eventual status as 'cultural icon'.

Dürer, Knight, Death and the Devil, 1513–14, 24.3 × 18.8 cm. Dürer (1471–1528), the foremost artist of the German Renaissance, was an outstanding painter, woodcut artist and engraver. Like the majority of artists prior to the nineteenth century, much of his output was inspired by biblical texts and themes (see for instance his ground-breaking *Apocalypse* series of 1498 and his *Small* and *Large Passion* cycles of 1508–1511, his *Life of the Virgin* of 1511 and his *Engraved Passion* of 1513). His *Knight, Death and the Devil* of 1513–4 is part of a set of three engravings (*The Meisterstiche*) widely regarded as his finest engravings (Fig. 12.8). The other images in the set are *St Jerome in his Study* (which stresses the contemplative aspect of the Christian life) and *Melancholia I*.[71]

There exists a wealth of scholarship on *Knight, Death and the Devil* which does not need to be rehearsed here.[72] A brief description will suffice. It is a well-balanced yet crowded image in which a fully armoured knight rides resolutely through a rocky landscape, adorned with sparse vegetation. A city on a hill in the background emphasizes the knight's isolation from the rest of society. Symbols of death surround him on all sides. There is a skull, a traditional *memento mori*, in the bottom left-hand corner of the image (just above Dürer's famous monogram, here placed in a manner resembling a gravestone).

---

70. As above, see Gillingham, *Psalms Through the Centuries*, 2:152–3; Roncace, 'Psalm 23 as Cultural Icon', and Jacobson, 'Through the Pistol Smoke Dimly', on the wider cultural reception of Ps. 23.4.

71. Martin Bailey, *Dürer*, Phaidon Colour Library (London: Phaidon, 1995), 15–16.

72. See, for instance, Erwin Panofsky, *The Life and Art of Albrecht Dürer*, 4th ed. (Princeton: Princeton University Press, 1955), 151–4; Henry Rox, 'On Dürer's Knight, Death, and Devil', *The Art Bulletin* 30 (1948): 67–70; Ursula Meyer, 'Political Implications of Dürer's "Knight, Death and Devil"', *The Print Collector's Newsletter* 9, no. 2 (1978): 35–9; Kate Heard and Lucy Whitaker, *The Northern Renaissance: Dürer to Holbein* (London: Royal Collections, 2011), 98.

Figure 12.8. *Dürer,* Knight, Death and the Devil, *24.3 × 18.8 cm. Credit: Cabinet des Estampes et des Dessins, Strasbourg, France/Bridgeman Images.*

A monstrous figure with a skull-like face and snakes for hair, a personification of Death, rides next to the knight on a worn-out horse, holding an hourglass (another *memento mori*). The knight's magnificent horse (probably based on a statue by Colleoni in Venice, which Dürer would have seen around 1505–7) is followed by a hybrid beast (presumably the devil) reminiscent of the Satanic beasts in Dürer's *Apocalypse* series. Under the horse's legs runs a faithful dog and a lizard, a symbol of danger. Despite all these deathly distractions the knight's pose and demeanour is determined and unflinching. The engraving is widely accepted as having been inspired both by Ps. 23.4 and by Erasmus' *Handbook of a Christian Knight* of 1504 in which he urged Christians to act as soldiers, fighting against 'the flesh, the devil and the world' with faith.[73] Thus we may venture that in this image the Christian Knight or soldier is traversing the 'valley of the shadow of death' with the confident trust of the Psalmist of Psalm 23. Panofsky argues that the 'enemies of man' (perhaps an oblique reference to the 'enemies' of Ps. 23.5) as conceived in this image (as devils and monsters) do not appear to be real and can therefore be ignored.[74] He further argues that the fact that the knight, horse and dog have been engraved in 'pure profile' creates the impression that they are not even aware of these dangers and are thus imperturbable.[75] I suggest that in fact the combination of 'Death', the monster and the various *momento mori* are a frightening visual metaphor for the dangers and temptations of life, to which the knight (the ideal Christian) is not impervious, but, in the spirit of Psalm 23, is able ultimately to deflect and resist as a consequence of his faith and trust in God.

Two Illustrations for The Pilgrim's Progress. The character of Christian in Bunyan's *Pilgrim's Progress* of 1678 represents the foremost literary exploration of the ideal Christian knight and pilgrim foreshadowed by Erasmus and visually by Dürer.[76] In short, *The Pilgrim's Progress* is the allegorical tale of Christian, an 'everyman' character who we follow as he journeys from his home (leaving his wife and children, although they later follow him in Part 2) towards the 'Celestial City' accompanied by various other allegorical characters along the way. The narrative is steeped in the Bible and Theology, both in a practical sense (there are notes highlighting biblical references throughout the text), and in a more metaphorical sense, via its references to pilgrimage and Protestant Theology (Bunyan was a strong believer in the concept of salvation by faith alone).[77] With regard to Bunyan's use of Psalm 23, its status as the inspiration for the valley of the shadow of death that Christian has to cross (as well as Jer. 2.6) is clearly signposted in the biblical note, as well as via the language of the passage itself.[78] Hamlin argues that Bunyan has borrowed from a 'biblical

73. Panofsky, *The Life and Art of Albrecht Dürer*, 152; Heard and Whitaker, *The Northern Renaissance*, 98.
74. Panofsky, *The Life and Art of Albrecht Dürer*, 152.
75. Ibid., 154.
76. For information on the reception history in particular, see William R. Owens and Stuart Sim, eds., *Reception, Appropriation, Recollection: Bunyan's Pilgrim's Progress*, Religions and Discourse 33 (Oxford: Peter Lang, 2007); see also William R. Owens and John Bunyan, *The Pilgrim's Progress* (Oxford: Oxford University Press, 2003).
77. Owens and Bunyan, *The Pilgrim's Progress*, xviii–xxxii.
78. Ibid., 65.

lyric' and imposed a narrative structure upon it, whereby a resting place and 'river of God' (surely a reference to the still waters and green pastures of Ps. 23.1-2), and secondly the Delectable Mountains complete with 'green pastures' are reached *after* Christian has traversed the Valley of the Shadow of Death.[79] Bunyan's interpretation or imposition of narrative is justified by the juxtaposition, inbuilt in the Psalm, between the pastures and the valley.[80] There are some similarities here with the approach taken to Psalm 23 (and the Psalms as a corpus more widely) in the illustrations for the *Utrecht Psalter*, whereby units of the Psalm are juxtaposed in unexpected ways and in so doing, new meanings created.

Figure 12.9. The Pilgrim's Progress.
Credit: Lebrecht Authors/Bridgeman Images.

79. Hamlin, *Psalm Culture and Early Modern English Literature*, 167.
80. Ibid.

By 1680 the text of *The Pilgrim's Progress* was issued with fifteen woodcut illustrations plus a frontispiece of Bunyan. These images have, according to Collé Bak, given the text a 'third dimension' and she critiques the disparaging tone with which the early 'inferior' woodcuts have often been spoken of.[81] In fact, in some periods of the text's history, *The Pilgrim's Progress* existed as a series of images without text, testament to the formational role that illustrations of this text have played, and to the bond that they helped to create with the text's audience, particularly the non-aristocratic audience.[82] Thus in this very early image of the Valley of the Shadow of Death (c. 1680) we see Christian attired in the style of an armoured knight with his sword drawn against the phantoms and monsters that surround him (Fig. 12.9). In the bottom left hand corner of the image is a traditional medieval-style hell-mouth breathing flames and there are three hybrid monsters to the left of Christian and three to the right. Despite the fact that in the text we are told that Christian 'perceived that God was with them' in the Valley of the Shadow of Death, in the accompanying image no such respite is obvious, although it may be hinted at. The bleakness of the 'valley of the shadow of death' is created by the (unknown) artist's use of chiaroscuro to create shadow and shade at the top and bottom of the image (as well as a sense of light around Christian himself, perhaps an indication of God's protection). Christian himself appears resolute against the threat (somewhat in the style of Dürer's knight) but in this image the darkness of Ps. 23.4 is frozen in time, without resolution.

Collé Bak treats the 'Southey edition' of 1830 as almost an entirely different genre of illustrated *Pilgrim's Progress*. The illustrations were engraved after drawings by the celebrated nineteenth-century artist John Martin. The edition was marketed by John Murray as one that would appeal to men of 'taste', with an introduction by the poet Robert Southey. The volume was well-reviewed and the illustrations particularly praised as almost a corrective to some of Bunyan's 'eminently faulty' passages.[83] Thus, these images helped to cement the work's reputation among the upper classes, as well as with the middle and working classes with which it was already extremely popular. In the 'Southey edition' image of 'The Shadow of the Valley of Death' (9.8 × 12.7 cm), one can immediately sense a shift in artistic ambition (Fig. 12.10).

---

81. Nathalie Collé Bak, 'The Role of Illustrations in the Reception of The Pilgrim's Progress', in Owens and Sim, eds., *Reception, Appropriation Recollection*, 81–98 (84).
82. Ibid., 87, 93.
83. Ibid., 94–5.

Figure 12.10. *W. R. Smith after John Martin,* The Valley of the Shadow of Death. © *Photo: Royal Academy of Arts, London.*

Gone is the tight focus on the figure Christian at the centre of his tormentors in favour of an almost panoramic view of the tiny figure of Christian (to the left of the image) walking through what appears to be a network of infinite caves. In the foreground we see an underground lake stretching backwards into the distance, reminiscent of the Styx, a detail that would not be out of keeping with Martin's grandiose style and love of classical references. Although there are no other living figures in the image, the presence of ghoulish creatures is suggested by the swirling rock formations at the roof of the cave. The cave structure in this image evokes a different type of claustrophobia to that experienced in the early image, although this is offset somewhat by the presence of a pale light source in the distance. Christian, hands held out before him, seems almost drawn towards the light, probably intended as a reminder of the presence of God, even in this valley of death. Thus the image manages to evoke the oppression of the 'valley of death', while maintaining the focus on the 'light' at the end of it.

Figure 12.11. Roger Fenton, The Valley of the Shadow of Death, *1854*, 27.6 × 34.9 cm. Credit: Private Collection/Bridgeman Images.

Roger Fenton's *The Valley of the Shadow of Death* of 1854 was one of the first battlefield photos (Fig. 12 11).[84] The photo, which was not exhibited until 1855, presents a panorama of a battlefield during the Crimean War.[85] It depicts the narrow ravine which ran between the British and Russian camps, known as the 'valley of death'.[86] There are no soldiers present, nor any sign of life, just bare boulders, a track along which guns and cannons were probably pulled and a vast number of cannon balls, a reminder of an earlier battle. Fenton was an amateur photographer who had gone to Crimea as much to experiment with the new technology of photography and techniques for developing photos, as to document the Crimean War

---

84. 'Valley of the Shadow of Death', *The J. Paul Getty Museum*, n.d., http://www.getty.edu/art/collection/objects/60602/roger-fenton-valley-of-the-shadow-of-death-english-april-23-1855/.

85. Helen Groth, 'Technological Mediations and the Public Sphere: Roger Fenton's Crimea Exhibition and "The Charge of the Light Brigade"', *Vic. Lit. Cult.* 30, no. 2 (2002): 553–70 (557).

86. Gillingham, *Psalms Through the Centuries*, 2:149.

(1853–56).[87] Although the image (alongside Fenton's entire Crimea catalogue) has variously been described as a propagandist attempt to 'sanitize' the war (as opposed to William Howard Russell's graphic reports from the frontline) and later as a symbol of the futility of war, what is most interesting for our purposes is the image's title.[88] The title was not given to the photo by Fenton but rather was appended to the image by the authors of the 1855 exhibition catalogue.[89] The title, *The Valley of the Shadow of Death*, almost certainly recalls Tennyson's, *The Charge of the Light Brigade*, which he had written after reading two reports of the battle in the *Times* in November 1854. Tennyson uses the reference to Ps. 23.4 (the valley of death) in Stanzas 1 and 2 of the poem and also refers to the 'jaws of Death' in stanzas 3 and 5. Fenton was aware of the poem while he was in Crimea and had been inspired by Tennyson's work prior to this. Groth asserts that the photo's exhibition-title presupposes an educated middle-class audience, someone who could make the 'appropriate associative link between Fenton's photograph, Tennyson's poem and the twenty-third Psalm'.[90] And yet, we might counter that thanks to the popularity of the illustrated *Pilgrim's Progress*, as well as Psalm 23 itself, references both textual and visual to Ps. 23.4's 'valley of the shadow of death' were so common in British culture that even if the reader/viewer was not aware of Tennyson's poem, they would have picked up on the allusion to the Psalm. As to the image itself, this is a very modern 'valley of the shadow of death', a post-Christian, post-apocalyptic one even. It evokes a world without God, but without humanity either.

Conclusion

Throughout our selective survey of the visual history of Psalm 23 we have kept the text in dialogue with the images (in line with Gillingham's emphasis on the need for the 'critical imagination' when 'doing' reception history). We will now summarize the ways in which the images explored help to expand and even challenge our understanding of the Psalm. For the purposes of this discussion I will discuss images from different time periods and different contexts (e.g. images from psalms cycles versus 'stand alone' images or images from different cycles altogether) together, as their historical context was discussed in detail above.

---

87. Groth, 'Technological Mediations and the Public Sphere', 557.
88. Ibid.
89. Ibid., 553.
90. Ibid., 558.

Psalm 23 is a poem with shades of both light and darkness, whose underlying theme is one of confident trust in God. The medieval illustrations engaged with the 'word images' found therein in a surprising variety of ways and place different degrees of emphasis on the 'light' and 'shade' found within the text. The *Utrecht* image juxtaposes all of the 'word images' found within Psalm 23 in one pictorial space. Thus while the pastoral idyll and the 'valley of the shadow of death' are both given space, the valley of death is almost cordoned off in the lower right-hand corner of the image, thus privileging the positive images of the Psalm as well as the idea of protection and prosperity in this life. As Noel argues, this form of 'charade illustration' finds its culmination in the *Luttrell Psalter*. I suggested that the images of St Christopher and St Edmund found in the margins of Psalm 23 of *Luttrell* serve to bring out the Psalm's themes of journeying, anointing and divine presence in an unorthodox yet effective way.

The single *Stuttgart* illustration for Psalm 23 promotes the image of Christ-as-Shepherd holding the serpent at bay over and above any of the pastoral imagery found in the text. Whether the Christ-Shepherd figure has defeated death in this life or eschatological death in this image, is ambiguous. In promoting v 4 of Psalm 23 in this way, over and above other aspects of the text, *Stuttgart* anticipates a long strand of engagement with this section of the Psalm, one that becomes increasingly decontextualized by the seventeenth century. This strand was explored via images from Dürer, illustrations to the *Pilgrim's Progress*, a photograph from the Crimean War (by James Fenton) and an image from Arthur Wragg's *Psalms for Modern Life*. While in Psalm 23, the Psalmist seems quite clear that despite his brush with the valley of death, evil need not be feared, the images we explored use the motif of the valley of death as a pretext to explore the notion of doubt (to greater and lesser extents). While Dürer's knight and the Christian of the 1680 *Pilgrim's Progress* woodcut version of the 'Valley of the Shadow of Death' have been represented as resolute figures, doubts seem to creep into the visualizations by the time of the Martin engraving for the same section of the *Pilgrim's Progress*. Here the tiny pilgrim is dwarfed by the deathly cave, itself reminiscent of Hades, although a light at the end of the cave evokes a glimmer of the hopefulness espoused by the rest of Psalm 23. This image of the lone figure in an actual 'valley of death' (whereas in the text of the psalm it is surely intended as a metaphor) paves the way for the more individualistic interpretations of the Psalm seen in popular culture, such as in Coolio's *Gangsta's Paradise* of 1995 in which he raps of his own 'shadow of death' moment during his career as a drug dealer. By the time of the

Fenton photograph, the glimmers of hope seen in the earlier visualizations of Ps. 23.4 seem spent and even God appears absent from this new world of warfare and technology. The Wragg image from 1933 is different again. As the title of the volume, *Psalms for Modern Life*, would suggest, Wragg was attempting to wrench the Psalms from their familiar iconography and place them in new visual contexts. Thus, his visualization of Ps. 23.4 is set on the operating table, as if answering the question of what 'the confident trust in God' espoused by Psalm 23 would look like in a self-consciously modern setting.

And finally, in a complete contrast to the preceding section, our two examples from the Jewish tradition, *The Parma Psalter* image and Chagall's image of Psalm 23, privilege the positive aspects of the Psalm at the expense of any visual reference at all to the 'valley of the shadow of death', the motif which had come to be such an integral part of the Christian visual tradition. The *Parma* image shows the Psalmist as a human figure with an animal head, a surreal touch which is echoed in spirit by Chagall's dreamlike vision of the Psalmist-as-painter, depicted here counting his many blessings (his skill as an artist, his wife, Vava, and God's protection in general). While Chagall was in all likelihood working from the Hebrew text of Psalm 23 (he was fluent in Hebrew), which refers only to a 'dark valley' in v. 4, the *Parma Psalter* is vocalised and so does indeed refer to the 'valley of the shadow of death'. Despite this, the *Parma* artist, working, we may presume, from within the tradition from which they came, presents the Psalm as a celebration of God's constant presence in this life.

Engaging with this selective survey of contrasting images from the visual history of Psalm 23 prompts us to consider afresh the imagery (the 'word pictures') of the Psalm and also its structure. When the horizon of the ancient text intersects with new horizons and eras, it is not just new art that can be created, but new meaning too. And like the medievals with their illustrated Psalters, when we return to the text itself, in study, prayer or song, our minds will come alive with some of these images, helping to illuminate, elucidate and animate this 'cultural icon' of a Psalm.

Bibliography

'The Annotated Utrecht Psalter'. Released 2015. www.utrechtpsalter.nl.
Bailey, Martin. *Dürer*. Phaidon Colour Library. London: Phaidon, 1995.
Bak, Nathalie Collé. 'The Role of Illustrations in the Reception of *The Pilgrim's Progress*'. Pages 81–98 in *Reception, Appropriation, Recollection: Bunyan's Pilgrim's Progress*. Edited by W. R. Owens and Stuart Sim. Religions and Discourse 33. Oxford: Peter Lang, 2007.

Barker, Ethel Ross. 'The Symbolism of Certain Catacomb Frescoes - I'. *The Burlington Magazine for Connoisseurs* 24, no. 127 (1913): 43–5, 47–50.

Beit-Arié, Malachi, Emanuel Silver, and Thérèse Metzger. *The Parma Psalter: A Thirteenth-Century Illuminated Hebrew Book of Psalms with a Commentary by Abraham Ibn Ezra.* London: Facsimile Editions, 1996.

Bradley, Jill. *"You Shall Surely Not Die": The Concepts of Sin and Death as Expressed in the Manuscript Art of Northwestern Europe, c. 800–1200.* Library of the Written Word 4. Leiden: Brill, 2008.

Brook, Judith. *Arthur Wragg: Twentieth-century Artist, Prophet and Jester.* Bristol: Sansom & Co., 2001.

Brown, Michelle. *The Luttrell Psalter: A Facsimile.* London: The British Library, 2006.

Bunyan, John. *The Pilgrim's Progress.* Edited with an introduction and notes by William R. Owens. Oxford: Oxford University Press, 2003.

Camille, Michael. *Mirror in Parchment: The Luttrell Psalter and the Making of Medieval England.* Picturing History. London: Reaktion, 1998.

Cassidy, Brendan and Rosemary Muir Wright, eds. *Studies in the Illustration of the Psalter.* Stamford, UK: Shaun Tyas, 2000.

Chagall, Marc. *L'Ancien Testament: La Genèse, l'Exode, le Cantique des Cantiques.* Paris: Chêne, 2005.

Dormer, Sally. 'Illuminated Psalter Manuscripts'. Transcript of Lecture given at the Museum of London on 29 May 2012. Accessed 14 November 2019. https://www.gresham.ac.uk/lectures-and-events/illuminated-psalter-manuscripts.

Exum, J. Cheryl. *Art as Biblical Commentary: Visual Criticism from Hagar the Wife of Abraham to Mary the Mother of Jesus.* LHBOTS 694. London: Bloomsbury T&T Clark, 2019.

Fenton, Roger. 'Valley of the Shadow of Death'. The J. Paul Getty Museum. Accessed 5 November 2019, http://www.getty.edu/art/collection/objects/60602/roger-fenton-valley-of-the-shadow-of-death-english-april-23-1855/.

Foray, Jean-Michel, and Françoise Rossini-Paquet. *National Museum Message Biblique Marc Chagall.* Paris: Réunion des musées nationaux, 2000.

Gillingham, Susan E. 'Biblical Studies on Holiday? A Personal View of Reception History'. Pages 17–30 in *Reception History and Biblical Studies: Theory and Practice.* Edited by Emma England and William John Lyons. LHBOTS 615/Scriptural Traces 6. London: T&T Clark, 2015.

Gillingham, Susan E., ed. *Jewish and Christian Approaches to the Psalms: Conflict and Convergence.* Oxford: Oxford University Press, 2015.

Gillingham, Susan E. *Psalms Through the Centuries.* 2 vols. Wiley Blackwell Bible Commentaries. Chichester: Wiley-Blackwell, 2008/2018.

Gillingham, Susan E. 'Reception History, Biblical Studies and the Issue of Multivalency. Annual Aquinas Lecture, Faculty of Theology, University of Malta'. *Melita Theoligica* 68 (2018b): 1–15.

Glueck, Grace. 'Chagall's Prints at Modern Museum'. *New York Times Archives*, 21 December 1979. Accessed 14 November 2019, https://www.nytimes.com/1979/12/21/archives/art-chagalls-prints-at-modern-museum.html.

Groth, Helen. 'Technological Mediations and the Public Sphere: Roger Fenton's Crimea Exhibition and "The Charge of the Light Brigade"'. *Victorian Literature and Culture* 30, no. 2 (2002): 553–70.

Hamlin, Hannibal. *Psalm Culture and Early Modern English Literature.* Cambridge: Cambridge University Press, 2004.

Heard, Kate, and Lucy Whitaker. *The Northern Renaissance: Dürer to Holbein*. London: Royal Collections, 2011.

Horst, Koert van der, William Noel, and Wilhelmina C. M. Wüstefeld. *The Utrecht Psalter in Medieval Art: Picturing the Psalms of David*. London: Harvey Miller, 1996.

Jacobson, Karl. 'Through the Pistol Smoke Dimly: Psalm 23 in Contemporary Film and Song'. *SBL Forum* (January 2009). Accessed 18 December 2020, http://sbl-site.org/Article.aspx?ArticleID=796.

Jaski, Bart. 'The Utrecht Psalter'. Utrecht Library Special Collections. Released 2015. Accessed 5 November 2019, https://www.uu.nl/en/utrecht-university-library-special-collections/the-treasury/manuscripts-from-the-treasury/the-utrecht-psalter.

Jasper, D. 'The Twenty-Third Psalm in English Literature'. *Religion and Literature* 30 (1998): 1–11.

Mayer, Klaus, and Marc Chagall. *Psalmen in Bildern*. Würzberg: Echter, 1995.

Meyer, Ursula. 'Political Implications of Dürer's "Knight, Death and Devil"'. *The Print Collectors Newsletter* 9, no. 2 (May–June 1978): 35–9.

Morgan, David. *Visual Piety: A History and Theory of Popular Religious Images*. Berkeley: University of California Press, 1998.

Noel, William. 'Medieval Charades and the Visual Syntax of the Utrecht Psalter'. Pages 34–41 in *Studies in the Illustration of the Psalter*. Edited by Brendan Cassidy and Rosemary Muir Wright. Stamford, UK: Shaun Tyas, 2000.

O'Hear, Natasha, and Anthony O'Hear. *Picturing the Apocalypse: The Book of Revelation in the Arts over Two Millennia*. Oxford: Oxford University Press, 2015.

Owens, William R., and Stuart Sim, eds. *Reception, Appropriation, Recollection: Bunyan's Pilgrim's Progress*. Religions and Discourse 33. Oxford: Peter Lang, 2007.

Panofsky, Erwin. *The Life and Art of Albrecht Dürer*. 4th ed. Princeton: Princeton University Press, 1955.

'Psalm 22'. The Annotated Utrecht Psalter. Released 2015. http://psalter.library.uu.nl/page?p=32&res=1&x=0&y=0.

Roncace, Mark. 'Psalm 23 as Cultural Icon'. *Bible Odyssey*. Accessed 5 November 2019, https://www.bibleodyssey.org:443/passages/main-articles/lord-is-my-shepherd.

Rox, Henry. 'On Dürer's Knight, Death, and Devil'. *The Art Bulletin* 30 (1948): 67–70.

Sandler, Lucy Freeman. '"The Images of Words in Gothic English Psalters": The Saunders Lecture 1997'. Pages 67–86 in *Studies in the Illustration of the Psalter*. Edited by Brendan Cassidy and Rosemary Muir Wright. Stamford, UK: Shaun Tyas, 2000.

Sandler, Lucy Freeman. 'The Word in the Text and the Image in the Margin: The Case of the Luttrell Psalter'. *The Journal of the Walters Art Gallery* 54 (1996): 87–99.

Strawn, Brent A. 'Lord is My Shepherd (Ps 23)'. *Bible Odyssey*. Accessed 5 November 2019, https://www.bibleodyssey.org:443/passages/main-articles/lord-is-my-shepherd.

Wagner, Roger. *The Book of Praises: A Translation of the Psalms*. Oxford: Besalel Press, 1994.

Werlin, Steve. 'Shepherds in the Bible and in Art'. *Bible Odyssey*. Accessed 5 November 2019, https://www.bibleodyssey.org:443/passages/related-articles/shepherds-in-the-bible-and-in-art.

Wragg, Arthur. *The Psalms for Modern Life*. London: Selwyn & Blount, 1933.

Wright, Rosemary Muir. 'Introducing the Medieval Psalter'. Pages 1–11 in *Studies in the Illustration of the Psalter*. Edited by Brendan Cassidy and Rosemary Muir Wright. Stamford, UK: Shaun Tyas, 2000.

Index of References

Hebrew Bible/ Old Testament		Deuteronomy		1.12	50
Genesis		1.37	45	1.13-16	50
2.17	204	4.21	45	3.20-30	54
4.2	166	26.6	45	3.39	55
12.3	124	32.42	17	7	71
15.18	124			7.12	72
24.12-14	114	*Joshua*		8	53, 55, 56, 58
41.40	29, 36	2	50		
		2.1-2	50	8.7-10	55
		2.3	50	8.13-14	55
Exodus		2.4-16	50	8.13	48, 52, 53
1.14	45	2.4	50	11.14-21	54
2.18-23	72	2.6	50	12.25	72
3.14	88	11.14	139	12.26-29	49, 59
6.7	72			12.28	49
6.9	45	*Judges*		12.31	49
15	47	8.13-16	58	14.33	37
15.12	47	15.14	17	15.5	37
15.13	47			15.7-8	103
15.14-16	47	*1 Samuel*		18.10-17	54
18.7	36	1.10-15	114	19.3	54
		1.12-18	104	19.13	54
Leviticus		2.2-10	115	20.8-10	54
14.6	185	2.4-7	17	22	11, 69
16.5-22	106	10.1	37		
21.6	33	17.32-40	50	*1 Kings*	
21.8	33	17.41-54	50	1–12	69
21.17	33	17.54	50	1.15-19	54
21.21	33	17.55-56	50	2.5-6	54
21.22	33	17.55	50	2.5	55
22.25	33	18.7	17	2.6	55
		19.5	59	2.28-34	54
Numbers		20.41	36, 37	3–11	72
5.11-28	104			3.9	74
19.17	185	*2 Samuel*		3.16-28	71
19.18	185	1 1-11	50	4.21	71
		1 11	50	4.34	70

Index of References

1 Kings (cont.)
5.4	75
6–7	4
8.46	45
10.1-13	71
10.10	75
11.15	48, 49

2 Kings
4.18-25	104
5.1	56
5.8-14	104
13.14-17	56

1 Chronicles
16	11
18.3-13	58
18.12	50, 52, 54, 56
22.7-9	54

Ezra
9.14	44

Nehemiah
8	114

Job
3.22	29
4.14	27
5.19	17
7.16	165
9.29	165
39.4	28

Psalms
1–41	11
1	25, 26, 78, 193, 198
1.6	26
2	25, 26, 57, 120, 141, 193
2.3	32
2.7	27
2.10-11	32
2.11-12	3, 25
2.11	26, 28, 31
2.12	26, 27, 29–31, 37, 38
4.3-5	105
5.4	103, 105
6.9	105
8	11, 141
9	11, 180
10	11
11	180, 182
11.1	180
11.6	182
12	180
13	64, 180
14	11, 64
15	103
15.4	204
16	143, 196
17.7	17
18	11, 69, 120, 151, 180, 182
18.7	182
18.8-16	62
18.13-14	182
19	11, 12, 14, 78, 94, 147–9, 152–4, 156, 157, 159
19.8-11	17
20	61, 120, 180
20.3	58
20.10	61
21	61, 120
22	196
22.9-10	85
22.23	103
23	4, 193–8, 200, 202–4, 206, 207, 211–15, 217, 218, 222–4
23.1-2	196, 213, 218
23.2	200, 201, 203, 206
23.3-4	207
23.3	204, 214
23.4	4, 194, 195, 198, 201, 204, 211, 214–16, 219, 222–4
23.5	202, 209, 214, 217
23.6	195, 201
24	94, 103
24.3	207
27	11, 180
27.7	186
27.10	85
28	13
29	12, 13, 180, 183
29.4	183
29.9	183
30	13, 56, 141, 142, 180
30.3	45
30.4	184
30.7	45
31	3, 82, 88, 94, 95
31.1-9	91, 92
31.2-5	90
31.6	90, 91
31.7	90, 92
31.8-9	91
31.9	91
31.10-14	92
31.10	91
31.12-14	91–3
31.14	92
31.15	91, 92
31.16	92

31.17	92	48.7	27		48, 50–62,
31.18	92	48.9-15	103		64, 65
31.19	92, 93	48.13	103	60.1	44, 53, 60,
31.20-21	93	50	58, 68		61
31.22	93	50.1	58	60.2	44, 49
31.23	93	50.3	103	60.3-7	44
31.24-25	93	50.9	58	60.3	44, 45, 55,
32	13	50.10	58		64
32.3	17	50.18	53	60.4-5	45
33	13	51–72	48	60.4	45, 65
33.13-14	17	51	10, 44, 49,	60.5	45
33.14	17		52, 53, 55,	60.6-7	60
34	13, 78, 180		75, 180,	60.6	46, 47, 52
35.5	104		181, 183,	60.7-12	62
37	78		186	60.7	44, 47, 61,
39	4, 163–8,	51.1	183		64
	170–2, 174	51.7	185, 186	60.8-10	44, 47, 56,
39.4-6	164, 168,	51.16	55		57, 59, 63
	170, 172	51.20-21	59	60.8-9	46
39.5	163, 164,	52–64	51	60.8	45, 58, 59,
	173	52–59	52		62, 64
39.6	163	52	65	60.9	46
39.10-11	164, 169,	52.2	65	60.10	46, 59, 61
	171	52.3-7	105	60.11-12	49, 60, 64
39.11	163, 164	53	11, 64	60.11	44, 47, 49,
39.13-14	171	53.5	59		59, 60, 64,
39.13	165	55	55, 64		65
40.13-17	11	55.13-15	55	60.12-14	44
41	198	55.21	55	60.12-13	49
42–83	11	55.24	55, 59	60.12	64
42–72	11	56	59	60.13-14	47, 60
42	180, 181	56.14	59	60.13	47, 52, 55,
42.4-5	184	57	11, 64		60, 61
43	44	57.1	59	60.14	47, 48, 60,
44	44, 47, 56,	57.7-11	62		61, 65, 94
	61	57.9	103	61–64	51, 56
44.6	47	58.2-3	105	61.3-4	59
44.7	47	58.11-12	59	61.7-8	59
44.8	47	59	57, 59, 64	62.4	105
44.9	48	59.6	57	62.9	167
44.14	57	59.9	57, 59	62.11	105
45	57, 62,	59.11	60	62.12	17
	120, 141,	59.14	59	63	51, 52
	180	59.17	59	63.3	58
45.16	103	59.18	59	65	151
46	56, 103	60	3, 11, 42,	65.13	103
48	13		43, 45, 47,	66.1-12	103

Psalms (cont.)		72.10		71, 129		95.1	103
66.15	103	72.11		71		96	11, 180,
67	19, 20, 103	72.12-14		71, 74, 75,			181, 184
67.1	20			124, 129		96.3	184
67.2	20	72.12		74		96.10	182, 184,
67.3	20	72.15		71, 76, 124			185
67.4	20	72.16-17		124		97	180, 181
67.5	20	72.16		72, 75		97.10	181, 184
67.6	20	72.17		75, 124,		98.4-6	103
67.7	20			129		99	180
67.8	20	72.18-19		72, 126		100	103, 180,
68	180, 181,	73–89		11			181
	188	73–83		68		101-113	106
68.1-4	189	73		74, 78		101	120
68.1	188	75		13		102.8	17
68.3	189	76		180, 188,		103	180
68.25	58			190		103.10-14	103
69–71	75	76.6		189, 190		105.20	17
70–71	76	77.18-19		17		106	198
70	11	79.4		57		106.5	103
71	76	80.7		57		107-150	11
71.3	76	81		57		107.4-32	103
71.6	76	82		57		107.21-22	103
71.14	76	85.7		103		108	11, 47, 60
72	3, 4, 51,	85.11		36		108.1-6	62
	52, 68,	88		83		108.7-14	62
	69, 71,	89		53, 180,		108.7	44, 57
	73–6, 78,			181, 198		108.14	94
	118–22,	89.1		181		110	120, 140,
	124–33,	89.5		181, 184			141, 143
	198	89.7		184		112	78
72.1-17	126	89.12		182		114	17
72.1-8	124	90-106		11		116	17
72.1-7	75, 129	91		104		116.13	104
72.1-4	71, 74	92.4		103		116.17	103
72.1	71, 130	93–99		53		117	180, 181,
72.2	71, 73	93		180, 182,			187
72.3	74, 125			183		117.1	17
72.4	73	93.3-6		17		118.1-4	103
72.5-11	74	93.5		183		118.27	103
72.5	74, 129	94-100		106		120-134	11, 71
72.6	72	94.1		17		121	151
72.7	125, 129	94.3		17		124	7, 8
72.8-11	75	95		11, 180		126	78
72.9-11	124	95.1-17		103			
72.9	32	95.1-7		103			

127	3, 68, 71–3, 76, 77, 79	31.1-7	27	52.4	45
		31.2	27	53.1-5	17
		31.3	27	53.2	17
127.1-2	76, 78			53.4	17
127.1	72, 77	*Ecclesiastes*		54.5	17
127.2	72	1.1	70, 71	54.7-8	17
127.3-5	72, 76–8	1.2	165, 174	60.1-3	17
127.3	77	1.3	174	60.5	61
127.4	78	1.12	71	60.6	124
127.5	78	1.14	166	60.14	124
128	77, 78	1.18	70	63	61
132	120	2.4-7	174	63.1-6	44, 60
133	77	2.11	166, 174	63.1-3	61
134.2	58	2.15	166	63.6	61
135	180, 181, 187	2.17	166		
		2.19	166	*Jeremiah*	
135.1-4	103	2.21	166	2.6	217
135.1-3	187	3.1-8	173	9.19	44
135.4	187	3.2	173	9.25	44
135.5	187	3.3	173	25.15-30	45
136	17	5.14	174	25.15	45
137	139–41	9.11	174	25.16	45
137.2	17	12.1-7	173	25.27	45
139.13-16	85	12.8	165	25.30	45
142	210			36	114
144	11, 180	*Song of Songs*			
144.1-11	120	1.5	17	*Lamentations*	
144.4	166, 167	2.3	72	3.29	32
145	180–2	2.16	72		
145.20	182	4.16	72	*Ezekiel*	
148	94, 180, 187			3.13	30, 36
		Isaiah			
150.1	58	2.7	17	*Daniel*	
150.3-5	103	14.4-9	17	7	141
		29.1-16	45		
Proverbs		30.1-7	52	*Hosea*	
2.9	27	30.7	52	6.1-2	17
7.13	37	31.1-9	52	10.5	29
13.7	17	31.4	52	13.2	36
16.15	72	31.9	52	14.6-7	17
19.12	72	33.14	27		
21.6	165	38	115	*Amos*	
24.26	36	49.7	124	1.3	17
25.1	73	49.23	32, 124		
27.6-7	17	51.17	45	*Jonah*	
28.11	17	51.22	45	2	115

Micah
7.17   32

Zechariah
1.16   45
8.15   45
9.5   17
9.9-10   124
10.6   44

Malachi
3.7   45

NEW TESTAMENT
Matthew
2.9-12   75

Mark
12.35-37   140

John
10   197
10.11   196

Acts
2.24-26   143
4.24-28   141
17   148

1 Corinthians
10.4   139

Hebrews
1.5   141
1.13   140

1 Peter
2.25   196
3.19   152
5.4   196

Revelation
6.2-8   199
7   197
7.17   196

MIDRASH
Canticles Rabbah
1.1   70

Josephus
Antiquities
7.109   54
7.386   55

CLASSICAL SOURCES
Origen
Commentary on Joshua
15.1   139

CHRISTIAN THEOLOGICAL
WRITINGS
Karl Barth
Church Dogmatics
I.1 ss8.3   148
I.1 ss8.3,
  326-9   148
II, 139   148
II, 99   148
II.1, 107-8 149
II.1, 107   150

*The Collected Works
of Gerard Manley
Hopkins*
I, 343-9   157
II, 308   155
II, 867-8   151
III, 592   154
IV, 287-91 153
IV, 311-17 153
IV, 313   154
V, 348   152
V, 349   153
V, 385-6   159
V, 392   158
V, 524   153
V, 525   153

ANCIENT NEAR EASTERN
SOURCES
namburbi-*prayer*
l. 15   107
l. 26   107
ll. 1-9   107
ll. 1-19   106
ll. 10-14   107
ll. 16-20   107
ll. 20-26   107
ll. 20-21   107
ll. 22-23   107
ll. 24-26   107

Index of Authors

Aejmelaeus, A. 84, 95
Allan, K. 83, 95
Allen, L. C. 30, 38, 77, 79
Alshekh, M. 60, 66
Alter, R. 64, 65, 115, 133, 134, 167, 171, 174
Anderson, B. 131, 134
Arneth, M. 123, 125, 134
Assis, E. 60, 66
Assmann, J. 126, 134
Attard, S. M. 45, 51, 54, 55, 66
Auffret, P. 32, 38
Augusti, J. C. W. 120, 137
Austin, J. L. 115
Auwers, J. M. 120, 134
Avioz, A. 36, 38

Baethgen, F. 27, 38
Bailey, M. 215, 224
Bak, N. C. 219, 224
Baker, C. H. C. 177, 191
Baker, M. I. 177, 191
Balentine, S. 82, 87, 94, 95
Barbiero, G. 51, 54, 66, 127, 134
Barker, E. R. 197, 225
Barnes, W. E. 27, 38
Barnstone, A. 115
Barnstone, W. 115
Barr, J. 29, 38, 148, 149, 159
Barth, K. 147, 159
Barthélemy, D. 34, 38
Barton, J. 14, 22, 43, 66
Bazylinski, S. 61, 66
Beaudoin, T. 110, 115
Beeks, G. 178, 179, 191
Begrich, J. 43, 60, 66, 100, 116, 122
Beit-Arie', M. 204, 205, 225
Bell, A. 83, 84, 95
Bellenberg, K. 115
Berlejung, A. 33, 38

Bertholet, A. 32, 38
Beyse, K. M. 30, 36
Bickell, G. 31, 38
Bland, D. 127, 134
Block, D. I. 30, 38
Bolin, T. 70
Bradley, J. 204, 225
Brady, N. 179, 192
Brandt, L. F. 167–9, 174
Bratcher, R. G. 90, 95
Braude, W. G. 55
Brettler, M. Z. 33, 39
Briggs, C. A. 28, 39, 58, 66
Briggs, E. G. 28, 39, 58, 66
Brockington, L. H. 30, 39
Brook, J. 210, 225
Brown, D. 154, 159
Brown, M. 206, 207, 225
Brown, W. P. 81, 89, 95
Broyles, C. C. 119, 120, 134
Brueggemann, W. 56, 57, 62, 66, 70, 72–4, 79, 85, 95
Bubel, K. 156, 159
Bundvad, M. 173, 174
Bunyan, J. 217, 225
Burkitt, F. C. 169, 174
Burrows, D. 178, 179, 191

Camille, M. 206, 225
Campbell, G. 184, 191
Carlson, T. B. 83, 95
Carr, D. M. 115, 124, 134
Carrière, J.-M. 119, 134
Carston, R. 135, 134
Cassidy, B. 225
Ceresko, A. R. 18, 22
Chagall, M. 212, 214, 225, 226
Chamness, N. O. 115
Cheyne, T. K. 31, 39
Childs, B. S. 48, 54, 66, 68, 79

Clark, H. H. 83, 95
Clarke, E. 167, 168, 171–5
Clines, D. J. A. 15, 22, 29, 39
Closen, G. E. 35, 39
Clutterbuck, J. 183, 185, 191
Cohen, J. M. 36, 39
Cohen, Y. 164, 175
Cole, R. L. 26, 32, 39
Collins, A. Y. 140, 145
Collins, C. J. 36
Collins, J. J. 140, 145
Colón, M. J. 167, 170, 171, 175
Cotter, J. F. 151, 152, 159
Cowley, A. E. 15
Cox, H. 178, 180, 189
Craigie, P. 12, 22, 27, 39, 88, 90, 95, 171, 175
Crane, M. T. 87, 95
Crenshaw, J. L. 71, 72, 78, 79, 165, 175
Croft, S. J. L. 165, 175

Daffern, M. I. J. 81, 95
Dahl, G. 119, 134
Dahood, M. J. 39, 58, 77, 79, 124, 134
deClaissé-Walford, N. 34, 39
Deissler, A. 31, 39
Delitzsch, F. 27, 34, 35, 39, 48, 56, 66, 119
Dell, K. J. 70, 73, 76, 77, 79
deSilva, D. A. 18, 22
Dewey, J. 134
Dietrich, J. 123, 134
Diller, C. 127
Doan, W. 82, 87, 95, 96
Dormer, S. 198, 225
Dorsey, D. A. 18, 22
Downes, K. 176, 177, 191
Downes, W. 86, 87, 95
Driver, G. R. 30, 39, 46, 66
Driver, S. R. 35, 39
Dubois, M. 151, 152, 159
Duhm, B. 31, 39
Dunlop, I. 176, 191
Dweck, Y. 8, 22
Dylan, B. 115

Eaton, J. H. 57, 60, 66
Eder, S. 115
Emerton, J. A. 33, 39
England, E. 7, 22

Erbele-Küster, D. 115
Estes, D. J. 76, 77, 79
Exum, J. C. 195, 225

Fabry, H.-J. 48, 66
Fenton, R. 225
Fiddes, P. 151, 160
Fischer-Lichte, E. 115, 116
FitzGerald, W. 116
Fleer, D. 127, 134
Foray, J.-M. 212, 225
Fox, M. V. 174, 175
Frankfort, H. 126, 134
Fraser, H. 156, 157, 160
Fredericks, D. C. 166, 175
Frost, D. L. 33, 39

Galling, K. 174, 175
Gardner, W. H. 151, 152, 154, 155, 158, 160
Gerstenberger, E. 88, 90, 95, 99, 104, 107, 116
Gesenius, W. 22, 32
Gibson, J. C. L. 37, 39
Giles, T. 82, 87, 95, 96
Gillingham, S. E. 2, 3, 7–9, 11, 12, 22, 23, 25, 39, 57, 61, 62, 73, 75, 76, 79, 81, 96, 99, 100, 114–16, 118–22, 124, 128–30, 132, 135, 141, 142, 145, 146, 149, 151, 157, 160, 164, 173, 175, 193–6, 202, 205, 212, 215, 221, 225
Glueck, G. 214, 225
Goldingay, J. 19, 23, 29, 39, 90, 96, 163, 175
Gordon, R. P. 37, 39
Goulder, M. D. 68, 69, 79
Greenberg, M. 30, 39
Gregory, G. 16, 17
Grelot, P. 122, 135
Gressmann, H. 122, 135
Groth, H. 221, 222, 225
Gruber, M. I. 32, 39
Gunkel, H. 35, 39, 43, 66, 71, 76, 79, 100, 116, 120, 122, 135

Hallo, W. 39
Hamlin, H. 196, 202, 218, 225
Harding, J. E. 7, 23
Hartenstein, F. 27, 40
Hartvigsen, K. M. 83, 96

Index of Authors

Hatch, L. C. 156, 160
Haupt, P. 28, 40
Heard, K. 215, 217, 226
Heeßel, N. 105, 116
Hempfer, K. W. 116
Herder, J. G. 101, 114, 116
Higgins, L. 150, 160
Hill, R. C. 13, 23, 141, 145
Holladay, W. L. 31, 40
Hooker, R. 139, 145
Horst, K. van der 199, 200, 226
Hossfeld, F.-L. 47, 67, 123, 135
Houston, W. J. 129, 130, 135
Human, D. J. 123, 130, 135

Jacobson, K. 194, 196, 215, 226
Jacobson, R. A. 34, 39, 163, 164, 175
Jaffe, Y. 119, 135
Janowski, B. 27, 40, 123, 125, 135
Janzen, J. G. 82, 94, 96
Jarick, J. 165, 173, 175
Jaski, B. 226
Jasper, D. 196, 226
Jobling, D. 74, 79, 129, 135
Johnson, A. R. 73, 79
Johnson, J. 176, 191
Johnson, V. L. 53, 55, 67
Joüon, P. 15, 23
Joyce, P. M. 9

Kaiser, W. 27, 119, 120, 135
Khan, G. 15, 23
Kirkpatrick, A. F. 27, 40, 46, 50, 55, 67
Kitchen, K. A. 36, 40
Knauf, E. A. 58, 67
Köbert, R. 34, 40
König, E. 116
Körting, C. 12, 23
Kopf, L. 30, 40
Kratz, R. G. 12, 23
Kraus, H.-J. 38, 40, 50, 57, 67, 71, 76, 80, 88, 92, 96, 123, 124, 135, 136
Kuntz, J. K. 77, 78, 80
Kynes, W. 76, 80

LaNeel Turner, B. 39
Lagrange, M. J. 32, 40
Lenzi, A. 107, 116
Levinas, E. 111, 116
Lewis, C. S. 140, 145

Lichtmann, M. 150, 156, 160
Lipton, D. 9, 23
Loretz, O. 122, 123, 136
Lowth, R. 16, 17, 23, 101-3, 115, 116
Lund, N. 16, 18, 23
Lyons, W. J. 7, 22

MacKenzie, N. H. 151, 152, 154, 155, 158, 160
Măcelaru, M. V. 121, 136
Macintosh, A. A. 29, 33, 39, 40
Mandolfo, C. 84, 96
Maré, L. P. 62, 67
Maul, S. M. 104–7, 116
May, H. G. 42, 43, 67
Mayer, K. 212, 214, 226
Mays, J. L. 124, 136
McKane, W. 27, 40
McKenzie, J. L. 120
Meek, R. L. 165, 166, 169, 173–5
Mein, A. 130, 136
Metzger, T. 204, 205, 225
Meyer, U. 215, 226
Meynet, R. 16, 23
Miller, D. B. 166, 175
Miller, P. D. Jr 76, 77, 80, 82, 86, 94, 96
Mitchell, D. C. 119, 136
Mitchell, S. 164, 175
Morgan, D. 197, 226
Morgenstern, J. 31, 40
Mowinckel, S. 73, 80, 82, 96, 116, 122, 136
Muilenburg, J. 95, 96
Muller, J. 156, 160
Murphy, R. E. 119, 123, 136

Németh, A. 123, 124, 136
Nielsen, K. 63
Nixon, J. V. 156, 160
Noel, W. 199, 200, 202, 207, 223, 226
Norton, G. J. 28, 40

O'Hear, A. 195, 226
O'Hear, N. 195, 226
Obiorah, M. J. 130, 136
Ogden, G. S. 43, 44, 60, 67
Olofsson, S. 28, 40
Otto, E. 123, 136
Owens, W. R. 217, 226

Palmer, D. G. 18, 23
Panksepp, J. 87, 96
Panofsky, E. 215, 217, 226
Pardee, D. 183, 191
Pardee, N. 183, 191
Paul, S. M. 122, 136
Pecklers, K. F. 8, 24
Pelt, M. V. van 27
Perdue, L. G. 78, 80
Phillips, C. 156, 160
Pickstock, C. J. C. 159, 160
Pietersma, A. 28, 40
Pomplun, T. 154, 160
Poorthuis, M. 119, 136
Prince, J. D. 31, 40

Ravasi, G. 50, 59, 67
Reibel, D. A. 16
Reid, W. S. 7, 24
Reider, J. 29, 40
Renaud, B. 125, 136
Rendtorff, R. 53, 67
Reyburn, W. D. 90, 95
Rhoads, D. 117
Ricoeur, P. 63, 67, 132, 136
Roberts, J. 8, 24
Robinson, A. 31, 40
Romero-Girón Deleito, J. 46, 67
Roncace, M. 194, 196, 215, 226
Rooke, D. W. 187, 191
Ross, A. P. 27, 40, 179, 191
Rossini-Paquet, F. 212
Rothenberg, J. 117
Rowley, H. H. 38, 40
Rox, H. 215, 226

Sabottka, L. 30, 40
Salo, R. S. 123–5, 137
Sandler, L. F. 199, 200, 206, 207, 226
Sargent, B. 140, 145
Saur, M. 120, 137
Sawyer, J. F. 9, 24, 48, 66
Schiffer, G. 117
Schmidt, H. 77, 80
Scholem, G. 8, 24
Seybold, K. 45, 59, 67, 101, 117, 174, 175
Sheppard, G. T. 120, 137
Sherwood, Y. 10, 24
Sievers, E. 32, 40

Silver, E. 204, 205, 225
Sim, S. 217, 226
Smith, J. K. A. 131, 137
Smith, R. 187, 192
Sneed, M. 174, 175
Sonne, I. 31, 40
Sperling, S. D. 32, 40
Starbuck, S. R. A. 123, 137
Steinberg, J. 52, 61, 67
Stocks, S. P. 77, 80
Strawn, B. A. 82, 85, 86, 91, 94, 96, 195, 196, 226
Stroud, F. 189, 192
Süssenbach, C. 60, 67
Suarez, M. 150, 160

Talmage, F. E. 7, 24
Tamez, E. 130, 137
Tanner, B. L. 34
Tate, M. E. 19, 24, 124, 137
Tate, N. 179, 192
Taylor, C. 131, 137
Taylor, D. J. 171, 175
Terrien, S. L. 68, 73, 75, 80, 164, 175
Tov, E. 34, 40

Uehlinger, C. 33, 40, 43, 67
Ulrich, E. 14, 24
Utzschneider, H. 117

Vang, C. 33, 40
VanGemeren, W. A. 19, 24
Vayntrub, J. 82, 96
Vermeylen, J. 31, 40, 60, 67
Volbers, J. 116

Wagner, R. 197, 226
Ward, B. W. 154, 160
Watson, J. R. 7, 8, 24
Wearing, C. 133, 134
Weiser, A. 45, 58, 67, 88, 96
Wendland, E. R. 90, 96
Werlin, S. 197, 226
Wesselschmidt, Q. E. 119, 137
West, T. M. 82, 96
Westermann, C. 62, 67
Wette, W. L. M. de 120, 137
Whitaker, L. 215, 217, 226
White, N. 154, 160
Whitley, C. F. 169, 175

Whybray, R. N. 36, 40, 75–8, 80
Wilcox, H. 157, 160, 191
Willgren Davage, D. 69, 140, 145
Willgren, D. 49, 100, 117, 123
Williams, D. 156, 160
Williamson, H. G. M. 25, 33, 35, 40
Wragg, A. 210, 226
Wright, D. 19, 24
Wright, J. W. 54, 67

Wright, R. M. 198, 199, 225
Wüstefeld, W. C. M. 199, 200, 226

Younger, K. L. 32

Zenger, E. 48, 67, 123, 125, 135, 137
Zimmerli, W. 30, 41
Zimmern, H. 32, 41

www.ingramcontent.com/pod-product-compliance
Lightning Source LLC
Chambersburg PA
CBHW062136300426
44115CB00012BA/1947